Get Buffed!™

Ian King's Guide to getting BIGGER, STRONGER & LEANER!

King Sports Publishing
www.getbuffed.net
Email : info@getbuffed.net
Ph +1-775-327-4550 Fax +1-240-465-4873
1135 Terminal Way, Suite 209, Reno NV 89502, USA

Published by :
King Sports Publishing
King Sports International
www.getbuffed.net
info@getbuffed.net
Ph +1-775-327-4550 Fax +1-240-465-4873
1135 Terminal Way, Suite 209, Reno NV 89502, USA

ISBN 1-920685-00-6
Title: Get Buffed!: Ian King's guide to getting bigger, stronger and leaner
Edition: 3rd
Author/Contributor: King, Ian
Date of Publication:.01 Jan 2002   Price: $ 39.95 USD / $69.95 AUD
Format:.PB Size:.295x210   No. of Pages: 301
Publisher: King Sports International

Disclaimer

This book is designed to provide information in regard to the subject matter covered. The purpose of this book it to educate. The author and publisher shall have neither liability nor responsibility to any person or entity with respect to any of the information contained in this book. It is recommend that you seek independent medical and training specialist advice before proceeding with any training method.

Get Buffed!

The words 'buffed' can mean a lot of things. We go to the gym to 'get buffed'. To a bodybuilder it may mean to get big and lean. To a powerlifter it might mean to get strong and big. To an Olympic lifter it might mean to get strong and explosive. To an athlete it means getting the strength and shape to optimize their performance. To the average person in a health club it may mean to get lean, muscular and fit.

Call it what you want – it's getting buffed!

Whatever your goals, getting buffed can be a lot of fun, and very rewarding. It can also mean a better quality or longer life; and greater social, personal and financial rewards.

Whatever 'getting buffed' means to or does for you, there will be something in this book that assists you to do it better!

Ian King

Table of Contents

Introduction

Meet the author

There's been a lot of books written about training, some of them excellent. So what makes this book different? This book is an accumulation of my personal and professional experiences. Lessons learned from training myself and from training others.

I first went into a gym in the 60's, when I was about 7 years of age. I had attached myself to the local strong-man, an islander by the name of Iwela Jacobs. He was my first mentor in what was an incredibly early-developed passion for physical preparation! The gym was the Port Moresby (Papua New Guinea - or the Territory of Papua and New Guinea as it was more correctly known at that time) YMCA. When I was 'discovered' by the staff they 'kicked' me out - too young, they claimed!

In secondary school I spent as much time in the gym as my schedule allowed. The equipment was really modern, in this Australian boarding school gym - the barbells were jam tins filled with cement connected with rusty bent iron bars! And you needed to skillfully side-step the holes in the wooden floor (not unlike the strength training facility at the Argentinean Institute of Sport I used during a visit there in the early 1990's!). This never slowed us down or made us feel that we were missing out. And it still wouldn't. Give me any equipment and the athletes and I will succeed!

I studied physical preparation at university - because I wanted to know more about training – not because I had any plans about what I was going to do professionally with this educa-

> *The equipment was really modern in this gym - the barbells were jam tins filled with cement connected with rusty bent iron bars!*

tion! Elite athletes who I trained with side by side in the gym in those years were the initial demand for what was to become one of the first commercial professional services in physical preparation of the elite athletes in Australia. Strength and conditioning in America was still in it's infancy then, in the early 80's. In fact, the National Strength and Conditioning Association at that time was titled the National Strength Coaches Association.

The initial demand for my services from my elite athlete training partners rapidly grew into a situation where I was working at an exhausting pace, servicing over 20 sports at national/international level, and working in over 10 different countries, during the subsequent decade.

This became my classroom, and I learned so much. It seems a trend to boast and maybe even exaggerate about the places one has been, the athlete one has worked with. I shy away from this. Suffice to say I worked with a significant number of athletes at international level continuously for that decade. The key is the word continuously. I was able to implement methods, watch the long-term results, and modify and improve my approach. This I believe was the greatest and most unique aspects of my education.

It is these experiences that allow me to write this book, and it is this that I believe makes the information in this book unique.

Let's get into it!

Chapter 1
What is training?
Training vs. the training effect

You've gone to the gym. You've pushed your body to the limit. You know you've worked hard – you're sweating profusely, your muscles are screaming, and by the end you feel smashed! There is no doubt about it - you have trained. But is that all there is to getting the result? To getting what is called the 'training effect'? The training effect is literally the end result of your training. In this case, getting bigger, stronger and/or leaner.

No. This is not all there is to it! But based on the behavior and attitudes of most, you could be forgiven for thinking that this is it - this is training- you have done all you need to do to get the end result.

Let me make it very clear for you - the training effect is not simply the training! Instead, it is the training followed by recovery.

So let me make it very clear for you - the training effect is not simply the training! Instead, it is the training **followed by recovery**. The addition of the 'recovery' to the 'training' is what gives you the training effect.

Yes, training is important - but it is not the complete picture. **If I teach you nothing else, then I have made a significant impact on not only how you train but also the results you'll get!**

I truly hope that you come to understand that optimal training is not about how much or hard or long or painful it can be; rather it is about the amount of training, which when combined with the recovery situation you are in, will give you the best training effect.

I am going to start out in this book by giving you the opportunity to learn some of the most powerful tools for analyzing and designing your own program. Techniques that until now were possessed only by professionals, and even then only a minority of these individuals have been able to successfully 'do what they know'.

In doing so, I am going to make it very clear the need to give the component of recovery the same respect as the component of training.

In summary, this book is going to give you the tools to ensure that your training is not only effective but safe, and that it allows you the balance and success in life that you seek and deserve.

Optimal training is not about how much or hard or long or painful it can be - but rather the amount of training, which when combined with the recovery situation you are in, will give you the best training effect.

Get Buffed!™

Chapter 2
The bottom line
The fatigue/recovery curve

How much should I train? How often? How hard? How long for? The answers to these typical questions are best provided through an understanding of the variables that affect us individually. Understanding our own 'fatigue curves'. Because there is no one answer. You are each individuals. And there is no one better placed to answer these questions than yourself - when you know how to interpret the answers that your body provides.

One of the most powerful tools in understanding the training process is what is often called the fatigue / recovery curve. It has been called many different things (e.g. the general adaptation syndrome) and been credited to many different authors.

One of the powerful tools in understanding the training process is what is often called the fatigue / recovery curve.

Is this fatigue curve a generalization? Yes, because there are many types of fatigue e.g. neural, metabolic, emotional etc., and they realistically take different times to recover. But let's keep it simple for now.

The scene is simple. You are cruising along at your current homeostasis, whatever that may be. Then you train (point A in Figure 1). Training, of no surprise to you, is **disruptive to the body**. It causes the body to 'crash'. You feel tired, lethargic etc. This response is called fatigue (point B in Figure 1).

Figure 1 - The fatigue curve.

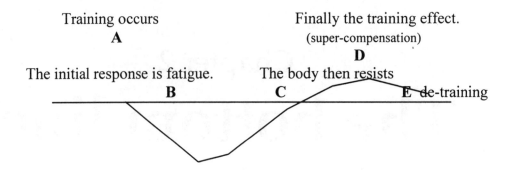

How low does the fatigue curve go down after training? That depends on some of the following :

- **your state of recovery prior to training** : if you were run down prior to starting that training session, the fatigue curve will probably go lower than it would have had you been fresher;
- **the intensity of the workout** : the 'harder' you train (expressed as a percentage of your maximal effort), expect the fatigue curve to go lower;
- **the volume of the training session** : the more sets and exercises you do, all things being equal, the deeper the fatigue curve will go;
- **the duration of the workout** : the longer the workout goes for, the deeper the fatigue curve may go;
- **the complexity of the exercises used** : exercises that include more of the body's musculature and nervous system may cause greater fatigue (e.g. squats opposed to leg press, chin ups versus lat pull-downs); each exercise has a metabolic/ neural cost which gives an indication of fatigue potential.

After a point in time your body **resists this fatigue**, and the recovery process commences (point C in Figure 1).

How fast does the fatigue curve recover after training? That depends on some of the following :

- **your conditioning to the exercise** : was it a type and intensity that you are used to (remember, it is unfamiliar exercise that causes a lot more fatigue and soreness);
- **your metabolic and neural recovery capacity** : how fast are the metabolic and neural systems being replenished. This is

Training is disruptive to the body. It causes the body to 'crash'. You feel tired, lethargic etc. This response is called fatigue.

Get Buffed!™

influenced by such things as diet, supplements, and drugs etc.

- **your exposure to other forms of training** : exposure to additional training during this recovery phase may slow down the recovery;
- **your exposure to specific recovery methods** : methods such as massage, hot and cold baths, stretching etc. are called recovery methods, and if used appropriately, may accelerate the rate of recovery;
- **lifestyle** : are the conditions in your lifestyle conducive or counter-productive to recovery? (e.g. having a job, money worries, families demands, etc. all detract from recovery potential. I am not suggesting that any of these are 'bad', but they must be recognized for their impact on recovery ability). Put simply, the professional athlete does not sit around for most of the day because they are lazy - they know that doing too much extra-curricular activity may hinder their recovery from training.

The fatigue curve has now reached the point of the previous level of homeostasis, your previous base-line. But it doesn't stop here. It wants to go above, go higher than the previous baseline. This phenomenon is often describe as **super or over compensation**, and is a biological survival instinct aimed at preparing the body for a subsequent exposure similar to the stimulus of the last training session. **This is the training effect!** You are now capable of doing more than you were able to do before - because of the cumulative effect of the training stimulus AND the recovery process (point D in Fig. 1).

This is the training effect! Where you are now capable of doing more than you were able to do before - because of the cumulative effect of the training stimulus AND the recovery process.

How do you know if you have recovered? : Quite simply, your performance should exceed the previous. If you could do 10 reps at 100 kgs in the bench press in the last workout, and you can do 11 or more this time - you have experienced the 'training effect'. You have made smart decisions.

There is one final step left in the fatigue curve, and that is what happens if there is no subsequent stimulus of a similar kind. You will slowly return to the baseline initially. If this baseline was supported by previous training and that training has ceased, your work capacity may retreat even lower than this earlier base-line. This is often called **'de-training'** (point E in Figure 1), quite simply 'if you don't use it, you lose it'.

What if you do less than last time? : Two possibilities - either you have not recovered, or you have detrained. I suspect the first possibility, as it can take somewhere between 7 -28 days (generally speaking) to detrain in strength. So if you are exposing your body to a similar stimulus in a time frame less than 7 days and you are 'weaker', it is safe to say you have not fully recovered.

What happens if you train with high intensity, volume and or duration? : Quite simply, you cause the fatigue curve to go down lower and for longer. This is in itself not bad, but it does mean that to experience the training effect, it will be a longer time before you can afford to return to a similar training session. Or you will need to implement what I call 'recovery methods' (as discussed on the previous page) to accelerate the recovery process.

Remember - if you commence a training session at point on the fatigue curve lower than your previous baseline, you have re-set your new baseline lower than it was previously.

Most aren't prepared to do this. **Most train hard and long, and with high frequency**. Unless one is supported by a incredibly higher recovery system (natural or chemically enhanced), this approach will result in over-training and non-achievement of goals. **Welcome to the most common training scenario (read error)!**

Remember - *if you commence a training session at a point on the fatigue curve lower than your previous baseline, you have re-set your new baseline lower than it was previously*. Every subsequent time you do this, you significantly lower your position on the fatigue curve. You'd better use a big sheet of paper because very quickly you will be off the bottom of the page!

What happens if I train with lower intensity, volume and or duration? Your fatigue curve will not go as low or take as long to recover. Based on what I see of most peoples intended training frequencies, this is what most should be doing!

So which approach should I use? The answer is simple - all of them! You just need to know when to use each of these methods, and for how long. You need to determine which method predominantly suits you and your recovery situation. And when things change—e.g. you get older, you get kids etc., you need to be able to change the dominant training protocols you are using.

Note that when I encourage lower intensity I mean specifically less use of what I call supra-maximal efforts e.g. forced reps (i. e. the balls-to-the-wall approach). You will learn as you read on that whilst I place more value on intensity than volume in training - I just want to see the more demanding methods used less often!

So what does it mean if I am not making the progress I believe I should be? : There are really only three possibilities -

1. **you have detrained** : this is unlikely as most train too much, not too little;
2. **you have over-trained** : this in my opinion is the most likely cause. I say this because everyone assumes that if they do what someone else is doing it will work. Crazy! You are all individuals physiologically and experience different life stresses. Don't question it! If it isn't happening - do less!!
3. **your training stimulus is inappropriate** : this is very possible, but not as likely as the over-training issue. In this case you need a 'better' program!

So what do you do about it? : Read this book very carefully, and be prepared to do things differently. Believe it or not, the failure in training is rarely through a lack of knowledge. Most people, deep down, have at least a sneaking suspicion of what they should do. They know what they should do! The challenge is getting people to do what they should do, not want they want to do!

Most people, deep down, have at least a sneaking suspicion of what they should do. The challenge is getting people to do what they should do, not want they want to do!

Remember - to keep doing the same thing and expect a different result is not much short of crazy! Another goal I have in writing this book is to inspire you to make changes in your training — changes that will bring great rewards!

Chapter 3
What is periodization?
And should I use it?

This would be a good discussion for someone wanting to exploit periodization - but I am not going to buy into that. I believe that this topic has been mystified to extract every last commercial drop out of it. Hey - do you have a training plan? Well, then you are using periodization! Because my definition of periodization is simple - a plan! But if you don't have a plan I guess you aren't using periodization!

Periodization is no more complex than working out a plan to optimize your training results. Initial western world focus on periodization of strength training began with sets and reps. But the reality is you should be considering the periodization of every variable - not just sets and reps (intensity and volume). The variables you can apply periodization to include, (not in any order or exclusively) :

speed of movement; rest period; exercise selection; sequence of exercises; order of muscle groups on each training day; allocation of muscle groups to training days; etc.

Each of these issues is discussed in the following chapters. This approach is not totally unique in that other authors are discussing these to various extents. But what is unique is my approach to periodizing training methods, which inherently involves periodization of many of the other variables. Another unique technique I use that is the way I alter the order in

Do you have a training plan? Well, then you are using periodization!

which muscle groups are sequenced in subsequent workouts. These techniques will become apparent in the sample workouts later in the book.

The three main generalized types of periodization of reps and sets that I will talk about in this book include standard, linear and alternating. The following outlines these three types of strength periodization. For the purposes of comparison, all examples use four three week stages to create 12 week blocks.

1. Standard periodization : involves holding all variables constant for a training block e.g. 12 weeks, with consideration for providing variety in subsequent blocks. The only training group I would even consider this for is the beginner, and even then ideally I would like to see at least some form of variation within that time. This approach was reinforced by the work of De Lorme in the 1960's, who showed research results confirming that multiple sets (of 10 reps in this case) were effective in developing muscle strength.

*Figure 2 - An example of **standard periodization**.*

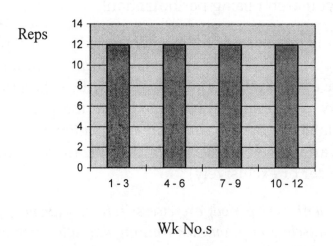

Reps

Wk No.s

2. Linear periodization : involves a linear progression in lowering reps and increasing load (representing the inverse relationship between volume and intensity). This method was developed (in literature at least) by North American sport scientists such as Stone and O'Bryant as a more effective alternative to standard periodization. I believe this method is suited to beginners, intermediate and in some cases advanced trainees.

The benefits of this method include that it makes it easier for the trainee to select the right appropriate loads as a function of the smooth progression towards lower reps. The disadvantages includes that the early stages may cause a detraining in neural adaptation, and the later stages may cause a detraining in metabolic adaptations. Despite this, I like this method because I believe it is effective for more trainees than the other two methods.

*Figure 3 - An example of **linear periodization**.*

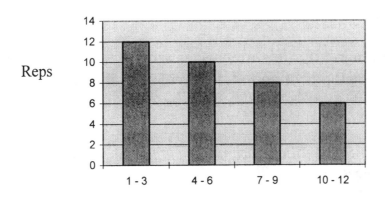

Week No.s

3. **Alternating periodization** : involves alternating between volume (another term used in this method is accumulation) and intensity (again, another term seen is intensification). This method was proposed by the West German strength researcher Schmidtbleicher in the early 1980's and further promoted by other North American strength coaches in later years.

I believe this method is suited predominantly to the advanced trainee. It's advantages includes that it avoids the detraining issues involved in linear progression (i.e. reduces the concern of detraining metabolic or neural adaptations because of more frequent exposure to each). Disadvantages include that it requires the trainee to be experienced in load selection as the reps drop and rise suddenly and significantly. I feel this method is used on some individuals who would perhaps be better off using linear periodization. I would consider only the advanced trainee for this method.

*Figure 4 - An example of **alternating periodization**.*

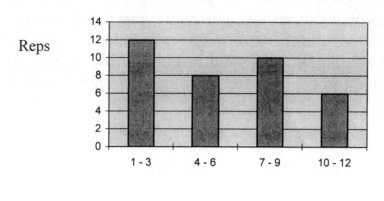

Wk No.s

The following figure summarizes who may benefit from each of these methods of periodization of reps and sets.

I feel this method is used on some individuals who would perhaps be better off using linear periodization.

Figure 5 - Suitability of each method of periodization to various training ages.

Method of Strength Periodization	Suitability to Training Age
Standard	Beginner
Linear	Beginner Intermediate Advanced
Alternating	Advanced

Chapter 4
How often should I train?

How to select frequency of training

From the discussion in Chapter 2 (the fatigue/recovery curve) you should now understand why I believe that frequency of training should be considered inverse to how 'hard' you train. The 'harder' you train, the less frequently you can afford to train with success. Vice versa, the 'easier' you train, the more frequently you can afford to train and succeed.

The first step in making the frequency decision is to decide whether you want to base your frequency on the day cycle method or the calendar week cycle method. The second step is to determine whether you wish to train using a form of a split routine or a total body workout. And thirdly, if using a split routine, which type of split routine.

But before I get down to explaining this, let me stress that the single biggest error I see in training frequency is overlooking the role of the central nervous system (CNS).

Take split training sessions (I will explain what these are shortly for those who aren't familiar with them) - the argument is that it allows you to train different muscle groups on subsequent days, therefore allowing them adequate time to rest and recover. That is fine if you only recognize the peripheral muscle physiology. But if you recognize the role of the CNS in the training of any and all muscle groups, you may gain a greater appreciation of the need to allow this system to recover, irrespective of which muscle groups comes next!

The single biggest error I see in training frequency is overlooking the role of the central nervous system.

Step 1 - Day Cycles or Calendar Week Cycles

Day cycles : ignore weekends. They rotate the training days based on how many days since the last training session. Day cycles work well for those whose lives revolve around training. My concern is that in many cases they encourage or lead to over-training.

Figure 6 - An example of a 3 part (A-C) split routine day cycle over 4 calendar weeks.

Week No.	Sun	Mon	Tue	Wed	Thu	Fri	Sat
1	A	B		C		A	B
2		C		A	B		C
3		A	B		C		A
4	B		C		A	B	

My concern is that in many cases they (day cycles splits) encourage or lead to over-training.

Calendar week cycles : revolve around the days of the week as we know them e.g. on Monday you repeat the previous Monday's workout and so on. Some find them limiting because each body part does not recover in a 7 day cycle. I don't see this a being as big a limiting factor however. *Most importantly, don't feel you need to use the day cycle method to show your commitment to training.* Unless training is the only commitment in your life, I would recommend the calendar week cycle for the majority.

Figure 7 - An example of a 4 part (A-D) split routine calendar week cycle over 4 calendar weeks.

Week No.	Sun	Mon	Tue	Wed	Thu	Fri	Sat
1		A	B		C	D	
2		A	B		C	D	
3		A	B		C	D	
4		A	B		C	D	

Get Buffed!™

Step 2 - Total body workouts or split routines

Total body workouts : mean doing the whole body in each and every workout. The advantage of them is time-efficiency e.g. you could train the whole body in 60 minutes. The flipside of this is the reduced inability to specialize. You cannot afford to spend much time on each muscle group (e.g. 10 major muscle groups in 60 minutes means 6 minutes per muscle group).

Total body workouts are ideal for beginners, those who wish to reduce their time commitment to training, and those who find their energy levels/recovery ability are not that high. For the average person, the total body workout has something of a time restriction between workouts - at the highest frequency, you are limited to 3 workouts per week or every 48 hours (although it could be argued that not all muscle groups are going to recover in 48 hrs!). Remember as a relative beginner, this short time between repeating the same muscle group may be less of an issue because of the inverse relationship I spoke of earlier between frequency and intensity - inexperienced lifters are less likely to train with high intensity, and therefore can tolerate a higher frequency.

Total body workouts are ideal for beginners, those who wish to reduce their time commitment to training, and find their energy levels/recovery ability not as high.

Figure 8 - An example of a 3/wk workout, using the same workout each time you train.

Week No.	Sun	Mon	Tue	Wed	Thu	Fri	Sat
1 - 3		A		A		A	

Split routines : means dividing the body up and doing a percentage of the body during each training session. They can involve (but don't have to) a greater total time commitment in the week, but do allow greater focus to be paid to each muscle group. I like this about them. But where I feel most go wrong is the old belief - *"it's OK to train 3 days in a row because I am training different muscle groups each time."* I question training 3 consecutive days (i.e. 3 days in a row). I believe that only certain people in certain conditions can get away with this approach. For the most, I recommend no more than 4 workouts per calendar week, and no more than 2 days consecutively.

Step 3 - Which type of split

I am going to show you what I believe to be the most effective split combinations for each of the three categories of training. This is by no means exhausting your options - it's only limited by your imagination! The muscle group allocation in the following examples is flexible - just get the feel for the overall concept.

The 'semi-total body' split routine : this takes the 'good' from the typical 3/wk total body workout (which is low time commitment) and reduces some of the 'bad' (which is the inadequate time for large muscle groups to recover, and the inability to specialize). The example in Figure 9 is a lower body priority program.

Figure 9 - An example of a 3/wk 'semi-total body' split routine. This split requires less of your time and allows more time for muscle recovery than a standard total body workout.

I am going to show you what I believe to be the most effective split combinations for three categories of training.

Monday (A)	Wednesday (B)	Friday (C)
Quad dominant (e.g. squat)	Horizontal push (e.g. bench)	Hip dominant (e.g. deadlift)
Lower back (e.g. good morning)	Horizontal pull (e.g. row)	Vertical push (e.g. shoulder press)
Vertical pull (e.g. chins)	Triceps	Biceps
Forearms	Calves	Upper traps

NB the allocation of muscle groups to training days is an example only.

The 4/wk calendar week split routine : this requires a greater commitment than the above 3/wk split routine, but allows for more specialization for each muscle group. The example in Figure 10 is an upper body priority program.

Figure 10 - An example of a 4/wk split routine. This split requires more of your time but also allows more time on muscle group.

Monday (A)	Tuesday (B)	Thursday (C)	Friday (D)
Horizontal push (e.g. bench press)	Hip dominant (e.g. deadlift)	Vertical pull (e.g. chin up)	Quad dominant (e.g. squat)
Horizontal pull (e.g. row)	Hip dominant (e.g. good morning)	Vertical push (e.g. shoulder press)	Quad dominant (e.g. lunge)
Triceps	Upper trap	Biceps	Calf

NB the allocation of muscle groups to training days is an example only.

The 5 day cycle split routine : this requires a greater commitment of time and the greatest specialization in muscle groups. I do however question how many people have the recovery capacity to find this optimal.

Fig 11 - An example of a 5 day cycle split routine. The cycle is repeated on the basis of how many days later, not the day of the week.

A - 2 days later	B - the next day	C - 2 days later	D - the next day	E - 2 days later
Quad dominant (e.g. squat)	Horizontal push (e.g. bench press)	Biceps	Hip dominant (e.g. deadlift)	Vertical pull (e.g. chin ups)
Quad dominant (e.g. lunge)	Horizontal pull (e.g. row)	Triceps	Hip dominant (e.g. stiff legged deadlift)	Vertical push (e.g. shoulder press)
Calves	Horizontal push (e.g. incline press)	Forearms	Upper traps	Vertical pull (e.g. lat p/down)

NB the allocation of muscle groups to training days is an example only.

What about double-day training? : Double day training means training twice in one day. This is a method I believe suited only to professional (or full time) athletes whose recovery circumstances are superior. Does double day training work? Nothing works if it exceeds your ability to recover from it!

Can I periodize training frequency? : You sure can! There is no end to the combinations that you can put together. As an (extreme) example simply working with the 3 examples from above, you may spend the first 3 weeks using the 5 part day cycle split routine, then the next 3 weeks using the 4/wk calendar week split routine, and the next 3 weeks using the 3/wk semi-total body calendar week split routine. This is just an example. You really can put any combination together but I stress the need to have some continuity in exercise selection.

Double day training means training twice in one day. This is a method I believe suited only to professional (or full time) athletes whose recovery circumstances are superior.

Chapter 5
How hard should I train?

Train smarter, not harder

Y ou've read the articles in the magazines and seen the pictures - the only way to go is 'balls to the wall' every training session. Or is it? Most people take this approach but that's perhaps got more to do with misinformation and misunderstanding than any thing else.

Consider this. Anabolic drug use in sport commenced sometime around the 1960's, and this was not the first ergogenic ever used. During the seventies, the medical profession, out of ignorance or whatever, maintained the line that anabolic drug use didn't have any positive effect on athletic performance or enhancement of lean muscle tissue. The elite athletes knew otherwise. During the 1980's, bodybuilding magazines chose not to discuss the drugs issue, insisting or inferring that the 40-60 set workouts that their star's were doing were 'clean'. It was taboo to write about drugs, but everyone reading the bodybuilding magazines were perhaps copying the training methods of those who had chemical assistance to raise their work/recovery capacity.

During the 1980's, bodybuilding magazines also refused to discuss the drugs issue, insisting or inferring that the 40-60 set workouts that their star's were doing were 'clean'.

It wasn't until the 90's that more honest articles on the use of drugs began appearing, perhaps led by publishers such as Bill Phillips (*Mile High Publishing* and *Muscle Media 2000*). This was a great advancement in honesty, but now that there were no limits the training articles, in my opinion, assumed that all readers were going to use drugs to support their training methods.

I don't believe this is the case. I know there are many trainers who for whatever reason chose not to use drugs. This is not a moral discussion. This is a reality. Drugs do increase your work and recovery capacity. If you are not using them, or only use low dosages, you cannot rely on drugs to overcome training error, or to ensure progress despite your training mistakes.

I would go so far as to say that there is not a power sport in the world that has not had the average training load expectations raised as a result of systematic drug use. So, for example, athletes in countries whose coach adopted the East German training methods minus the drugs do it tough!

In effect, this situation in bodybuilding has led recreational bodybuilders to believe that there is no other way than to use drugs. Their use of conventional, traditional bodybuilding methods have left them with minimal results. It may be difficult to get the extreme results that certain drug programs may be able to provide, but smart application of training methods outlined in this book will give you an alternative. I can make this statement because of the thousands of drug-free athletes whose training I have had the opportunity to experiment with, and learn the cause-effect relationships of my training methods.

It would be difficult to get the extreme results that certain drug programs may be able to provide, but smart application of training methods outlined in this book will give you an alternative.

Training intensity can be defined in a number of ways :

- **the shortening of the rest period** : the focus in this method is to reduce the rest periods between sets as a form of progression. This is from the metabolic perspective, focusing on the discomfort of working under lactic acid. This method ignores the neural component, but is effective for certain hypertrophy components (e.g. increase size of slow twitch or Type 1 muscle fibers, increased capillarization, short-term elevation of hormones including Growth Hormone);
- **the percentage of the maximum lift** : is usually based on a 1RM (one repetition maximum - how much weight you can lift for 1 rep). For example, you may have 100 kgs 1 RM - 80% of that is 80 kgs, and there may be say an expectation to perform 5 reps at this 80%. This method focuses more on the neural training effect, but is not reliable unless you

know your RM for each lift, and on each training day - which for anyone other than competitive lifters, is not practical. The chances of over-training or under-training using this method of load prescription is high;

- **the perceived exertion matched with number of reps :** this method uses a perception of effort matched with a number of reps e.g. do 5 reps with a load that causes high level fatigue but not total failure. Provided the communication is clear, this is the method I prefer.

There is nothing wrong with using a period of time dedicated to reducing the time frame of the rest period. I just wouldn't use this for too long. This would negate two very important realities of strength training - the neural component (which is still under-exploited by most), and that strength training is for my mind an anaerobic activity, not an aerobic activity. Improving aerobic work capacity or muscle endurance has limited impact on strength, power and hypertrophy of the larger and more responsive muscle fibers, the fast twitch or Type ll fibers. The majority of time should be spent with longer rest periods, and manipulating the variable of load and perceived effort, not reducing the rest periods.

So what is the answer to the question - how hard should I train? : Periodize intensity! That's right - cycle it, vary it according to a plan. And what is a plan that you can use to periodize intensity?

If you commence a training cycle at 100% of your maximum, I suggest that the subsequent fatigue may exceed your ability to recover.

Consider this - in week 1 of a new cycle, you face in most cases an unfamiliar exercise. This in itself will cause adequate muscle micro-trauma from which to recover. Realize also that your neural intra and inter-muscular coordination on this exercise will not be optimal. Therefore any attempts to lift maximally will compromise adherence to any pre-determined technique (I hope there is a pre-determined technique plan!).

If you commence a training cycle at 100% of your maximum, I suggest that the subsequent fatigue may exceed your ability to recover, and under most circumstances, you may not be able to carry improvements beyond the first or second week (this limitation has historically been overcome by increasing dosage of ergogenic aids, an option not available to or chosen by all). Put simply, you may feel like you are getting weaker in this lift over the subsequent weeks.

Figure 12 - Load selection and outcome over a 3 week cycle using 100 % effort each week (based on a 6 RM of 100 kgs, and assuming increases in this RM weekly or per micro-cycle).

	Week / Micro-cycle No.		
	1	2	3
Plan	100 kg @ 6	105 kg @ 6	105 kg @ 6
% of starting RM	*100 %*	*105 %*	*105 %*
Probable Outcome	100 kg @ 6	105 kg @ 5-6	105 kg @ 4-5

In brief, I suggest that the first week or micro-cycle of any new training cycle be treated as an 'exposure week', not a maximum effort week.

I believe that for most people most of the time the above model is excessive, and gains stagnate as a result. Of course, if you never experience what I have described in the above table, you need not read any further. However for those who can identify with this situation, I have created a more progressive model (see Figure 13) which allows for super-compensation of strength (i.e. elevated ability) by avoiding excessive stress on the recovery system.

Figure 13 - Load selection and outcome over a 3 week cycle using a progressive effort each week (based on a 6 RM of 100 kgs, and assuming increases in this RM weekly or per micro-cycle).

	Week Micro-cycle No.		
	1	2	3
Plan	95 kg @ 6	100 kg @ 6	105 kg @ 6
% of starting RM	*95 %*	*100 %*	*105 %*
Probable Outcome	95 kg @ 6	100 kg @ 6	105 kg @ 6

In brief, I suggest that the first week of any new training cycle be treated as an 'exposure week', not a maximum effort week. What is often overlooked is the adaptation that results simply from the exposure - **not only is a maximum effort unnecessary, it may also be counterproductive!** Additionally, this sub-maximal approach in the first week allows for greater focus on technique. The aim of the second week is to work to the current limit, and the aim of the third week may be to create new levels of strength (see Figure 14). This progressive intensity approach can be modified to suit a training block of various weeks (e.g. 2, 4 or more weeks etc.).

Figure 14 - Key concepts and aims of progressive application of intensity within a cycle.

Week or Micro-cycle Number	Key Concepts and Aims
1	• sub-maximal load • definitely no missed reps • focus on and exaggerate technique • get technique feedback if available (from spotter, instructor or coach); make sure you get it in this week
2	• work to prior maximum levels as estimated at the commencement of the cycle • use a spotter where necessary but preferably no missed reps • maintain technique from previous week
3	• work to supra-maximal levels • the start-cycle maximum may now be higher, in which case you are really only working to your new maximum levels • some missed reps may occur (but don't aim for them), or you may use overload methods - so use spotters • minimize technique breakdown

Another method of cycling intensity is to alter speed of movement from week to week (see Figure 15). I believe this is only suited for advanced strength athletes or those solely pursuing hypertrophy i.e. that are not wanting to build strength in any specific exercise. This method involves the manipulation of at least two major variables from week to week - load and speed of movement. I believe that this interferes with continuity or building on previous work. In addition it become a challenge to determine the cause effect relationship as you are moving two variables—load and speed. For those wishing to accurately monitor strength change in specific exercises I would discourage this method.

Figure 15 - The manipulation of speed of movement to shift intensity levels from week to week (or micro-cycle to micro-cycle).

Week/Micro-cycle No.	Average Speed of Movement	Guideline Intensities (based on %MVC)
1	421	80 - 90 %
2	311	85 - 95 %
3	201	90 - 100 %

NB The average speed of movement and guideline intensities are examples only.

What about forced and assisted reps to increase intensity? : These are methods that present a stimulus that is either greater than a 1RM (e.g. eccentric overload) or greater in effort than a maximum voluntary contraction involves (e.g. assisted reps). You can call them 'supra-maximal' efforts. They are in themselves effective, but how often should they be used? If you use them for more than 2 weeks consecutively and you progress, great. Perhaps you have superior recovery ability. I suggest that they present fatigue levels that are excessive, and therefore if your recovery ability is anything less than superior, they are only effective if used sparingly e.g. 1-2 sets per week per exercise, for no more than 2 weeks consecutively. In total, I see their role in perspective of less than 10 % of your total training program. However, generally speaking, the more advanced you become, the more you may need to use these methods.

In total, I see their role (forced and assisted reps) in perspective of less than 10 % of your total training program.

In the above example I use a three week cycle, which will be the cycle that most of you will probably be using. And if you aren't, just adjust the above example to suit the number of weeks in your cycle. If your training cycle is longer, use smaller increments of intensity progression, so that the first

Get Buffed!™

and last week emphasis is the same. And if you use a shorter number of weeks in your cycle (e.g. 2 wks), condense the progressions.

Note that whilst I chose to control the use of intensity, I believe intensity to be more important than volume in strength training. In fact, in any athletic endeavor where neural adaptations dominate (e.g. speed training, power sports) , I will prioritize intensity over volume.

I believe intensity to be more important than volume in strength training.

As I have stressed throughout - don't focus on how hard you can train - rather focus on how hard you should train so that, **when combined with the amount of time and type of recovery you have available before repeating the same workout,** will give you the best result. And don't blindly assume you should train as hard as you 'imagine' others do!

Rather focus on how hard you should train so that, when combined with the amount of time and type of recovery you have available before repeating the same workout, will give you the best result.

Chapter 6
How long should I train for?

Optimal training durations

You've read the muscle magazines. Some of those workouts take about 2 hours. That's great, because the more time you spend in the gym the better. Or is it?

I define the workout duration as the time in minutes between the start of the warm up sets for the first exercise and the end of the last work set of the last exercise. I do not include the warm up or stretching or the control drills in the workout time. Is duration of workout the same as the number of sets in a workout? Not really. If you know the number of sets, number of reps, speed of each rep, duration of rest periods between sets, and number of exercises, you can work out duration of workout. Of course this is assuming no social interaction is added to the duration!

I am a big believer in short workouts. By this I mean workouts of an hour or less duration.

I am a big believer in short workouts. By this I mean workouts of an hour or less duration. Why? To get an insight into my beliefs on duration of workout, consider the following.

The **main factors that influence or are influenced by the duration of the workout** include :

1. Metabolic/neural stores : there is only limited amount of resting stores of ATP-CP and neuro-transmitters. Whilst not being able to precisely say how long they will last, one indicator of diminishment of these stores may be a decrement in strength. Training beyond this point may result in a further shift from neural adaptations to metabolic adaptations. In brief, if you want to exploit the neural components of strength training adaptations, stop at or before this point of depletion. If you wish to extend into strength endurance, go just beyond this point. If you wish to extend into total body endurance, keep going even further. I recommend using strength training only for the first option – stopping before the decrement.

2. Hormonal response : there is a lot of discussion in certain literature about the elevation of androgen levels during the early stages of training, and the lowering of them at a certain point. Testosterone levels are linked to androgen levels, and cortisol levels act inversely to testosterone levels. Cortisol is considered a catabolic agent. The time frame that it is believed that testosterone may lower and cortisol rise is between the forty and sixty (40-60) minute mark. In brief, if you wish to avoid / minimize catabolism (muscle breakdown), don't train beyond 40-60 minutes.

3. Multiple day training : refers to the training system of training more than once in a day. This system may have been influenced by the concerns that arise out of the understanding of the hormone response to training duration. It is believed that the hormone balance is restored within a few hours of training. The Bulgarian weightlifting team (amongst others) reportedly exploited this training method during the 1980's e.g. they allegedly trained for 20-40 minutes, 2-4 times a day. I am still not convinced that the average recreational bodybuilder relying on his natural hormone system will find this method any more effective than smart single day training.

4. Training adaptations : short training sessions may be more effective for neural adaptations (e.g. 20-40 minutes). Longer training sessions may be more suited to metabolic adaptations (e.g. 40-60 minutes).

I am still not convinced that the average recreational bodybuilder relying on his natural hormone system will find this (multiple day training) method any more effective than smart single day training.

Figure 16 - The relationship between duration and training adaptation.

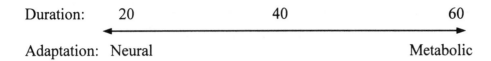

Duration: 20   40   60

Adaptation: Neural   Metabolic

So what duration is best? : I suggest strength training sessions that last somewhere between 20 and 60 minutes. Theoretically, the desired training effect (i.e. neural vs. metabolic) would have the greatest bearing on which end of this time frame range to train. However I suspect that other variables play a bigger role - perhaps non more so than recovery ability. In other words, if a person chasing metabolic adaptations has poor recovery (e.g. work related stress), I would still train them between 20-40 minutes.

When I talk about metabolic adaptations I am talking about changes in structure e.g. increase size in muscle fiber and other connective tissues, increased substrate stores giving a 'fuller' look, increased size and function of blood vessels etc. Metabolic training is another way of saying size training. When I talk about neural adaptations I am referring to increase function e.g. increased ability to recruit muscle fibers, increased co-ordination between different muscles etc. Neural training is another way of saying strength training.

Are there any times when training duration may vary? : Periodization of duration, as with all strength training variables, is definitely an option. It provides another way of experiencing varying training effects. With the inverse relationship between volume and intensity, longer workouts may provide more metabolic adaptations, shorter workouts more neural adaptations. The following figures give examples of periodization of duration.

I suggest strength training sessions that last somewhere between 20 and 60 minutes.

*Figure 17 - An example of **linear periodization of duration.***

Wk No.	Duration of Each Workout
1-3	60 minutes
4-6	50 minutes
7-9	40 minutes
10-12	30 minutes

*Figure 18 - An example of **alternating periodization of duration**.*

Wk No.	Duration of Each Workout
1-3	60 minutes
4-6	40 minutes
7-9	50 minutes
10-12	30 minutes

How can I measure or anticipate the duration of a workout when I am assessing the training program? : In advance, you can calculate the estimated duration of the planned workout by using the following method. In reality, most over-training (from a time and volume perspective) commences at the time the program is written. It is easy for the person designing the program to get carried away - add this exercise, do this number of sets etc. - oblivious to the impact of total duration.

In reality, most over-training (from a time and volume perspective) commences at the time the program is written.

Figure 19 - Steps to calculating total workout duration.

Step No	Step	Example	Calculation
1	Determine average number of reps per set	6	6 reps
2	Determine average speed of movement per rep	311	3+1+1=5
	Total time per set (TUT)		**30 secs**
3	Determine rest period duration per set	1 minutes 30 seconds	**1 min 30 sec**
	Total time per set		**2 minutes**
4	Determine total number of sets per workout	20 sets	
	Total Workout Duration		20 sets x 2 minutes = **40 minutes**

Chapter 7

How many sets should I do in the workout?

More is not always better

Counting the number of sets is a very valuable way to ensure that you are not over-training. Or at least it is in my opinion. But you don't see too many other people writing or talking about it. In fact, you will have to look hard to find written reference to this topic. Most focus on the number of sets per exercise or the reps or similar.

I have very firm beliefs on this topic. Volume and intensity are inversely related. When one is up, the other is forced down. You cannot do a high volume workout (i.e. a high number of sets) and have as high an intensity as you would have with a lower number of sets. Many kid themselves on this, but you cannot avoid reality.

I have very firm beliefs on this topic. Volume and intensity are inversely related. When one is up, the other is forced down.

Is one better than the other? High volume (high set numbers) training has specific training effect that are beneficial (including an association with muscle hypertrophy); lower volume (low number of sets) training also has specific training effects that are beneficial (including an association with neuro-muscular strength gains).

But let me share something with you that few have picked up

on. The belief that high volume (high number of sets) is more effective for hypertrophy than low volume (low number of sets) is based primarily on :

1. the observation of typical bodybuilding training
2. muscle biopsy of advanced bodybuilders

Remember what I have stressed - don't expect the methods of others to work unless you are adopting their entire approach. I have no doubt that anabolic steroids have been involved in influencing this ability to gain muscle mass from high volume training in most cases. So if you are using these drugs, sure, the volume may work. If you aren't, I strongly suggest you forget the dominant beliefs and use a much lower training volume - even if your primary goal is hypertrophy!

So what are my preferred number of sets per workout? Check out Figure 20.

Figure 20 - Guidelines for optimal number of sets per training session for each generalized training method.

Training Method	Range of Optimal Number of Sets*	Rationale
Stability/control & General Fitness	20-30	can do more sets because intensity will be low and rest periods short
General Strength & Hypertrophy	15-25	increasing intensity requires lowered volume
Maximal Strength	5-15	even higher levels of intensity require further reduction in volume
Explosive Power	5-15	similar levels of intensity to above, so similar volume
Quickness / Stretch-shortening Cycle	5-20	the range of intensity may be broader, requiring a broader range of volume

* these are guidelines for non-ergogenic drug situations. They have been developed over years of training the 'clean' athlete.

So how can you work out which number of sets is best for your training? Try this step-by-step method (see Figure 21).

Get Buffed!™

Figure 21 - Steps to determining optimal number of sets.

1. Determine **duration** of training session.
2. Determine what **number of total sets** for the training session may be optimal.
3. Determine **training method**, which will dictate the length of the **rest periods**.
4. Determine how many/which **muscle groups** to be trained.
5. Determine how many **sets per muscle group** you wish to do.
6. Determine how many **exercises per muscle group** you wish to do.
7. Determine how many **sets per exercise** you wish to do.

1. Determine duration of training session : work out how long you want to train - the total number of sets per training session is influenced by total duration desired and rest periods to be used. The duration in minutes of a training session will be a product of number of sets and rest periods used between sets.

2. Determine what number of total sets for the training session may be optimal : I believe the most important component of this equation is the 'bigger picture'. That is, decide how many total sets per workout you deem to be optimal, before considering how many sets per exercise. Figures 20 and 21 provide my guidelines on determining optimal number of sets.

I believe the most important component of this equation is the 'bigger picture'. That is, decide how many total sets per workout you deem to be optimal.

3. Determine training method, which will dictate the length of the rest periods : determining the desired training method will assist in selecting what duration rest periods are likely to be employed e.g. neural training will require longer rest periods, metabolic shorter rest periods. Refer to Chapter 17 to learn about which training method to use, and Chapter 13 to learn more about the relationship between rest periods and training methods.

4. Determine how many/which muscle groups to be trained : this will determine how you distribute your effort. For example, if you have decided to perform twenty to twenty-five (20-25) sets, and you have now chosen to do four (4) muscle groups, you know you have to divide your energies into four directions. The question of how many muscle groups to do in a workout is further discussed in Chapter 8.

5. Determine how many sets per muscle group you wish to do : this will be influenced by what percentage of effort you wish to allocate to that muscle group. For example, (following on from the above example) if you had decided to perform twenty to twenty-five (20-25) sets, and you knew you had four (4) muscle groups to address, and you decided to give equal attention to each muscle group - you would know to do about five to six (5-6) sets per muscle group.

6. Determine how many exercises per muscle group you wish to do: the number of sets per exercise per muscle group is now determined. Continuing on with the above example, you find you could do about five to six (5-6) sets per each of the four muscle groups to be trained. Note that there should be an inverse relationship between the number of exercises and the number of sets. The more exercises you chose to do, the less number of sets per exercise you should do, and vice versa. This is further discussed in Chapter 9.

If you are doing 2's you are obviously chasing intensity - don't fully negate it by maintaining a high volume.

7. Determine how many sets per exercise you wish to do: If you are specializing in the maximal strength of a particular exercise, you will benefit from doing a higher number of sets at that exercise. If you are simply attempting to create muscle breakdown as you may in hypertrophy training, the number of exercises may be more important than the number of sets per exercise. Therefore you may find yourself doing a higher number of different exercises with a lower number of sets per exercise. This is further discussed in Chapter 10.

What other factors influence the optimal number of sets? The following factors give you a greater insight into the issue of optimal number of sets.

1. The inverse relationship between reps and sets : as the reps decrease, you may benefit from doing more sets (to achieve adequate volume). For example, 2 sets of 10 reps = 20 reps and 2 sets of 2 reps = 4 reps - a significant volume difference. Some would suggest that you need to raise the volume of the 2's workout to 10 sets of 2 reps, to create equal volume as earlier. Whilst this may appear wise on paper, is there really any need to maintain the higher volume? I suggest not, in fact I suggest in doing so you will compromise the intensity based on the inverse relationship between volume and intensity. If you are doing 2's you are obviously chasing intensity - don't fully negate it by maintaining a high volume. I would suggest that half the volume would be adequate e.g. no more than 5 sets of 2 reps, in this example.

2. The influence of training age on number of sets : a beginner is not likely to need any more than one to two sets per exercise to gain a training effect. It could be argued that the more advanced a trainee becomes, the more sets required. I believe this is true up to a point. There is a point in time where further increases in volume (no. of sets) will not benefit, and the search for further training effects is limited to increases in intensity.

3. The influence of the size of the muscle : there is an argument that a smaller muscle group recovers more quickly than larger ones, and can therefore be subject to more sets than the larger muscle groups. This rationale suggests that exercises for the upper arm can be performed in a greater number of sets than exercises for the upper legs. The question remains - whilst they may be capable of this, does this mean that the higher volume for smaller muscle groups is superior? There may be other factors that contribute to the answer e.g. all the above in this section. Therefore don't blindly follow this guideline at the expense of ignoring the other issues discussed e.g. why do more sets of arms if your arm response to lower volume training is excellent? (this is more likely to apply to a beginner).

There is a point in time where further increases in volume will not benefit.

4. Number of sets is a recovery dependant : Ultimately one of the greatest effects on number of sets is recovery ability. Only do large numbers of sets if a) you can recover from them and b) you are convinced that this approach is superior to lower volume training.

5. Recovery capacity influences the end of the range of optimal number of sets : if you identify that the trainee has a superior recovery capacity, use the upper end of the range of the number of sets recommended in Figure 20. If you determine that they have less effective recovery ability, use the lower end of the range. Factors that contribute to recovery ability include genetics, age, maturation, sex, training condition, occupation, stress levels, nutrition, nutritional supplements, ergogenic aids, lifestyle, other recovery methods, etc.

6.   The intended adaptation influences which end of the range of optimal number of sets to use : if the trainee is primarily pursing intensity (neural) adaptations within any given training method or rep range, use the lower end of the range of number of sets. If the trainee is primarily pursuing volume (metabolic) adaptations, use the upper end of the range of recommended optimal number of sets. For example, a bodybuilder using 8-12 reps but more interested in volume may use 15-25 sets per workout, whereas a bodybuilder using 8-12 reps but who believes his/her best adaptations occur when more weight is able to be used (greater intensity) would lean towards using 10-15 sets (as per the ranges provided in Figure 20).

If you see someone in the gym doing set after set after set and they are growing from week to week, it is probably more a reflection of their drug program than their training program.

7. Number of sets in strength training has been influenced by anabolic steroids : I firmly believe that strength training program design has been historically influenced by anabolic steroids. If you accept the influence that bodybuilding, weightlifting and powerlifting have had on program design, and you understand the role drugs play in these sports, you may gain a fuller appreciation of this influence. In brief if you take drugs you can handle higher volumes (higher number of sets). If you see someone in the gym doing set after set after set and they are growing from week to week, it is probably more a reflection of their drug program than their training program.

8.   Number of sets in strength training has been influenced by hype : there are many interesting stories told of how bodybuilding editors have paid elite bodybuilders to allow the editor to write and publish a story about their training - that in reality is far from accurate, usually exaggerated. Do not blindly accept what you read in a bodybuilding magazine!

9.   Do no more sets than you know to be absolutely necessary : why do three sets per exercise? I will tell you why - because in the 1960's a sport scientist did a study and found that number of sets to be effective in his study - and you are still copying that influence! Do only one set - if and only after you find it is either ineffective or loses its effectiveness (most programs lose their effectiveness after 2-3 weeks) change, with a consideration to increasing the number of sets.

10. If in doubt - do less : if you are unsure how many sets is optimal - do less. You are more likely to obtain a training effect by finding out how little you need to do to benefit than finding out how much you can tolerate without benefiting.

11. Capable versus optimal : most people in strength training perform a number of sets that they have the energy to do. This is endurance training, not strength training. Strength training effectiveness is not judged by what you did (i.e. how many sets you did), but rather how much change occurred as a result (i.e. size or strength). This training effect is a combination of the workout plus the rest / recovery until the next workout. You will not know what is optimal during the session unless you have indicators based on prior experience. Don't work to metabolic signals such as total fatigue. And only use past indicators for number of sets if they have been effective. The day you realize they don't work - change the indicator - I suggest to lower volume until further indicators suggest otherwise.

Most people in strength training perform a number of sets that they have the energy to do. This is endurance training, not strength training.

12. Don't count warm up sets in total number of sets : do not count warm up sets in total volume. Other exercises of similarly low intensity e.g. maintenance stabilizer drills need not be counted also. To count them would be misleading.

13. There is no one correct protocol for number of sets : the 'heavy-duty one set to failure' (influenced by people such as the late Mike Mentzler) sub-culture will tell you that this is the only way to go, and the multiple set sub-culture will tell you that one set is inadequate to fatigue all motor units; the reality is simple - both methods have their advantages and disadvantages and both should be used. Again it is simply a question of how much time spent in each. The effects of varying from one method to another in itself usually guarantees a further training effect.

14. Periodize number of sets : number of sets, as with any training variable, can and should be periodized. This is more applicable as the trainee becomes more advanced. An example of periodization of number of sets is shown in Figure 23. Not only should the total number of sets per workout be periodized. The number of sets per exercise should also be periodized, to ensure the benefits and negate the disadvantages of both methods (i.e. high and low number of sets per exercise). This technique is also reflected in Figure 23.

Figure 22 - Factors that contribute to recovery ability and will therefore influence the number of sets you select per workout.

Factor	Interpretation
Genetics	Some people are born with greater capacity to recover. This will become evident from their previous training history e.g. check their training diaries.
Age	Whilst very young people (e.g. <12 yrs) will not be able to tolerate high work loads, those between 12-22 yrs may actually have greater recovery capacity than those older than 22 yrs. The message here is - take into account the reduced work capacity of the older trainee (due to reduced hormone levels such as growth hormone).
Maturation and Aging	Rate of human development and rate of aging have variance. A young person (e.g. a teenager) may be more or less advanced for his/her age. Conversely, a person in their 40's may show less effects of aging than others.
Sex	Comparisons between males and females have shown typically lower muscle masses in upper body for females. Other factors to be mindful are culture influenced training background, and typically lower testosterone levels in females. Women have been found to be able to do a greater no. of reps at a given %age of their RM than men, and therefore may benefit from doing less sets than the male at any given intensity (due to the inverse relationship between volume and intensity).
Training Condition	Those who present in 'better shape' may have greater recovery capacity than say a person who has been physically inactive for an extended period of time.
Occupation	If a person is in a manual occupation, whilst perhaps in 'better shape' than others, may not have the same recovery capacity as a white collar worker; a shift worker may not have the same recovery capacity as a day time worker because of the negative effect on sleep.
Stress levels	Stress in life can come from many directions. It may be family or work induced, caused by excessive travel to work, financial etc. Persons with greater non-physical stress levels may have lower capacity to recovery from physical training.
Nutrition	Nutritional habits will have a large bearing on recovery ability. Don't expect as much recovery ability from someone with poorer eating habits.
Nutritional supplements	Nutritional supplements, when used correctly, can have a powerful positive effect on recovery.
Ergogenic aids	If the trainee is using ergogenic aids (read drugs), expect an enhanced recovery capacity.
Lifestyle	Factors in lifestyle influence recovery capacity e.g. if the person is in the surfing sub-culture, frequent surfing may reduce recovery capacity from in particular upper body strength training; someone in the night-club sub-culture may have negative effects on recovery from the sleep habits used.
Other recovery methods	If other recovery methods are being used e.g. massage, relaxation techniques etc., expect recovery capacity to be enhanced.

Figure 23 - Periodization of number of sets per workout - using the alternating periodization method as an example applicable to the more advanced trainee.

Week No.s	No. of Sets Per Workout	Number of Exercises Per Workout	Number of Sets Per Exercise
1-2	20	10	2
3-4	12	3	4
5-6	16	5	3
7-8	10	2	5

Chapter 8

How many muscle groups should I do in the workout?

Splitting the body parts up

How many muscle groups are there? We can keep it simple and list 12 major muscle groups.

Figure 24 - A list of major muscle groups.

---

horizontal pulling (i.e. scapula retractors e.g. rows)
horizontal pushing (i.e. horizontal flexion e.g. bench press)
vertical pulling (i.e. scapula depressors e.g. chin ups)
vertical pushing (i.e. arm abduction e.g. shoulder press)
upper arm (bicep / tricep)
lower arm (forearm flexors and extensors)
neck (e.g. upper traps)
lower back
abdominals
hip dominant (e.g. deadlift and its variations)
quad dominant (e.g. squats and its variations)
lower legs (e.g. front and back of calves)

NB there is no order of priority in the above

The answer to the question of 'how many muscle groups should I do in the workout?' is relatively simple. Here are some of the issues involved :

1. generality vs. specificity : broadly speaking, it is a trade-off between generality and specificity. If you want to specialize in any muscle groups, you will probably not get them all done in one session. If you want a general training effect, you could probably do them all in one.

2. number of sessions per week : if you want to train more than three times a week, you had best split the muscle groups up i.e. create a split routine. Otherwise they may not recover in time. Conversely, if you only have time or interest to train once or twice, you may want to do them all in the one workout. But just because you may use the same muscle groups more than once in the week in a 2 or 3 workouts/week program, doesn't mean you don't have to use the same exercises each time! Unless you were needing to develop the skill of any given exercise (e.g. a clean for an Olympic lifter) I strongly recommend not using exactly the same exercise more than once in a week. This means when training the same muscle group twice or more in the week, look for variations of these exercises (see Fig. 25).

3. an AB split : an AB split means dividing the body into two, and performing half of the muscle groups of the body in each session. There are a number of variations of an AB split, and some of these are shown in Figures 26–28.

4. an ABC split : an ABC split means either dividing the body into three, or creating three different workouts using the same muscle groups. Refer to Figures 29-30 for an example of the first option. As far as splitting the body into three, this can be all the workouts for the week, or this ABC cycle can be repeated again (i.e. 6 sessions/wk). I don't find much use for the latter option (see Fig. 31).

5. an ABCD split : an ABCD split means creating four different workouts or dividing the body into four. Refer to Figures 32 and 33 for an example of the latter. This example involves training each muscle group only once directly each week. This is one of my favorite four day splits.

If you want to train more than three times a week, you had best split the muscle groups up i.e. create a split routine.

Get Buffed!™

Figure 25 - An example of the same muscle groups being used three times in one week, with different exercises.

Major Muscle Groups	A Day e.g. Monday	B Day e.g. Wednesday	C Day e.g. Friday
horizontal pulling (i.e. scapula retractors e.g. rows)	Seated row	DB row	Bent-over row
horizontal pushing (i.e. horizontal flexion e.g. bench press)	Bench press	Decline DB press	Incline DB Press
vertical pulling (i.e. scapula depressors e.g. chin ups)	Chin up	DB pullover	Lat pull-down
vertical pushing (i.e. arm abduction e.g. shoulder press)	Shoulder press	Lat DB raise	Upright row
upper arm (bicep / tricep)	Bar bicep curl	Tricep press-down	Incline DB curl
lower arm (forearm flexors and extensors)	Forearm extensors -bar	Forearm flexors -bar	Forearm extensors-DB
hip dominant (e.g. deadlift and its variations)	Leg abduction	Deadlift	Leg adduction
quad dominant (e.g. squats and its variations)	Squats	Leg curls/extensions	Lunges
lower back	Back extension	Hip/thigh extensions	Good morning
lower legs (e.g. front and back of calves)	Standing calf press	Toe ups	Seated calf press
abdominals	Knee ups	Curl ups + twists	Curl ups
neck (e.g. upper traps)	Bar shrugs-front	DB shrugs	Bar shrugs-back

NB to keep volume down, which is a challenge in a total body workout, I have used only one upper arm and one lower arm exercise per session. Note however that when the forearm flexors are involved in the upper arm workouts (i.e. bicep curls), the forearm extensors are trained and vice versa.

Figure 26 - An example of a AB split with a total frequency of 2/wk. Half the body is trained in each workout, and therefore each muscle group is only trained once per week. This is a effective low volume method for 'hard gainer's or an appropriate maintenance program for a more advanced trainee.

Sun	Mon	Tue	Wed	Thu	Fri	Sat
	A			B		

Figure 27 - An example of a AB split with a total frequency of 3/wk. In one week, half the muscle get trained twice and the other half once per week. In the next week, this is reversed. This is also an effective low volume method for 'hard gainer's or an appropriate maintenance program for a more advanced trainee.

Wk No	Sun	Mon	Tue	Wed	Thu	Fri	Sat
1		A		B		A	
2		B		A		B	

Figure 28 - An example of a AB split with a total frequency of 4/wk. The second A and B in the week are repeats of the first A and B workouts. Therefore each muscle group is trained twice per week every week. This method is suitable for the early split routines of a relative beginner, but I do not recommend it for a more advanced trainer. It presents too frequent exposure to the same muscle groups and exercises.

Wk No	Sun	Mon	Tue	Wed	Thu	Fri	Sat
		A	B		A	B	

NB. As a progression from the above, different exercises and/or intensities could be used in the second A's and B's of the week. e.g. the heavy/light method. I would prefer the different exercise approach.

*Figure 29 - An example of an ABC split with a total frequency of 3/
wk. This would mean each muscle group is only trained once a week,
and that only 1/3 of the body is trained each workout. This is probably one of my favorite options for those training 3/wk.*

Wk No	Sun	Mon	Tue	Wed	Thu	Fri	Sat
		A		B		C	

*Figure 30 - An example of muscle group allocation in the above 3/wk
split, no repeating the same muscle group in the one week.*

A Day e.g. Monday	B Day e.g. Wednesday	C Day e.g. Friday
Hip dominant (deadlifts)	Lower back (back extensions)	Quad dominant (squats)
Horizontal pull (row)	Bicep (curl)	Vertical push (shoulder press)
Horizontal push (bench)	Tricep (extension)	Vertical pull (chin)
Forearm (flexion)	Neck (shrugs)	Forearm (extension)
Gastrocnemius (stand calf press)	Tibialis Anterior (toes ups)	Soleus (seated calf press)
Lower Abdominal (knee ups)	Oblique Abdominal (Russian twists)	Upper Abdominal (sit ups)

*Figure 31 - An example of an ABC split with a total frequency of 6/
wk. This would mean each muscle group is trained twice a week.
Despite it's popularity in bodybuilding, this is not a method I am
fond of. You would need a superior 'recovery' system to benefit from
it.*

Wk No	Sun	Mon	Tue	Wed	Thu	Fri	Sat
		A	B	C	A	B	C

Figure 32 - An example of an ABCD split with a total frequency of 4/wk. This could mean each muscle group is only trained once a week, and that only 1/4 of the body is trained each workout. This is one of my favorite options for those training 4/wk.

Wk No	Sun	Mon	Tue	Wed	Thu	Fri	Sat
		A	B		C	D	

Figure 33 - An example of muscle group allocation in the above 4/wk ABCD split, with no repeating the same muscle group in the one week.

A Day e.g. Monday	B Day e.g. Tuesday	C Day e.g. Thursday	D Day e.g. Friday
Quad Dominant	Horizontal Push	Hip Dominant	Vertical Push
Lower back	Horizontal Pull	Upper traps	Vertical Pull
Calf-seated	Triceps	Calf - standing	Biceps
Abdominal	F/arm flexion	Abdominal	F/arm extension

Get Buffed!™

Chapter 9

How many exercises should I do per muscle group?

Specializing or spreading the effect.

This question cannot be answered in isolation. For example, you may have a predetermined opinion that says four exercises per muscle group are required. But you may not have taken into account (in this example) that you have six muscle groups. Which would mean a twenty-four (24) exercise workout, which in my opinion would be a ridiculous volume.

So, firstly determine how many total sets in the workout you want to do. Then determine how many muscle groups you have to do. Then work with this figure.

In the below example we have four sets per muscle group. Now we decide - how many exercises per muscle group. The trade-off goes like this : if you want to specialize in an exercise, you need to do more sets of less exercises e.g. if you are at a point in the program where you were peaking on your bench press - you would probably take all four sets for this one exercise. On the other hand, if you wanted to gain a variety effect -

overload the muscle from different angles - as you would do in the early stages of a program or during a hypertrophy phase - you would do as many as 4 exercises for that muscle group, using 1 set per exercise.

Figure 34 - An example of determining how many sets available for each muscle group.

Total number of sets permissible	16 sets
Total number of muscle groups to be worked in that session	4
Number of sets available to each muscle group *	4

* assuming the sets are to be spread evenly amongst each muscle group - which is not necessarily the case

Chapter 10

How many sets should I do per exercise?

An inverse relationship with the number of exercises

There should be an inverse relationship between the number of exercises and the number of sets. The more exercises you want to do, the less the number of sets per exercise you can afford to do. If you are specializing in the maximal strength of a particular exercise, you may benefit from doing higher a number of sets at that exercise. If you are simply attempting to create muscle breakdown as you may in hypertrophy training, you may benefit from doing a higher number of different exercises, with a lower number of sets per exercise.

The more exercises you want to do, the less the number of sets per exercise you can afford to do.

Figure 35 - The inverse relationship between number of exercises and number of sets and the rationale. In this example there are only six (6) sets available for the particular muscle group.

No. of Exercise/ Muscle Group	No. of Sets per Exercise	Rationale
6	1	Allows for the greatest variety in overloading various lines of movement and joint angles, but does not specialize in the skill of any one exercise.
3	2	Is a balance of the above and below - provides a mixture of variety in lines / joint angles and specialization.
1	6	Provides for the greatest skill development/ specialization in one exercise, but provides no variety in exercise line or joint angle overload.

Note :There are variations on the above available. For example, you may use 4 sets on one exercise and 2 sets on a second. This would provide specialization on the first exercise and variety in line/angle in the second exercise.

If you hold the total number of sets per workout as a constant or fixed number, the more exercises you select, the lower number of sets per exercise you will be able to do.

Figure 36 - An example of the inverse relationship between number of exercises and number of sets per exercise, where the total number of sets for the training session ranges from 18-24.

No of Exercises	Total Number of Sets Per Exercise Possible	Most Suited Training Methods *
1	10-20	Maximal Strength
2	5-10	Explosive Power
3	4-8	Quickness/SSC
4	3-6	
5	2-4	General Strength
6	2-4	&
7	1-3	Hypertrophy
8	1-3	Stability / Control
9-12	1-2	& General
13-20	1	Fitness

* this is a generalization only - don't be afraid to work outside these boundaries

There is an incredible trend in strength training to do three sets of every exercises. Why is this?

There is an incredible trend in strength training to do three sets of every exercises. More specifically, three (or more) sets at the same weight on the same exercise -most commonly, 3 sets of 10! Why is this? I've asked myself that question many times, and the only answer I come up with is the power of tradition. You see, these magic numbers were 'validated' way back in the late '40's and early '50's by an American army surgeon by the name of De Lorme when he presented research evidence supporting the use of three sets of ten reps. All credit to the contribution De Lorme made to the science of training, but that was fifty years ago. Yet what do you see almost every time you look at a training program? 3 x 10 (or 15 or 12 or 8, or 6 etc.) ! What do you see every time you browse (I say browse, because invariably there's nothing that warrants reading) through a mainstream bodybuilding magazine? 3 x 10!

Get Buffed!™

Subsequent research data from American sports scientists and strength training habits of those with influence further burnt this standard set mentality into the psyche of American (read the rest of the world, such is the influence of American culture) strength training.

Do I believe the use of 'standard sets' is warranted? On occasion, yes, including the following :

- when the athlete/trainee requires sub-maximal intensity for rehearsal (this is not uncommon in the strength sports of weightlifting and powerlifting);
- where volume is required, and the quality of this volume is less relevant.

To understand why I am critical of standards sets (i.e. three or more sets of the same reps and load), lets take a street-language look at the 'anatomy of the multiple sets workout'.

The first work set

The primary effect of the first work set is shock. The body, subject to the laws of homeostasis and innate protective mechanisms, rarely functions optimally during the first work set. Psychologically you may be shocked by the apparent 'heaviness' of the load. The exposure to this load is to some extent unfamiliar (depending of course on how long since this load was last applied). You may struggle a bit on this set. You may even panic and question your current strength levels. Don't panic. The first set is really a 'settler'. The message is that this first set may not be the appropriate time to attempt to achieve your highest load of the workout. Sure you are at your freshest - but neurally you are not at your most efficient.

The primary effect of the first work set is shock. The body, subject to the laws of homeostasis and innate protective mechanisms, rarely functions optimally during the first work set.

This point should not be ignored. A second message that we can take from the analysis of the first set is don't go too close to fatigue in the first set - any residual fatigue may negate the neural benefits from the first set that augment the next set.

The second work set

This set is potentially the 'best' set. The second work set benefits from the first work set - in what can be described as
'neural arousal', or greater neuro-muscular innervation. Provided the rest periods between sets has been adequate
(relative to your training goal), your nervous system is 'woken
up' by the exposure to load in the first. The neural inhibition
level (the loading level at which the body automatically shuts
down to prevent injury) is raised. Psychologically, you have
benefited from the exposure to the load of the first set - now
you are ready, anticipating the load. There will be no surprises. Because of the shock the first set presented, you may
be more emotionally/psychologically aroused. This second
set, I find in most cases, is potentially your best set. If it isn't
you either went too heavy in the first set, or didn't rest long
enough, or are suffering from over-training.

*I am not talking
about whether it
is possible, I am
q u e s t i o n i n g
whether it is the
most efficient!*

The third and subsequent work sets

How you respond to the third and subsequent work sets may
be influenced by many factors including

- your entry level recovery (as reflected by your resting
  stores of metabolic and neural substrates);
- your level of specific conditioning (ability to tolerate this
  volume);
- nutritional/ergogenic effects on your rate of substrate/
  neural chemical replacement; and
- how close to maximum effort and fatigue you went on
  the prior two work sets.

These factors aside, I believe that in most cases, the application of a third or more work set of the same load are affected
by residual fatigue. And therefore they are perhaps not the
most efficient method of overload.

In a nut-shell, if you are lifting the same load for say three sets
of ten, it is unlikely it was your maximum in set one. In fact, if
you are able to complete three sets of ten at the same load,
even if you reach exhaustion on the tenth rep of the third set,
it is unlikely that even the second set was at or near your

Get Buffed!™

maximum. Probably the only time you are at your maximum is on the third set - and even then that maximum may be more of a metabolic maximum than a neural maximum.

I know that this is contentious. I realize that one of the most influential text books in American strength and conditioning states that *"...sets at the same 10-RM load can be repeated using the same resistance...."*. Let me clarify this - I am not talking about whether it is possible, I am questioning whether it is the optimal! In my opinion, it is difficult to do more than two sets at the same reps and load if the effort is maximal. In most cases of standard sets, I feel that each set is performed sub-maximally from either a load or fatigue perspective. Figure 37 illustrates my point using estimations.

Figure 37 - Percentage of maximal neural and metabolic work expressed in standard sets (percentages are only estimates or generalizations).

Loading Parameters	Set No.		
	1	2	3
Reps used	10	10	10
Load used	100 kg	100 kgs	100 kgs
%age of 10 RM neuro-muscular work capacity used in each set	80%	75%	80%
%age of 10RM metabolic work capacity used in each set	80%	90%	100%
%age of averaged work ca pacity used in each set	80%	82%	90%

Any number of work sets exceeding a total of 12 for the workout should only be contemplated by those with optimal lifestyles and recovery conditions.

A final point on why I immediately lose faith in a program upon sighting '3x' is that unless you don't plan on doing many exercises in the workout (e.g. six or less), this protocol locks you into over-training. At least over-training from my perspective. Generally speaking, any number of work sets exceeding a total of 12 for the workout (yes, that right, 12 sets for the total workout, not per muscle group!) should only be contemplated by those with optimal lifestyles and recovery conditions. If you have a day job and/or consider your recovery average, this rules you out. So when you put together your program, and you chose eight or more exercises for the workout, and combine them with the old '3x', you automatically have a number of sets equaling twenty-four (24) or more for the workout.

Chapter 11

How many reps should I do?

Benefit from a variety of reps!

There is a common belief in training literature (the scientifically influenced writings at least) that specific repetitions will give specific adaptations. This perspective of the relationship between reps and training methods is based mainly on observation and linking muscle biopsy to training method.

How accurate is this? I cannot say this any clearer - you and your response to training are the only real guides. For example, consensus suggests that optimal hypertrophy occurs when using 8-12 reps (see Figure 38). However, you may find that you get a better hypertrophy result from 4 reps than you do from 12!

I cannot say this any clearer - you and your response to training are the only real guides.

An interesting comment I will make here is that the longer one has been training for, I have observed a shift down in the optimal number of reps. Put simply, a beginner may grow on 12's, but 10 years later, find that 6's are more effective.

Generally speaking, I do believe that the repetition continuum goes from a dominant metabolic effect (increased slow twitch muscle size, substrate stores, capillaries etc.) to a dominant neural effect (increased size of fast twitch muscle fibers, ability to contract more motor units etc.). This is illustrated in Figure 39.

Reps	Dominant Training Effect	Specific Adaptations
1	N	
2	E	increased relative
3	U	strength
4	R	
5	A	
	L	
6	A MIX OF NEURAL	increases in absolute
7	AND	strength and
8	METABOLIC	hypertrophy
9		
10		optimal hypertrophy
11	M	repetitions
12	E	
	T	
13	A	
14	B	specific muscle
15	0	endurance and
16	L	some contribution
17	I	to hypertrophy
18	C	
19		
20		

Note : The above figure works on the assumption that the repetitions shown above were the limit of the number of reps possible - that is that the trainee is working to fatigue or failure at those particular reps.

The longer one has been training for, I have observed a shift down in the optimal number of reps. Put simply, a beginner may grow on 12's, but 10 years later, find that 6's are more effective.

Figure 39 - The repetition continuum versus training effect (King and Poliquin, 1991, Optimal Strength Training, unpublished).

1	3	5	7	9	11	13	15	17	19	21

100%   50%
Neural Adaptations   Metabolic Adaptations
(neuro-muscular)   (cellular)

So how do you know which reps to use? : This is what I recommend you do :

1. Start out using the reps as they appear in Figure 38 : That is, match your training goal to the generalized rep bracket. For example, if you are aiming for size only, use 8-12's. If you want strength only, use 1-5's. If you want both, use mainly 6-8's.

2. Unless you are young or inexperienced : if your body has not physically matured (e.g. <18 years of age), you may need to over-ride the above with age-related guidelines of using lighter load/higher reps as a younger person. This is influenced by training age as well, and training age also influences whether you should apply step 1. Training age means how long you have been doing a particular training, in this case strength training. Relative beginners will find higher reps more optimal irrespective of their specific training goal. So if you are a relative beginner, ignore step 1!

3. Change if you find this doesn't work : If you find the initial method ineffective, and you believe it is because of the reps you are using, look to change the reps.

4. Periodize reps : in both short-term cycles (e.g. 12 weeks) as well as longer time frames (e.g. 12 years) from higher reps to lower reps. There is a significant amount of evidence supporting the methods of progressing from metabolic (higher reps) to neural (lower reps) training in strength training. I do also support the belief in general that maximal strength is served by developing a degree of hypertrophy first. You could periodize from lower to higher reps but that's another discussion!

Periodize reps in both short-term cycles (e.g. 12 weeks) as well as longer time frames (e.g. 12 years) from higher reps to lower reps.

5. The need for variety : will also influence the use of various reps brackets. In fact, just the use of this variety in itself can present bonus strength or hypertrophy gains. For example if you have been pursuing hypertrophy, and after spending considerable time training in classic hypertrophy brackets (e.g. 8-12), you may experience further significant hypertrophy when changing to a lower rep bracket. Whilst this appears to contradict the above table, it shows that variety alone can accelerate gains. Note this can apply both ways - in strength (neural) and size (metabolic) training.

The message is clear - irrespective of the specific goal, training in too narrow a rep bracket may not be as effective as alternating or mixing the different rep brackets. The key is not which reps to use, rather how much time to spend in each different rep bracket.

I spoke earlier in the book of periodization of reps, and the two most popular methods. The following figures give specific examples of the reps in each method.

Figure 40 - Linear periodization of repetitions.

Week No.	Repetitions
1-4	10-12
5-8	8-10
9-12	6-8
13-16	4-6

Note : the early proponents of this method used four week blocks.

Figure 41 - Alternating periodization of repetitions.

Week No.	Repetitions
1-2	10-12
3-4	4-6
5-6	8-10
7-8	3-5
9-10	5-7
11-12	2-3

Note : the early proponents of this method used two week blocks.

Chapter 12

What speed of movement should I use?

Most of them!

Had I asked this question ten years ago no-one would have know what I was talking about (except the athletes I trained at that time)! There was simply no focus on speed of movement, or the term tempo which has been popularized in the US.

However it seems now that so many people are familiar with and use the number system I created in the 80's. It is also appears to me that no-one is using speed timings and the periodization of these in the manner that I had intended.

The speed of the movement determines a number of things, including the amount of tension developed, the use of mechanical energy and the load.

The speed of the movement determines a number of things, including the amount of tension developed, the use of mechanical energy (such as the stretch-shortening cycle), and the load. Put simply, the slower the movement, the lower the load but greater the muscular work. The faster the movement, the greater the load potential, but the muscle load is reduced (relatively speaking) and mechanical energy is increased. If you want to maximizes the load lifted, you use the mechanical energy to your benefit. If you want the muscles to do more of the work, you negate the mechanical energy by techniques such as slowing down the speed of movement.

The time from the start to the end of a set can be called the 'time under tension' (TUT). The speed of movement is one factor that determines the TUT (reps and range are others). The common interpretation of training effects from 'time under tension' is as follows :

Figure 42 - Common interpretation of time under tension (TUT).

TUT	Dominant Training Effect
1-20 seconds	Speed strength/maximal strength
20-40 seconds	Maximal strength/hypertrophy
40-70 seconds	Hypertrophy/muscle endurance

To communicate how fast or slow I wanted an athlete to move the load in strength training, I developed a numbering system in the 80's. I was first influenced by Arthur Jones and Ellington Darden. They were the first I had seen to attach numbers to training programs. It was my recognition of the pause between eccentric and concentric, and the impact varying this has on the training effect, that completed the picture. The primary role of controlling the pause between lifting and lowering weights is simply to negate or exploit the effects of the stretch shortening cycle (SSC).

Maybe you don't know what the stretch shortening cycle is. As an example, walking employs the stretch shortening cycle. When your foot hits the ground, the quads go through an eccentric (lengthening) cycle, an isometric cycle, and then a concentric (shortening) cycle. If the transition from eccentric to isometric to concentric is performed quickly, the resultant concentric contraction is a lot more powerful than if no prior eccentric action was performed. If the transition is long, the elastic energy is dissipated.

Another way I use to impress what impact the stretch shortening role has is to get someone to bend at the knees and hips as if they were going to jump, pause for a few seconds and then jump. Then I get them to do it again, without the pause. You would expect them to jump higher without the pause, as this allows them to use the elastic energy available .

Taking advantage of the stretch shortening cycle is a great thing if you're an athlete doing specific speed or speed-strength training. But for optimal muscle hypertrophy, taking

> *To communicate how fast or slow I wanted an athlete to move the load in strength training, I developed a numbering system in the 80's.*

Get Buffed!™

advantage of it is **not** always optimal.

Australian biomechanist Greg Wilson did some great research in the 1990s in quantifying the role of the SSC. He found that if you do a conventional bench press with an eccentric or lowering phase that was about a second, it took a full four second pause in between the eccentric and concentric to completely eliminate the stretch shortening cycle i.e. if you lower the bar and you rest it on top of your chest for a period of less than four seconds, you're still getting an added boost from all the elastic energy. The only real work you'll do is during the last third of the concentric movement! If, however, you negated all that elastic energy by taking a four-second pause, you had to work all that much harder—recruit that many more muscle fibers—to lift the bar. All things being equal, this may mean more muscle growth.

So why don't more people do it this way? Because using the elastic energy offers 'fools gold' - when you take advantage of the stretch shortening cycle, you can lift more weight. And if you focus on what load you are lifting at the expense of an awareness of what the muscles are doing - don't expect the best results in terms of muscle growth. Basically I don't want to know how much you lift – this really tells me nothing as I don't know what percentage of the lift is mechanical energy! What is more important is whether the muscle is being trained optimally in the lift! And this usually has more to do with a controlled speed than the load.

The critical issue is how you periodize the speed and which speed you spend the most time at.

So is using elastic energy bad? Of course not. I recommend using all speeds - the real issue is how you periodize the speed (I tend to go from slow to fast over time) and which speed you spend the most time at. This is critical. You need to know which speed of movement you respond best to. Which ever one you use, a little rule of thumb is this - the lowering time should be longer than the lifting time. So don't be lazy - control that lowering!

Another important point to remember is that being aware of the movement speed allows you also to control this variable. There is little value in increasing the load in a subsequent workout if you also change the speed - who knows whether you are getting stronger or working harder. You may well be just using more elastic energy!

An example of using inappropriate movement speeds was when athletes started doing weight training in the '60s and '70s, using traditional bodybuilding movements and traditional bodybuilding speeds. They typically did slow concentric movements. Unfortunately, doing a slow lift didn't always transfer over to the sports they were playing. They should have been using more explosive concentric movements.

I believe that bodybuilders also can benefit from using explosive concentric movements. If you intentionally accelerate a weight, you'll develop more functional power, and you'll also possibly recruit more muscle fibers, leading to greater hypertrophy. This is not to suggest explosive concentric movements need to dominate the bodybuilders training—just that there is a place for it.

> *Dorian Yates uses quite a controlled lifting speed. In fact he appears to be attempting to avoid acceleration. This is definitely an option.*

I have watched English bodybuilder and former Mr. Olympia Dorian Yates train on video and he uses quite a controlled lifting speed. In fact he appears to be attempting to avoid acceleration during the concentric phase. This is definitely an option, but I lean to spending more time with an explosive concentric. Maybe it is my sport involvement that influences this.

I use a three (3) number system to communicate speed of movement in strength training. More recently there have been moves by some to use four (4) numbers. I am not sure if this is borne out of need, or a desire to be able to claim the concept! Whilst you can argue the technical correctness of four numbers, from my experiences, until the basics are perfected I don't like to finesse too much! The middle number generally applies to the pause at both end of the eccentric and concentric movements. More information is not always needed—what is needed is something that works!

An example would be 3:1:1. All the numbers refer to seconds. The first number relates to the eccentric phase. The second or middle number to the pause or isometric contraction duration between the eccentric and concentric contraction. The third number refers to the concentric phase.

The fact that the first number always refers to the eccentric contraction can cause some confusion in the trainee as a percentage of strength exercises commence with the concentric contraction, especially the pulling movements such as the chin

Get Buffed!™

ups. However once they become familiar with the system it works excellently. In brief, most pushing movements commence with the eccentric contraction, and most pulling movements commence with the concentric contraction.

Another less common criticism (one I used to get more so in the early 1990s) is that it is too complex and the movements should be 'just done'. Yes, the system does need to be understood by the program writer (I suspect this to be the greatest challenge to these critics); and yes, it does need to be explained to the trainee. No, it doesn't have to be executed with perfection - it is just a guideline (so don't get out your metronome!). And finally, ignoring the varying training effects that arise from varying movement speed is like throwing out 25% of your potential strength adaptations. As you please....

Where I believe most get it wrong is this. For those concerned about power (rate of force development), I don't recommend using anything less than a fast or attempted-to-be-fast concentric contraction for some 80-90% of total training time. A lack of awareness of the 'need for speed' (attempted acceleration) in the concentric phase in the power athlete may result in an adaptation to a non-specific rate of force development. This is the same non-effective and perhaps detrimental training effect that occurred when athletes first started using strength training and using the bodybuilding methods way back decades ago – a total lack of awareness of the need for a fast/ attempted-to-be-fast concentric contraction.   Therefore the power athlete cannot afford to spend more than 10-20 % (as a generalization) of their total strength training time using numbers greater than 1 as the third number.

For those concerned about power I do not recommend using anything less than a fast or attempted-to-be-fast concentric contraction for some 80-90% of total training time.

Additionally, when the number one does appear as the third number, the power athlete must have it reinforced - this means to try and go fast! And when the asterisk (*) is used - it must look fast!

The second most common error is for the program writer to compile a sequence of numbers which, when combined with the reps written, result in a time under tension that is not specific to their intended training outcome e.g. 421 x 10 reps (=70 sec) for maximal strength!? The major groups of speed combinations I use are as follows (see Figure 43). You may note that only one out of five (or 20%) of the combinations use a deliberately slow concentric phase.

Figure 43 - The major groups of speed of movement combinations I use in my strength training program design.

Eccentric Speed/Time	**Pause** Speed/Time	**Concentric** Speed/Time
very slow and controlled	long	slow and controlled
slow controlled	medium	fast/attempt to be fast
medium controlled	short	fast/attempt to be fast
fast controlled	nil	fast/attempt to be fast
fast	nil	fast/attempt to be fast

These are some of the keys to my unique numbering system that I feel are overlooked or not understood by some who have copied it. To provide guidelines as to the training methods that these speed of movement combinations are most suited to, the following figure is provided. This figure also provides ranges of speeds that are suited.

Figure 44 - The speed of movement combinations suited to various strength training methods.

Eccentric Speed/Time (seconds)	**Pause** Speed/Time (seconds)	**Concentric** Speed/Time (seconds)	**Training Methods** Most Suited to these Speed Combinations	**Examples of SOM** Combinations
very slow and controlled	long	slow and controlled	stability/control & general fitness; metabolic-end hypertrophy	8:0:4 6:1:3 4:2:1 3:1:3
slow controlled	medium	fast/attempt to be fast	general fitness; metabolic-end hypertrophy;	3:2:1
medium controlled	short	fast/attempt to be fast	neural-end hypertrophy; metabolic-end maximal strength	3:1:1 2:1:1
fast controlled	nil	fast/attempt to be fast	neural-end maximal strength; explosive power	2:0:1 1:0:1
fast	nil	fast/attempt to be fast	explosive power; quickness/SSC	10* *0*

Finally, I want to stress this - it is not so much a matter of finding out which is the best speed. Rather, finding out the most effective way to periodize the speed, and which speed to spend most of the time doing. If you take time to check out my program design examples later in this book you will see I tend to periodize from slow to fast, and that a rep TUT of about 5-6 seconds (3:1:1) is about my average.

I want to stress this - it is not so much a matter of finding out which is the best speed. Rather, finding out the most effective way to periodize the speed, and which speed to spend most of the time doing.

Chapter 13

How long should I rest between sets?

Metabolic vs. neural

T he reason we rest between sets is to allow recovery. There is more than one type of recovery, and we will discuss two of them. Metabolic and neural.

The major source of metabolic energy in strength training is adenosine triphosphate (ATP), and the textbook interpretation for recovery of ATP is as follows : 50% is recovered in the first thirty (30) seconds, and half or 50% of the outstanding balance is recovered every subsequent thirty (30) seconds.

There is more than one type of recovery, and we will discuss two of them. Metabolic and neural.

Figure 45 - The textbook interpretation of recovery from a replacement of ATP perspective.

Number of Seconds / Minutes Elapsed in Rest Period	% age of ATP replenished
30 sec	50%
1 minutes	75%
1 minutes 30 sec	87%
2 minutes	93%
2 minutes 30 sec	97%
3 minutes	98.5%

Whilst this table is a generalization, it is clear that for anywhere near full recovery of ATP, 2-3 minutes is required.

Neural recovery has not received as much attention as metabolic recovery in literature, and therefore an equivalent equation to the above table is not available. Most sources quote neural recovery to be between **five and six (5-6) times longer than metabolic recovery**. Taking into account the above table, this theory sheds light on why some power athletes take upwards of 10 minutes between efforts or sets.

There are other factors that you need to consider and these include :

1. **Work: rest ratios :** recovery is not simply time based, but also related to the duration and intensity of the work that preceded. Therefore another way to view rest periods is to consider the ratio of work time (time duration of the set in strength training) and rest time. A mainstream belief is that a work:rest ratio of about 1:5 is adequate when training the ATP-CP energy system. However if one is to consider neural recovery, this is inadequate. If neural adaptations are desired, work:rest ratios in excess of 1:20 are more effective. This may go as high as 1:60.

2. **Training age :** theoretically speaking beginners or young people lack the tolerance to lactic acid and may require longer rest periods. I would argue that they are not capable of intensity, and should not be lifting high loads, which negates this concern. Provided the intensity is commensurate with their age and experience, I believe a beginner can and should work with shorter rest periods. On the other hand, as the trainee becomes more advanced, their ability to increase the level of intensity improves, and they will require longer rest periods. Whilst intensity or neural training may not always be the focus at any given time, I lean towards respecting intensity as being one of if not the most important variable in training.

3. **Bodyweight :** it does appear that heavier trainees require longer rest periods than lighter trainees. There is no doubt that their body has to work harder to support the greater body mass. This is more relevant when the trainee is exceeding 100 kgs in total bodyweight, and is not always apparent until over

Most sources quote neural recovery to be between five and six (5-6) times longer than metabolic recovery.

110-120 kgs. This would also be influenced by strength levels - all things being equal the heavier person is stronger, and in training creates greater inroads into his/her fatigue curve.

4. Aerobic Fitness : you may notice that those with high levels of aerobic fitness (or pre-disposed psychologically to aerobic activities) feel that they do not need to take the longer rest periods. This is usually the 'little person on their shoulder' saying *'come on, you are perpetual motion'*. If it was accurate that they didn't need the longer rest it is only because they lack the psychological and mechanical skills to lift with intensity. Ignore their desires - make them rest longer! Their metabolic system needs no further help. Their neural systems needs all the help it can get!

5. Repetitions and rest periods : there is an inverse relationship between reps and rest period - generally speaking the lower the reps, the longer the rest you should take. The higher the reps, the shorter the rest periods required. This is illustrated in Figure 46.

There is an inverse relationship between reps and rest period - generally speaking the lower the reps, the longer the rest you should take.

Figure 46 - The inverse relationship between reps and rest period.

Reps :	1	10	20
Rest Period:			
	5-10 minutes		30-60 sec

6. Rest periods and training methods : the following table provides guidelines for the appropriate matching of rest periods to training methods.

Figure 47 - The matching of rest periods to training methods.

Rest Period	What's Happened	Training Methods Suited
0-30 sec	<=50% metabolic recovery	General fitness Stability/control General Strength Metabolic-end hypertrophy
30 sec - 2 min	>90% metabolic recovery	General Strength Metabolic-end hypertrophy
2-3 min	Near complete metabolic recovery	Mixed metabolic-neural Hypertrophy
3-5 min	Near complete neural recovery	Neural-end Hypertrophy Metabolic End Maximal Strength, Explosive Power and Quickness/SSC
5-10 min	Complete neural recovery	Neural-end Maximal Strength, Explosive Power and Quickness/SSC

7. Periodization of Rest Periods : periodization of rest periods is simple and, considering the rest period-repetition relationship as discussed above, should be implemented as the reps are varied. Periodization of rest periods may be linked to the style of periodization used. The following tables are examples of rest period periodization in the framework of linear and alternating periodization.

Figure 48 - Periodization of rest period with **linear** periodization of strength training.

Week No.	Reps	Rest Periods
1-3	10-12	1 m
4-6	8-10	2 m
7-9	6-8	3 m
10-12	4-6	4 m

*Figure 49 - Periodization of rest period with **alternating** periodization of strength training.*

Week No.	Reps	Rest Periods
1-3	10-12	1 m
4-6	6-8	3 m
7-9	8-10	2 m
10-12	4-6	4 m

8. Long rest periods and what to do in them : this is what I recommend. Walk around for the first ½ to 1 minute, to accelerate recovery. Load the weight for your next set. Sit down and record what you just did in your training diary, confirm the weight for the next set. Then put a towel around your shoulders to maintain body temperature. Sit with reasonable posture, so as not to induce feelings of fatigue. Do not sit on the device or in the area in which you are training. Sit at least a few meters away from your work station. The workout area should be associated with a high level of arousal, not the level of arousal of the rest period. Do not get distracted from your set rest period or focus on training by meaningless conversation. Then begin the arousal process for the next set.

The workout area should be associated with a high level of arousal.

Chapter 14

How do I know which exercise to use?

Do the ones you need, not the ones you want!

$\mathbf{P}$icking exercises comes second to picking which muscle groups, and will be influenced by what order you intend to do the muscle groups. You need also take into account your aims.

So briefly on picking muscle groups. Here are my main concerns. Select muscle groups that :

- **reflect your imbalance** e.g. if you are less developed in the legs than in the upper body - increase the amount of lower body training. If your chest is more developed than your upper back, focus more on upper back; and
- **reflect your needs** - if you are a powerlifter, there is not a lot of value focusing on biceps at the expense of the more specific muscle groups, or spending the year leg pressing instead of squatting.

I support the use of big muscle group exercises. They are not only more effective for size and strength, they are more time efficient.

For the most part I support the use of big muscle group exercises. Some call them basic movements. They are the foundation of most strength sports. I believe they are not only more effective for size and strength, they are more time efficient i.e. they train more muscle mass in a shorter period of time.

If I had to pick a few basic movements that I believe you should base your training around they would include the exercises listed in Figure 50.

There is a time for everything of course and I will tend to use more isolated exercises in the earlier stage of a training program, year and / or career.

Figure 50 - The basic exercises for each major muscle group.

Major muscle group	Preferred basic movements
horizontal pulling (i.e. scapula retractors e.g. rows)	seated and bent over rows
horizontal pushing (i.e. horizontal flexion e.g. bench press)	bench press and it's variation (incline, decline etc.)
vertical pulling (i.e. scapula depressors e.g. chin ups)	chin ups and it's variations
vertical pushing (i.e. arm abduction e.g. shoulder press)	shoulder press and it's variations
upper arm (bicep / tricep)	underhand, overhand and neutral bicep curls; dips, close grip benches and overhead tri ext
lower arm (forearm flexors and extensors)	forearm flexion and extension
hip dominant (e.g. deadlift and its variations)	deadlift, cleans and their variations
quad dominant (e.g. squats and its variations)	squats and it's variations
lower back	deadlifts, cleans, good morning, stiff legged deadlift
lower legs (e.g. front and back of calves)	standing, seated, and leg press calf
abdominals	lower, upper, lateral and rotational abdominals
neck (e.g. upper traps)	shrugs and it's variations

Other issues to consider include :

• **unilateral vs. bilateral** : if you have an imbalance in size or strength from right to left arm or leg, select unilateral (one limb at a time) exercises. Doing bilateral (two limb) exercises will only make it worse;

- **need for specificity** : if you have a need to develop a specific type of strength, this may influence your exercise selection e.g. power movements for a power athlete;
- **suitability to training method** : some exercises just don't suit certain training methods e.g. it is difficult to perform a power clean in a slow manner! And I wouldn't give a maximum loaded good morning to anyone other than an experienced Olympic lifter, as another example;
- **suitability to level of ability** : I wouldn't give a chin up or a power clean to a raw beginner;
- **suitability to stage of program** : I tend to use more isolated exercises early in a training program, and then phase to more complex or compound exercises in the later stages of the program;
- **equipment availability** : if that is all the equipment you have, you need to either change gyms or allow this equipment availability to influence your exercise selection;
- **don't get caught up in trends** : for example, the Swiss ball is currently experiencing heightened popularity. But don't just jump on this bandwagon unless you really have a good reason to. In the early stages of any trend there is a tendency to over-react in the short term, and under-react in the long term.

Most programs I see lack balance. They focus too much on one exercise or muscle group at the expense of others. Or they may even have totally neglected a muscle group.

There is a time for everything of course and I will tend to use more isolated exercises in the earlier stage of a training program.

Most programs I see lack balance. They focus too much on one exercise or muscle group at the expense of others. Or they may even have totally neglected a muscle group.

Chapter 15

What order should I do my exercises in?

Put first things first!

There is really one simple rule here. The exercises you do first in the workout and first in the training week are the exercises that get the best effort, and therefore the best result. It is human nature to put one's favorite exercises first in the week and first in the workout - year in and year out - and then wonder why muscle imbalances occur!

So here is what I suggest : start every 12 week cycle with an workout order which is the reverse of what you want in the final stages of the program. And slowly revert that order during the 3 or 4 stages of the 12 week program, until the final stage is the order you really prefer.

The exercises you do first in the workout and first in the training week are the exercises that get the best effort, and therefore the best result.

The advantages of doing this include :

- you give priority training to muscle groups you would normally neglect, and gain added size and strength from doing this;
- you address muscle imbalances and reduce the incidence of injuries;
- you train the smaller muscle groups in isolation; and
- you create extra variety in your training.

The following is an example of a 4 stage, 3 week blocks over 12 weeks training program, where I do exactly this.

Figure 51 - Stage 1 (e.g. weeks 1-3) of an example of altering the sequence of muscle groups and exercises, using a typical 4/wk ABCD split routine.

A Day e.g. Mon		B Day e.g. Tue		C Day e.g. Thur		D Day e.g. Fri	
M/G	e.g. Exer	M/G	e.g. Exer	M/G	e.g. Exer	M/G	e.g. Exer
Lower abdom	Leg cycles	Upper abdom	Curls ups	Lower abdom	Toes to sky	Upper abdom	Rope p/down
Rotation abdom	Russian twist	Lateral abdom	Side Raises	Rotation abdom	Lateral leg lower	Lateral abdom	Side DB raises
Upper trap	shrugs	Biceps	DB bicep curl	Lower leg	Calf presses	Triceps	DB tricep extension
Hip dominant	Leg abduct /adduct	Vertical pulling	DB pull-over	Quad dominant	Leg flex / ext.	Horizont. pulling	Prone fly
	Hip/thigh ext.		Front DB raise		Ski squats		Supine fly
	Single leg back ext.	alternated with	Lat pull-down		Single leg squat	alternated with	DB row
	Single leg Good morn.	Vertical pushing	Lat DB Raise		Bulgarian squat	Horizont. pushing	Incline DB Press
	Single leg deadlift		Chin up		Single leg leg press		Seated row
	2 leg deadlift		Shoulder press		2 leg squat		Bench press

Stage 1 Rationale :
- strength trainees typically train their upper body first — this is very common in strength training (would you believe epidemic!) - so I have trained legs first in the week in this stage;
- the abdominals are usually done last in the workout so I have done them first in this stage;
- the upper abdominals are usually stronger than the lower (from being ordered in this way or from total neglect of lower) so I have prioritized them from lower to upper;
- in the leg department, they would usually train their quad dominant exercises (e.g. squats) ahead of their hip dominant exercises (e.g. deadlifts), so I have placed hip dominants earlier in the week than quad dominant exercises;
- the smaller muscle groups such as calves and upper traps are typically done towards the end of the programs - so I place them first in the workout in this stage;

Stage 1 : strength trainees typically train their upper body first — this is very common in strength training - so I have trained legs first in the week in this stage.

Get Buffed!™

- the upper and lower body exercises are predominantly iso-lated exercises as opposed to compound or multi-joint, which will be returned later;
- and are mostly unilateral (i.e. one limb at a time or limbs working independently). The more conventional bi-lateral movements will also be returned in later stages;
- as most programs prioritize horizontal pushing (bench) over pulling (rows), this has been reversed;
- as most programs prioritize horizontal pushing and pulling (e.g. bench and rows) over vertical pushing and pulling (e.g. shoulder press and chins) this has also been reversed.

Stage 2 : The order of hip dominant before quad dominant in this stage of the program has been maintained, but the order of exercises within each work-out is more conventional.

Figure 52 - Stage 2 (e.g. weeks 4-6) of an example of altering the sequence of muscle groups and exercises, using a typical 4/wk ABCD split routine.

A Day e.g. Mon		B Day e.g. Tue		C Day e.g. Thur		D Day e.g. Fri	
M/G	e.g. Exer	M/G	e.g. Exer	M/G	e.g. Exer	M/G	e.g.Exer
Hip dominant	2 leg deadlift	Vertical pulling	Chin up	Quad dominant	2 leg squat	Horizontal pulling	Seated row
	Clean pull		Shoulder press		Static lunge		Bench press
	Single leg deadlift	alternated	Lat pull-down		Single leg squat	alternated	Bent over row
	Good Morning	with	DB should. press		Leg Curl/ ext	with	Incline bar press
Upper trap	Shrugs		DB p/over	Lower leg	Calf presses		DB row
Lower abdom	Leg cycles	Vertical pushing	Lateral DB raise	Lower abdom	Toes to sky	Horizontal pushing	Decline DB press
Rotation abdom	Russian twist	Biceps	Bar bicep curl	Rotation abdom	Lateral leg lower	Triceps	Bar tricep exten.
		Upper abdom	Curls ups			Upper abdom	Rope p/down
		Lateral abdom	Side Raises			Lateral abdom	Side DB raises

Stage 2 Rationale :
- the order of hip dominant before quad dominant in this stage of the program has been maintained, but the order of exercises within each workout is more conventional i.e. now back to bigger exercises/muscle groups before smaller;
- similarly, the order of vertical pulling and pushing ahead of horizontal pushing and pulling has been maintained, but

the order within the workout has been returned to a more conventional sequence of bigger exercises/muscle groups before smaller;

- I haven't shown variation in the abdomen exercises because it is difficult to explain the variations in the space provided. Of course, they would be different from stage to stage.

Figure 53 - Stage 3 (e.g. weeks 7-9) of an example of altering the sequence of muscle groups and exercises, using a typical 4/wk ABCD split routine.

A Day e.g. Mon		B Day e.g. Tue		C Day e.g. Thur		D Day e.g. Fri	
M/G	e.g. Exer	M/G	e.g. Exer	M/G	e.g. Exer	M/G	e.g. Exer
Quad dominant	2 leg squat	Horizontal pulling	Seated row	Hip dominant	2 leg deadlift	Vertical pushing	Shoulder press
	Dynamic lunge	Horizontal pushing	Bench press		Clean pull	Vertical pulling	Chin up
Lower leg	Calf press	Biceps	Bar bicep curl	Upper trap	Shrugs	Triceps	Dips
Lower abdom	Leg cycles	Upper abdomen	Rope Pull-down	Lower abdom	Toes to sky	Upper abdomen	Curls ups
Rotation abdom	Russian twist	Lateral abdom	Side DB raises	Rotation abdom	Lateral leg lower	Lateral abdom	Side Raises

Stage 3 Rationale :
- the order of lower body ahead of upper body has been retained, but the order of hip dominant before quad dominant has been swapped over;
- the horizontal pulling and pushing has been moved back ahead of vertical pushing and pulling;
- but the horizontal pulling is still prioritized over the horizontal pushing;
- less exercises are being used, with more sets on each exercise;
- most if not all exercises are now bilateral;
- again I haven't shown variation in the abdomen exercises because it is difficult to explain the variations in the space provided. Of course, they would be different from stage to stage.

Stage 3 : The order of lower body ahead of upper body has been retained, but the order of hip dominant before quad dominant has been swapped over.

Figure 54 - Stage 4 (e.g. weeks 10-12) of an example of altering the sequence of muscle groups and exercises, using a typical 4/wk ABCD split routine.

A Day e.g. Mon		B Day e.g. Tue		C Day e.g. Thur		D Day e.g. Fri	
M/G	e.g. Exer	M/G	e.g. Exer	M/G	e.g. Exer	M/G	e.g. Exer
Horizontal pushing	Bench press	Quad dominant	2 leg squat	Vertical pulling	Chin up	Hip dominant	Two leg deadlift
Biceps	Bar bicep curl		Quarter squat	Triceps	Cl. grip bench		Deadlift off block
Upper abdom	Rope pull-down	Lower abdom	Leg cy-cles	Upper abdom	Curls ups	Rotation abdom	Russian twist

Stage 4 Rationale :
- the order of lower body ahead of upper body has been reversed;
- horizontal pushing takes priority of pulling;
- many of the smaller muscle group exercises have been eliminated, and there are less exercises - this is because more sets are being done on the exercises that are retained;
- again I haven't shown variation in the abdomen exercises because it is difficult to explain the variations in the space provided. Of course, they would be different from stage to stage.

Stage 4 : The order of lower body ahead of upper body has been reversed.

Chapter 16

Which muscle groups do I put together?

There are no rules!

This is one of the most common questions I get asked - is it OK or best to do 'x' muscle group with 'y' muscle group? My simple answer is this - anything is possible! There are up-sides and down-sides to which ever combination you come up with. The following discusses some of these options.

Which combination is best? Again it is not a matter of which is best, but how to skillfully use all methods over time in a balance that suits your needs.

There are advantages and disadvantages to every combination of muscle groups. The key is knowing what they are and exploiting the up-sides and minimizing the down-sides.

An example is doing all pushing movements on one day e.g. bench, shoulders and triceps. This has the advantage of restricting pushing fatigue to one day, but the disadvantage that the shoulders (if done after the chest) are probably not being overloaded optimally due to tricep fatigue from the chest exercises.

Another example is doing arms last in the workout. This makes sense as they are the weak link in many upper body compound movements. If they are pre-fatigued, the bigger

There are advantages and disadvantages to every combination of muscle groups. The key is knowing what they are and exploiting the up-sides and minimizing the down-sides.

muscle groups of the upper body are not fully overloaded (at least in exercises involving elbow flexion and extension). And there is further argument that the arms are getting worked all the way through the other push-pull movements, so the issue of pre-fatigue doesn't affect them. But my perspective is that the CNS and energy levels can be so fatigued by the end of the workout that justice is often not done to the specific training of the arms. If this is an issue (e.g. you like your guns!), arms will need to be done earlier in the workout for at least some stages.

So don't be hesitant to try different combinations. I can very safely say that if you aren't using a variety of combinations you will not maximizes your potential!

There really is no 'perfect combination'.

If you are stuck in a pattern of grouping certain muscle groups together you may be missing out on opportunities to exploit other training effects, and therefore to get greater gains from your training. So don't be hesitant to try different combinations. I can very safely say that if you aren't using a variety of combinations you will not maximizes your potential!

Figure 55 - An analysis of the pro's and con's of various combinations of muscle groups.

Combinations	Advantages	Disadvantages
Splitting upper and lower	• reduces the number of different muscles that you need to warm up/stretch • reduces the frequency of exposure to each	• can be a bit limiting - there are times when you may need to mix upper and lower in the one workout
Doing all upper body pushing exercises one day and all upper body pulling another day	• isolates fatigue to the one day, therefore allowing more days between exposure	• prevents each muscle from getting trained fresh e.g. if shoulder press comes after bench, the shoulder press loading is reduced as is the shoulder training effect
Doing opposite push-pull upper body exercises in the one workout	• ensures muscle balance in the training program • allows the use of opposite muscle super-sets or full recovery alternating sets	• means less recovery from pushing and pulling, and it is done on all upper body days (however this mainly affects the arms, which can recover relatively quickly)

Get Buffed!™

Chapter 17
What training methods are available?

There are no excuses for lacking variety in training!

There are so many different methods available, and this is one of the great aspects of training - you have so much variety to chose from. To help you understand the aims and potential benefits of each of these methods, I have summarized them in the following. They are discussed under sub-categories of dominant training goals, including :

There are so many different methods available, and this is one of the great aspects of training - you have so much variety to chose from.

- Methods suited to technique development (control) and rehabilitation
- Methods suited to general strength and hypertrophy
- Methods suited to hypertrophy, maximal strength and explosive power
- Methods suited to lowering body fat

Methods suited to technique development (control) and rehabilitation

Isometric training : this is perhaps the first stage of rehab and control training. Using isometric contractions to learn selective muscle recruitment e.g. early stage abdomen exercises, quad contractions when leg is in cast etc. The duration of the contraction is usually dependant on the ability to maintain a pre-determined quality of contraction. Initially this may not be long e.g. less than 10 seconds. The number of reps is determined in the same way - the ability to contract at a standard, and again can be typically low to start with. When this ability rises, the training effect of this type of training diminishes and it may be time to move on. This is a point that many clinically based therapists miss, and their patients are usually performing non-productive exercises over a long period of time.

Limited range for control, pain avoidance, or weak joint angles : this may be the next step in rehab and technique development. Using a portion of the total range. For example, where scapula retraction may be poor in a rowing movement, you could focus on the end part of the concentric contraction - from full contraction out until the scapula move - which for someone in this situation will not be very far out! An example of pain avoidance would be to use only the end of extension in the leg extension or leg press with someone with advanced osteo-arthritis. Where someone has been identified as having a control or strength problem at any other specific joint angles, this range could be isolated. Because the loading is usually low in these methods, you may do either higher reps (e.g. 10-30) or use a slower speed with lower reps (e.g. 6-15 @ 515 - 313)

In the progression from isometric contractions to dynamic contractions I like to start with slow speed movements.

Slow speed methods : in the progression from isometric contractions to dynamic contractions I like to start with slow speed movements. Slow speed movements ensure a reduced load, but more importantly give time for you to adjust / control the movement. Very important! The TUT of each rep may dictate the number of reps e.g. a rep TUT of 18 seconds (828) will mean 5 or less reps. My favorites here are 515 (5-10 reps) and 313 (10-20 reps).

Isometric stops during the eccentric contraction : the next progression may be to use isometric stops during the eccentric phase. There are two benefits. Firstly, it allows focus on a given joint angle, developing strength in a controlled manner at this joint angle. Secondly, it recognizes that the eccentric phase can tolerate greater stresses to achieve equal fatigue to the weaker concentric phase. My favorite is three 3 second pauses during the eccentric, varying the stopping point, showing more acceleration in the concentric, using 6-10 reps.

1 ½'s : One and a halves are perhaps the next step. For example, in a leg extension, you would fully extend the leg, pause, lower ½ way (or less) down, pause, return to full extension, pause, and then lower all the way down. This is one rep. This technique keeps the load down, and creates extra fatigue in the half that you are repeating. I like to do between 10-20 reps with this method. To get a feeling for this method, try it in the squat!

Pre-fatigue method : this is an excellent method for where you may want to keep loading down in a multi-joint movement, due to the presence or risk of injury or poor technique. For example, if you do one or more single joint movements before a multi-joint movement, where the single joint movements involves muscles that act as assistant muscle groups to the multi-joint movement—such as leg extension and curl prior to squatting. I like this method, and often use a lot more pre-fatigue isolated exercises than this prior to being exposed to the primary exercise in programs of this nature.

Multiple sets of the same exercise have a number of benefits, including increased power endurance and the opportunity to develop the skills required e.g. Olympic lifts, etc.

Short rest period training : using short rest periods ensure that the load used is less which may suit specific training aims.

Methods suited to general strength and hyper-trophy

Standard sets : this is perhaps the starter method for this training goal. Where you may do 2 or more sets using the same load on an exercise. The advantage for a beginner with this method is the loading is not maximal (how can you go to fatigue with a load, and repeat the same load with the same reps in a subsequent set?). This method provides volume for rehearsal and hypertrophy. However when you become more advanced and need greater intensity, I believe this method becomes of less value.

One set to failure : this method involves doing only one set per exercise, but going all out on this one set. This means that you can use a lot of different exercises, which is great for hypertrophy, but not as valuable for maximal strength training. A concern with this method is if you are going to total failure all the time i.e. every exercise, every workout - I doubt whether the average person will recover and therefore whether this is optimal for extended periods. Another concern is for the athlete – multiple sets of the same exercise have a number of benefits, including increased power endurance (required in many sports) and the opportunity to develop the skills required e.g. Olympic lifts, etc.

Step loading : this is the next progression from standard sets, where the reps in subsequent sets on the same exercise remain constant, but the load increases e.g. 1x10@90 kgs, 1x10@95 kgs, 1x10@100 kgs. This method recognizes that your neural firing potentially increases from set to set (until fatigue negates this). This is a method more suited to someone whose technique is not totally stable, as it allows them to improve from set to set, as opposed to needing to have the ideal technique with maximal loading in the first set. A good example of this is in the Olympic lifts (cleans, snatches and their variations - the reps would be a lot lower in this situation e.g. 4-6 reps). The down-side is similar to standard sets - when higher levels of intensity are required, it is not as an efficient method.

There is of course the option to pyramid both ways. The down-side with this is unless you are doing a very small number of exercises, you risk having excessive volume by number of sets.

Pyramiding : this is perhaps the next progression in these methods. An example of a basic pyramid would be : 1x10@60kgs, 1x8@70kgs, 1x6@80kgs. Any number can be used, there is no obligation to use the 10/8/6 - they are just a good beginners combination. This is pyramiding down. The advantage is the allowance for technique and neural firing to occur prior to exposure to higher loading - and this suits the less advanced person or muscle group; and the exposure to typical hypertrophy reps (10's) before exposure to more maximal strength reps (6's) favors a hypertrophy response. The reverse pyramid may look like this : 1x6@85kgs, 1x8@75kgs, 1x10@65kgs, and favors more of a strength response over a hypertrophy response. Note I used higher loads in the second example, illustrating that this method has more load potential. There is of course the option to pyramid both ways e.g. 10/8/6/8/10 or 6/8/10/8/6 (the former being more common). The down-side with this is unless you are doing a very small number of exercises, you risk having excessive volume by number of sets. A variation of this I do like is the 10/8/6/10 method, which allows what I call a 'back-off' set at the end - in this set you will use more weight or do more reps than you would have if you had done this set prior to experiencing neural elevation. American magazine owner *(Muscle Media)* Bill Phillips used this method extensively in his book *(Body for Life)*. Unlike the programs in that book, I would not recommend using a back off set on every exercise in a workout, especially if there were more than four exercises in the workout.

Slow speed methods : this method is also valuable for hypertrophy, as despite the reduced loading involved, creates a high level of tension and fatigue in the muscle. My favorite combinations for pursuing hyertrophy with this training method include 814 (4-6 reps), 613 (6-8 reps), and 412 (8-12 reps). However I feel that there was an over-reaction when these methods were promoted in North America in the 1990s, and they were being over-used and over-promoted. They need to kept in context, and for me, that is a limited use.

21's are an old favorite in bodybuilding and they are extremely effective!

Rest-pause methods at the end of the eccentric contraction : this method requires coming to a complete halt and for a period of time at the end of each eccentric contraction. The aim is to totally eliminate the elastic energy generated by the stretch-shortening cycle. This means that during the concentric phase, in the absence of mechanical energy, the muscles have to do all the work. My favorite combinations include 442, 442 and 421 for 6-10 reps.

1 ½'s : One and a halves are an excellent hypertrophy method. As the load increases, I like to see the reps come down from the previously mentioned 10-20, but no lower than say 6-10.

Isometric stops during the eccentric contraction : these can also be used very effectively for hypertrophy, but again as the load increases the reps need to come down.

21's : these are an old favorite in bodybuilding and they are extremely effective! There are a number of ways of doing 21's but my favorite is to do 7 half reps in the weakest half, followed immediately by 7 full reps, followed immediately by 7 half reps in the strongest half. Make sure you pause every time you change direction - this further increases the desired training effect.

Super-sets : the aim of supersets is to do a set of 2 different exercises back to back i.e. with no rest. The super-set may be of antagonist (opposite) muscle groups e.g. leg extension/leg curl; or of the same muscle group e.g. DB supine flye followed by bench press. The aim is to cause total fatigue in the area being trained, and the no rest between sets contributes to this.

Multi-sets : this is an extension of supersets, where 3 or more exercises are performed back to back with no rest between. I find this method extremely effective for muscle groups that don't respond to more conventional methods, including calves and upper arm. However you can use this method on any muscle group.

When you fail in a set it is usually in the concentric phase, and the eccentric phase can keep working.

Pre-fatigue method : are described in the earlier training goal, and have an equal role to play in this training goal. They really do make you work!

Strip sets : are not really general strength methods, more hypertrophy methods. They involve going to fatigue with a load, reducing the load, going again immediately to fatigue, reducing the load and going again etc. I usually use a total of 3 sets (with somewhere from 0-10 seconds rest between) of descending load, and the reps I tend to use are between the 6-10's on each set. But this is of course flexible.

Assisted or forced reps : like strip sets, these are not for general strength! They involve going to concentric fatigue followed by eccentric fatigue. When you fail in a set it is usually in the concentric phase, and the eccentric phase can keep working. There are a number of options here and here are two of them :

- when concentric failure occurs, the spotter helps complete the concentric phase and the lifter controls the eccentric phase, repeating a number of times until complete eccentric fatigue occurs;

- when concentric failure occurs, the spotter help complete the concentric phase, and then during the eccentric phase, the spotter pushes down, making the eccentric phase harder; this continues until complete eccentric fatigue occurs.

The advantage with these methods is that they do create high level fatigue. This can also be a down-side unless used sparingly. I feel they are over-used, and don't normally recommend planning to go to complete failure too often.

Short rest period training : short rest periods between sets creates greater fatigue of the metabolic system, which is supportive of hypertrophy. It also has been shown to cause higher testosterone and growth hormone release.

Methods suited to hypertrophy, maximal strength and explosive power

Contrast training is also an explosive power training method, but can be used to great effect in bodybuilding.

Standard sets : can work, but obviously the reps are lower e.g. 3x5reps @ 100 kgs. However I don't find them as effective, especially for the more advanced lifter.

Step loading : again these can work for this training goal, and are more effective I believe than standard sets. They still have their limitations for this training goal however. An example may be 1x5@100 kgs, 1x5@105 kgs, 1x5@110kgs.

Pyramids : these can also work for these training goals, with of course lower reps e.g. 1x5@100 kgs, 1x4@110 kgs, 1x3@120 kgs. They are much more effective than the above methods.

Wave loading : wave loading is like repeating a pyramid e.g.

Wave #1 :   5@100 kgs, 1x4@110 kgs, 1x3@120 kgs
Wave #2 :   5@105 kgs, 1x4@115 kgs, 1x3@125 kgs

The second wave should be higher in load for the same reps than the first. This will only work if you avoid excessive fatigue in the first wave. A case of not going too hard in the first wave. This is a very popular method for explosive power development, as it exposes to a contrast of speeds (the heavier the load the slower the speed and vice versa).

Complex training : this is also an excellent explosive power method, and involves progressing from a heavier slower movement to lighter faster movements.

Squat	2x5@ 130 kgs
Explosive squat	2x8@90 kgs
Depth jumps	2x10-15 @ bodyweight

Contrast training : is also an explosive power training method, but can be used to great effect in bodybuilding. It involves alternating from a high load/slow movement to a lower load/faster movement. You can see the speed training (explosive power) benefits, but the following example is a highly effective maximum strength/hypertrophy method.

1x6@100kgs / 1x1@120kgs / 1x6@105kgs / 1x1 @125kgs / 1x10-20 @80kgs

This is a highly effective method that will only work if you avoid excessive fatigue in the first 6's and 1's. The aim of the 1's is to expose the body to a higher load, and when you come back to the 6 the 6 should feel lighter than it otherwise would have. Note the goal is to lift heavier in the second 6 and 1 than in the first 6 and 1.

Limited range for load. This is a very effective way of exposing the body to a greater load, which helps from both a neuro-muscular perspective as well as a psychological perspective.

Alternated full recovery : involves working two exercises together, alternating sets from each one, but unlike a super-set, having a complete recovery between sets e.g. bench press and bicep curl. Do one set of bench, rest fully (e.g. 2 minutes), do 1 set of bicep curls, rest fully, do 1 set of bench, rest fully, etc.

There are many benefits to this method including:

- you are getting to rest for about 5 minutes between sets of the same exercise, which is adequate recovery;
- this method creates a shorter workout in total time than the conventional set, rest, repeat the same exercise;
- the theory that the antagonist muscle (the opposite muscle) inhibits the contraction is negated by working (neurally arousing) the antagonist, provided it is in fact

an antagonist that you are alternating with.

When using this method, I tend to match a small muscle group exercise with a bigger muscle group exercise (as in the example above), and it works best if they are opposite muscle groups - which means this method has less application for lower body training.

Rest-pause methods at the end of the concentric contraction : in this method a short rest (2-6 seconds) is taken after each rep, at the end of the concentric phase. This has no bearing on the stretch-shortening cycle, but rather on the recovery of the working muscle. 6 reps of this method compared to 6 reps of a normal set is significantly different. The training effect in terms of strength and what fiber type may hypertrophy (more fast twitch hypertrophy in this method) is greater with this method.

The higher intensity methods may interfere with recovery and growth, so I suggest staying with the lower intensity steady state exercises.

Limited range for load : this involves using a greater than normal load, and less than full range of movement - usually the stronger half. This is a very effective way of exposing the body to a greater load, which helps from both a neuro-muscular perspective as well as a psychological perspective. Loads 20-40% greater than your usual for this number of reps are possible, and I recommend using between 4-6 reps. I strongly recommend an experienced spotter or lift within the power rack with safety bars in place.

Isometric training : has been used in maximal strength training to address weaknesses at a given joint angle e.g. using the power rack. Contraction durations are relatively short e.g. 3-6 seconds, and reps low e.g. 4-10.

Eccentric training : eccentric training recognizes that the eccentric contraction is significantly stronger (by approximately 20-40%) than the concentric contraction, and that failure to train this contraction may deny full development of strength potential. Unlike the forced reps methods described above, maximal strength training of the eccentric phase should be done in a fresh state. An example may be to take a load in the bench press which is 20-30% more than what you can normally do for 4 conventional reps, and under the watchful eye of an experienced spotter, lower this load down in a pre-determined time of between 4-8 seconds. I say predetermined because if you are unable to maintain the pre-determined speed, terminate the set. Then the spotter should take as much weight as they can during the concentric phase, keeping you neurally and metabolically fresh for the eccentric phase. I tend to use low reps in this method e.g. 2-4 reps. This training method is for the experienced, advanced lifter only.

Other forms of eccentric overload include the hooks or chains used to increase the load during the eccentric phase, and drop off, disconnect, or reduce in load for the concentric phase.

Methods suited to lowering body fat

Some argue that higher intensity energy system training has a greater metabolic cost. The answer is academic to a strength athlete - the higher intensity methods may interfere with recovery and growth.

Aerobic training : aerobic training is often described as being the training method most likely to use fat as a dominant energy source. Some argue that higher intensity energy system training has a greater metabolic cost. The answer is academic to a strength athlete - the higher intensity methods may interfere with recovery and growth, so I suggest staying with the lower intensity steady state exercises such as cycling. This exercise has minimal loading through the joints. Running will burn more calories, but can be harsher on the body. Which ever mode of exercise you choose (bike, run, swim, blade etc.), short, frequent exposure to low level steady state aerobic training may be most effective in times when it is critical to lower body fat.

Circuit training : this is a very simple form of training that could also be used in general strength training. The aim of a circuit is to complete one set on a number of exercises, with no rest between sets, before considering subsequent repeats of the 'circuit'. As with any method of short rest, this places greater metabolic demand on the energy system.

Short rest periods between sets : short rest periods, as I have explained above, creates greater fatigue of the metabolic system, which is supportive of hypertrophy, and also has been shown to cause higher testosterone and growth hormone release. Higher GH (growth hormone) release has been related to lowering body fat.

Chapter 18

How should I periodize the training methods?

This really will change the way you train!

Earlier in the book I spoke of methods of periodization of reps and sets, but what about periodization of training methods? Most experts in this area will recommend progressing from methods that develop hypertrophy through to methods that develop maximal strength. This is a solid concept. What I have added is the awareness and the method of developing a number of specific aspects prior to increasing the loading. These include :

- muscle balance
- joint control and stability
- appropriate technique

I develop these in what I call a control/hypertrophy phase. An example of this is laid out in the sample program later in this book (Stage 1).

I use this periodization of training methods throughout the ca-

What I have added is the awareness and the method of developing a number of specific aspects prior to increasing the loading.

reer, year, and short term training programs (e.g. 12 weeks). Remember also, when prioritizing one component (in this case method), always be considering ways to maintain the remaining qualities.

Figure 56 - Periodization of training methods for bodybuilding.

Control/hypertrophy phase

↓

General Strength & hypertrophy phase

↓

Hypertrophy & maximal strength phase

↓

Maximal strength & power phase

From using this method I have found that the short term benefits of hypertrophy and maximal strength are delayed. But the long term benefits are significantly enhanced.

From using this method I have found that the short term benefits of hypertrophy and maximal strength are delayed (because of the lower loading in the control stage), but the long term benefits are significantly enhanced. These 'longer term' benefits may be apparent as early as towards the end of the 12 week program.

Chapter 19

How long should I stay on the same program?

Only you hold the answer!

This is a question that I often get asked. I can guess at it, but only you can really answer it. My answer is simple - use a program for as long as it continues to see results. As soon as you feel the results are diminishing, change.

Unfortunately, many fail to accept that the method has ceased being productive, ignore the warning signs and push on with it. By the time they accept it is no longer working, they are in an over-trained or plateau state. It is best to move just before the method loses it effectiveness, not after. This can take some experience. But more importantly, be prepared to let the formerly successful training method go – move on!

The key is knowing not only when to change, but how much change to use.

Don't kill the goose that laid the golden egg!

The key is knowing not only when to change, but how much change to use.

The following figure provides guidelines in this.

Figure 57 - Rate of change of program appropriate for varying training levels.

Training Age *	Rate of Change (weeks)	Additional Comments
Beginners	at least every 4-12 weeks	changes can be mild e.g. slight changes in exercise or reps
Intermediate	at least ever 2-4 weeks	changes can be more aggressive
Advanced	at least every 1-3 weeks	changes should be at there greatest in this stage

* I will let you place your own definition (in terms of years of training or whatever) to beginner, intermediate and advanced.

The following give examples of not only how often to change, but what to change and by how much.

Figure 58 - An example of rate of change suitable for a beginner trainee.

Variables	Week No.s		
	1-4	5-8	9-12
No of Exercises	10	10	10
Sets x Reps	2x12	2x10	2x8
Speed	321	311	211
Rest Per. (m)	1	1-2	2-3

Note in the above example the change was not as often or as significant.

Figure 59 - An example of rate of change suitable for an intermediate to advanced trainee.

Vari-ables	Week No.s					
	1-2	3-4	5-6	7-8	9-10	11-12
No of Exerc.	10	6	8	4	6	2
Sets x Reps	2x10	3x6	2x8	3x4	3x6	4x2
Speed	421	311	321	211	311	201
Rest Per.(m)	2	4	3	4-5	4	5-6

Note in the above example the change is happening in a shorter time frame and is more significant.

Figure 60 - An example of rate of change suitable for an advanced trainee.

Vari-ables	Week No.s					
	1	2	3	4	5	6
No of Exerc.	8	6	4	8	6	4
Sets x Reps	4x6	3x6	2x6	4x4	3x4	2x4
Speed	421	311	201	321	211	201
Rest Per.(m)	2	3	4	2	3	4

Note in the above example the change was quite rapid and significant.

Chapter 20

How much variety should I use?

Don't get carried away – continuity is still

Now that more lifters know about the importance of variety and change, the trend has swung from not enough variety to too much variety. How can I say too much? If you are simply training for hypertrophy, with no desire too get strong, then perhaps there is no such thing as too much variety. After all, all you want to do is cause muscle damage.

But if you have any desire to develop strength (and I believe this really is a significant part of optimal hypertrophy!), then **there can be too much variety!**

If you have any desire to develop strength then there can be too much variety.

I believe too much variety damages continuity. I want to see continuity in a program through the various stages. If you don't have a common thread running through the program, the strength development does not necessarily continue from stage to stage.

If you have a close look at the sample program later in the book, you will see continuity in the most important exercises e.g. the squat, chin, bench, row etc. They appear in all programs, with perhaps subtle variations. They provide the continuity, because in these programs it is these exercises I am wanting to base my strength and size training on.

But if you don't have something significant such as an exercise that is giving you continuity in your training, you may be negatively affecting your strength development.

Chapter 21
Techniques to raise intensity

Lift more when it counts!

I want to talk to you about a topic that few discuss. Why isn't it discussed more often? I don't know – for it's a powerful issue. The strength athletes who have mastered this aspect of training are the competitive lifters – whose success is dependant on how successfully they overcome the greatest load possible. Now we are seeing a trend to put it in a bottle – nice concept, but sometimes our actions are more powerful than what we can get in a bottle!

I believe that the main reason most fail in achieving their goals is that they over-train. They do too much for their specific recovery situation. Now for another major reason that most don't achieve – they lack the ability to elevate their expression of force. Have you heard about the proverbial women who lifted the car off her baby? The message is simple. When we are able to fully harness our strength potential, we are incredibly strong. When it is time to lift more, using the techniques I describe below will mean you will lift more and therefore increase the training effect – in brief, you will get bigger and stronger than you would have if you hadn't mastered these techniques!

What I'm talking about is **focus** and **intensity.** And remember my viewpoint – intensity is perhaps the most important training variable, of far greater importance to the strength athlete than volume.

When we are able to fully harness our strength potential, we are incredibly strong.

Remember this - effort is relative to perception. If you attempt a load that you would normally use in one of your early work sets but do it without warm up sets, it may feel heavy. If you are sitting on the bench press you just used, engaged in meaningless chat, and then ly down and immediately commence a set, it may feel heavy, and you will probably be lifting way down on your true potential. You may even fail a rep. With a change in approach, you can lift a lot heavier.

These are some of the techniques I use and recommend to raise the focus and intensity of your training session (and get better results!) :

- **never sit/stand on/near the device you are using** : sit/ stand a few meters away; develop the subconscious awareness that once you enter that area, you will need a higher level of focus or aggression (the less complex the lift, the more aggression will work);
- **never allow your focus to deviate far from the reason you are in the gym** : even during extended rest periods, as it will jeopardize your ability to return to the desired level of intensity; and this includes your conversation!;
- **use a towel over your shoulders during the rest periods** : this will maintain body temperature. Take it off immediately prior to the work set. The sudden exposure to a lower room temperature will cause a fight or flight response, aiding your challenge of raising your arousal level;
- **place the towel over your head in the last 30 seconds or so prior to lifting** : this will isolates you more, bringing your focus in, and has a greater temperature effect (flight-fight) when you remove it from the face than even the shoulders;
- **rehearse the lift in your mind** : especially in this last 30 seconds or so prior to approaching the device/area for the work set; develop a higher level of arousal, urgency and aggression;
- **mentally rehearse a successful lift** : focus on the end result, and remove any lingering doubts with determination and positiveness!
- **use imagery cues to assist your arousal** : I found focusing on someone I am determined to out-lift helps, reminding you of the urgency of now - to take the opportu-

nity to be stronger;

- **make a conscious decision to not give up** : or more importantly to succeed in the lift. The outcome is usually determined in the head before you even take the weight;
- **always use the same path from your pre-effort area to the work area** : don't change approach paths. Develop an association with a certain number of steps and physical surrounds;
- **get in 'the zone' before you start your approach to the bar** : the onus is on you to raise your level of arousal to a pre-determined point prior to moving to the bar. Don't act like you have forever, but consider holding back a moment if you are not convinced you are 'up' or 'in the zone';
- **start to hold your breath to a greater extent** : especially as you commence your walk approach to the bar. This will help maintain tension in the major muscles of the body, so vital in the squat and bench and other lifts where the bar load is compressing on the body. Don't allow a full exhalation. Exhaling lowers muscle tension and power potential; stay 'tight'!
- **hold the breath when you take the bar load in the first instance** : ff you don't use these techniques, your strength potential is lowered. The bar weight will compress you and you will feel / think 'this is heavy'. Not a good start!
- And if anyone 'pisses you off' during the workout, use this to your benefit. Apply that aggression to your max sets!

The optimal level arousal may be inverse to the motor complexity of the lift.

An important key to remember is that the optimal level of arousal may be inverse to the motor complexity of the lift. The less complex the lift, the more effective are higher levels of arousal. The more complex the lift, the less effective are the highest levels of arousal. You may have seen a competitive powerlifter head butt the bar prior to a squat – and get the lift. An Olympic weightlifter, prior to attempting a competitive lift, is usually more restrained, but you can see the internal efforts to focus and arouse. It is simply a matter of degrees. For simple movements you can get more fired up than for complex movements. Each lift and lifter has an optimum.

The above techniques don't need to be used all the time. They have a big role to play in maximal strength and power phases. And don't fake it – there is nothing worse than someone who

108

Chapter 22

Injury prevention

Insuring your training!

You have been training hard for months or years. You feel that you are just about to reach the goals you set. Then you get a little niggle in the joint. You ignore it. It doesn't go away. You push through it. It gets worse. Before you know it, you are out of serious training for a few months. You are forced to watch all those hard-earned gains disappear.

Sound familiar? It does to me. I have seen it more times than I wish to remember. The amazing thing is when you take that brand new car off the sale lot, do you do so without insurance? Or do you have it insured before you drive it onto the street? The common sense approach is to insure the car before it leaves the car dealers yard. So what is different about your body? Is the car more valuable? What have you done to insure the time and effort you have invested in training?

Before you know it, you are out of serious training for a few months. You are forced to watch all those hard-earned gains disappear.

What I aim to teach you is how to provide insurance against injuries. Which is even more important if you accept my belief that most training programs cause more long term damage than good. I also aim to teach this concept in a simple manner. Simple so you can understand at least the basics. But what I can never do and never aim to do is to convince you of the value of this concept. After all, it is your body. The great thing about you making the decisions is you take the responsibility. The reward or the loss rest with you. But there is no doubt in my mind that the bodybuilding fraternity is more receptive to new information than ever before, thanks largely to the new wave of bodybuilding magazine editors. Bodybuilding magazines were such a closed shop in the 80's. I doubt there was any commercial drive to provide quality information – nice pictures were doing enough for sales. Now to get sales people are demanding solid information – after all, this is the Information Age!

My 'training insurance against injuries' policy is simple. It's built around five key concepts :

- Flexibility
- Tension
- Muscle balance
- Joint control
- Appropriate warm up

My 'training insurance against injuries' policy is simple. It's built around five key concepts.

Flexibility refers to length in connective tissue. Tension refers to the tone of the connective tissue. Muscle balance refers to the relative strength development of related muscle groups. Joint control refers to the ability to control the interaction of muscles that affect any joint. Appropriate warm ups include general and specific components, stretching and control drills. They aim to reduce the risk of injury. It is an optimal development of these key concepts that make the greatest contribution to reducing the incidence of use (some like to call it 'over-use) injuries. The other type of injury, traumatic injury, is more affected by other factors, such as technique and load selection.

When approached to create a training program for an athlete, I listen intently to what the athlete says. Of equal importance I look at how the athlete presents - their flexibility, tension, muscle balance, and joint control. I can give them what they verbally request - but preferably after they get 'their house in order'. I see no sense on building on shaky foundations.

There are many therapists that can give excellent information and direction in this area. However what I am talking about is injury prevention, not injury rehabilitation (although the same principles are used). Therefore most trainees don't get exposed to these concepts until AFTER the injury has occurred. I teach these up front so as to avoid the injury. There are no shortage of 'how to train' articles, and articles about near miraculous injury rehab are becoming more common. But I see a void in both literature and practical application - 'how to train to avoid injury as well as achieving other specific goals'.

In brief you and I have choices. We can enhance performance, or we can prevent injury, or we can do both. If we are going to do both, I like to do injury prevention first.

Flexibility

Flexibility is in my opinion the 'last-frontier of training'. It is so misunderstood and neglected. When the extent of it's contribution to performance and injury prevention is fully understood, it's status will be elevated. That will eventually happen - maybe around the year 2010 or even later! But you don't have to wait till then!

Flexibility is in my opinion the 'last-frontier of training'. It is so misunderstood and neglected.

What does flexibility offer? Optimal flexibility enhances function and length. Function is the ability to recruit the muscle. Length is the range of movement available. The end result includes the potential for greater rates of gain in muscle size and strength. A small number of studies are verifying this hypothesis. But if you accept that sport science and sport historians have much in common, you wouldn't be waiting for full confirmation. (The message is clear - we are getting close to the secret getting out – unless you want to wait until the masses are doing it, you had better get into it now!)

But perhaps more importantly is the reduced incidence of training-related injuries with optimal flexibility. What is optimal, you ask? To answer this, you could enter into protracted and abstract philosophical debates with your learned colleagues, or you could simply monitor the transfer or benefits from increased flexibility to strength and size - and when the returns finally ceased, consider the possibility that optimum has been reached. I would lean towards the latter. And take it from me - there aren't too many people or athletes whose flexibility is optimal or above!

An Example of Flexibility : perhaps the most classical example of the effects of flexibility on injury prevention and performance is the hip flexor and quadriceps muscles. Apply the physiological principle that the greater the length of the muscle fiber, the greater the potential to contract. Shortened hip flexor/quadriceps muscles may not only have impaired strength potential, but also my be limited in their hypertrophy potential. I have not seen any objective analysis of this, but I have noted that many of the biggest and best shaped quads in bodybuilding over the last few decades have belonged to individuals with above average hip flexibility. Doing the splits was invariably one of their party tricks!

What about the role of injury prevention? It is a matter of where do I start! I describe the length (and tension - more on that shortly) of the hip flexor/quadriceps group as being the key to the lower body health of the athlete. Here is how I believe it works. Tight hip flexors/quads pull the top of the pelvis forward excessively (anterior rotation). This then causes the nerves coming out of the lower spine to be pinched. This in turn results in nerve irritation and muscle spasm in the muscles that these nerves innervate. The symptoms are often pains down the leg, apparent strains in the hamstrings or calves and so on. The symptoms are many. The cause is simple - excessive anterior rotation of the pelvis due to tight muscles. Relief is rapid when the cause is treated!

> *I describe the length (and tension) of the hip flexor/quadriceps group as being the key to the lower body health of the athlete.*

A simple test for hip flexor/quadriceps flexibility : Lay on your back on a high bench or massage table, with your hips at the edge of the table, legs off the table. Have a partner lift one of your legs up and place the sole of this lifted leg on your partner's chest. Bend this leg to 90 degrees at the knee and hip.

Let the lower leg hang. If the hanging leg is above parallel to the ground, you have very tight hip flexors! If the leg is hanging outwards (relative to the long axis of the trunk), you have tight thigh abductors/external rotators. Now have your partner bend the knee of the hanging leg by pushing the heel under the table. If you cannot bend the knee is this manner past 90 degrees you have extremely tight quads. In brief, a high score in this position would be the knee depressed so that the upper leg is angled downwards, the hanging leg is pulled inwards by the partner so that it angles across the midline of the body, and the heel is tucked up under the body to the point the heel touches under the table or bed – and this feels comfortable. This is what I want!

How can I improve this : There are a number of stretches that can be used effectively to lengthen the hip flexors and quadriceps, but the above described test position is amongst the best of them. It does require a partner, but that drawback is compensated for by the power of passive partner stretching. It is very effective. Ten to twenty minutes per leg, 2-4 times a week, should get great results! You can learn more about my favorite stretching routines my video tape *Ian King's Guide To Individual Stretching.* If you are seeking more advanced information on flexibility I have also recorded my two day 'Flexibility Specialization' seminar on video, available at www. kingsports.net.

What to expect if this flexibility is improved : Try the above immediately before a leg workout. You will have range in your exercises like never before. You may experience less knee pain (if you had some before). You will cause muscle breakdown and strength overload at joint angles never experienced before. You will immediately know the benefits. And this is only half - keep up the flexibility work and you will have the benefits of reduced training time and gains lost due to injury.

Optimal tension also enhances function and length. It doesn't replace it. Rather it has synergy with flexibility.

Tension

Tension is the domain of the massage therapist. Of all people, they have the best grasp of this topic. Or at least they should. They are in the best position to make these judgments when massage treatment is frequent and continual. But how many trainee's get regular and long term massage?

What does tension offer? Optimal tension also enhances function and length. It can be seen as a parallel contribution with flexibility. It doesn't replace it. Rather it has synergy with flexibility. Again what is optimal? You know what I think - find out for your self by finding the point of diminished return. Different people, different actions, different muscles - all may have differing levels of optimal.

An Example of Tension : To continue on the example of above with the hips, consider the iliotibial band (ITB). This connective tissue runs on the lateral or outside of the upper leg, from hip to knee. When the tension of this tissue is high, amongst other things, it may contribute to pulling the kneecap in such a way that you may experience a low-level non-specific knee pain. You would be amazed to know how many cases of knee pain like this can be resolved simply by lowering the tension of the ITB.

A simple test for ITB tension : In addition to the information provided by the position of the upper leg in the 'end-of-bench' flex test used in the above, try this. Sit on the end of a chair or table and place your thumbs (right thumb on right side, left thumb on left, simultaneously) on the ITB, starting at the hip end. Close your eyes. You are going to assess the level of discomfort that arises from applying pressure through your thumbs to your ITB. You are also going to assess any differences in discomfort right to left. Push in with your thumbs - hard - now move the thumbs up and down (floor to head) over a range of an inch or so, maintaining this pressure. Do this at inch intervals all the way down the ITB (i.e. to just above the knee joint). Were the ITB sensitive? It may be normal for them to have a degree of discomfort, but if you were literally jumping out your chair, they are too tight! Were there any patches that were tighter than others? This identifies areas in need of say massage. Was there any difference right to left? This may give early warning of impending knee pain. You can also get a partner to apply the thumb pressure. They are less likely to be kind!

> *Massage is even more important for treating tension in tissue such as the ITB because of the difficulty in stretching it.*

How can I improve this : Stretching contributes to lowering tension in connective tissue. Massage has a very direct contribution also. However, massage may be even more important for treating tension in tissue such as the ITB because of the difficulty in stretching it. You can learn to self-massage (self-massage techniques are explained in *Sports Massage and Stretching*, by W. Cleys, 1990, Bantam, Aust.) or seek regular professional massage (you can tell whether your masseur is switched on to this concept by whether they specifically assess and treat ITB tension each session). I find the ITB most effectively massaged whilst lying on your side, bend the top side knee and take top-side knee forward so it is resting on the bed.

Get Buffed!™

What to expect if this tension is improved : The most obvious thing is that you will be able to apply the above test with lowered discomfort. Additionally, you may notice less crepitus or other discomfort in the knee during leg training. You may also find that you are able to stand with your feet parallel in normal stance and not feel uncomfortable ! (which is how you should be standing!)

Muscle Balance

Muscle balance is perhaps discussed more often in training literature than the above two concepts. But do you understand it? Have you applied it to your training program design? What does muscle balance offer? Optimal muscle balance also enhances function and length, and reduces the incidence of training related injuries. Sound familiar? It should by now!

In a discussion of optimal muscle balance I draw your attention to this. The statistics that are generally applied may not suit you, or the activity you are involved in. So don't get hung up on general opinions of optimal muscle balance. For example, the hamstring: quadriceps ratio is often quoted in terms of strength (even then most figures miss the mark). But what about muscle length? What is the optimum relative length of these two? Or tension? What is the optimum relative tension of the two muscles? What I am stressing here is broaden your awareness from the simple focus on power output (which is usually measured using resistance modes and positions of dubious relevance to human function anyway!).

Don't get hung up on general opinions of optimal muscle balance.

An Example of Muscle Balance: I will continue with the hip as the example. We have discussed the way in which the hip flexor/quadriceps muscles serve to pull the top of the hips forward (anteriorly rotate them). Which muscles counteract this? The gluteals and abdominals work synergistically to posteriorly rotate the pelvis (pull the top of the hip backwards). The balance (in length, tension and function/strength) between these four muscle groups will largely dictate the average position of the pelvis.

A simple test for hip muscle balance : Lay on the your back on the ground. Bend your knees up until your feet are flat on the ground. Now try to slide your hands under the curve of your lower back. Ideally, this curve will have disappeared with the raising of the feet. So you shouldn't be able to slide your hand under your lower back. Now stand back on to a wall, with your knees only slightly bent, and your heels about 4 inches from the wall. Again, try to slide your hand between the wall and your lower back. You are more likely to be able to in this test, as it is a tougher test. Now try to squeeze your lower back against your hand as hard as you can. Ideally, you are able to literally hurt your hand. But don't be surprised if you fail this test. Most do. And most need to do some work here.

How can I improve this : There are a number of ways to improve this muscle balance. The most common imbalance is the hip anterior rotators (hip flexors and quads) are dominant over the hip posterior rotators (gluts and abdominals). The keys to this imbalance are to lengthen and lower the tension of the hip flexors and quads, and to strengthen, shorten, and raise the tension of the gluteals and abdominals.

What to expect if this muscle balance is improved : You are less likely to experience lower back pain and any of the related nerve symptoms. You will have a greater appreciation of this if you are currently experiencing back pain. Relief will be rapid. You will also be able to place your pelvis in positions during lower body training that you may not have been in since you were in nappies. And the resultant strength and size improvements will be pleasing. For example, the way I teach the squat (in particular) requires this muscle balance around the hip. And it is extremely effective!

Joint control

Joint control has been popular for at least a decade in many conventional physical therapy teachings, but has yet to gain exposure in bodybuilding. The closest it has come is the use of exercises such as the external rotation of the upper arm. But this application appears sporadic. Many therapists place premium attention on joint control, placing less value on flexibility. I reverse this. I don't believe that control is worth the primary focus until length, tension and muscle balance have been addressed at least initially. They provide enhanced

> *One of the reasons I believe joint control has not taken off in bodybuilding is the way it is taught by some therapists.*

Get Buffed!™

function. Without function, control drills are redundant.

One of the reasons I believe the concept and training of joint control has not taken off in bodybuilding is the way it is taught by some therapists. Familiar more-so with the general population, the control drills used by some therapists lack progression from the initial non-loading/total control focus. Most trainee's will do these drills about twice and then say "Where are the weights?". The way I provide control drills, and progress them, you will not only develop control, you have opportunity to develop hypertrophy and consolidate technique, which a short time later translates into new levels of strength.

What does joint control offer? The ability to control the joint is conventionally viewed primarily as an injury prevention issue. I support this contribution, but take it a step further. The ability to control the joint allows the use of new technique. The way I teach a deadlift and squat, you need hip control. And whilst learning this new technique and joint control, you can be the recipient of hypertrophy in a way you will not have felt before. How do I know? Because every time I give this type of workout to an athlete, they will experience muscle pain like never before! If it was a leg workout, walking will become a challenge for a few days! And this was the 'control' program!

Because every time I give this type of workout to an athlete, they will experience muscle pain like never before! And this was the 'control' program!

An Example of Joint Control : It would be easiest to give you an abdominal drill as an example of hip control. But you have read about that before. So I will get more advanced. When I teach the deadlift, the first half of the lift (the 'first pull') is characterized by no change in trunk angle. Additionally, I want no change in pelvis positioning relative to the spine from start to the end of the 'first pull'. To achieve this, you will need to be able to fire your four major hip stabilizers (hip flexors, quadriceps, gluteals, abdominal) in a manner that prevents anterior or posterior rotation of the pelvis. Considering the usual muscle balances at play, this is a challenge for most. You can see my favorite upper and lower body control drills on my video tape *Ian King's Guide To Control Drills*.

A simple test for hip joint control : Lay on your back on the ground. Raise your legs until they are perpendicular to the ground (90 degrees at the hip). Tighten your abdominals until your lower back is squeezed against the ground. Now slowly lower your legs, noting the leg angle at which the pressure from the lower back onto the ground diminished in the first instance. Numerous authors throw numbers around for norms here. Put simply, a minimum desirable level may be at least say 45 degrees of control down from the 90 degree start. This is only one of the many tests available – I used it because it is easy to describe more than any other reason. There are others tests I prefer. You can see my favorite (the 'thin tummy' drill on my video tape *Ian King's Guide To Abdominal Training*.

How can I improve this : There are a number of drills you can do to improve this. However no amount of drilling will work if your muscle length or tension is preventing you from achieving the ideal joint angle. You need to improve your flexibility to a point where it is no longer the limiting factor, then you can work on the control drills. Examples of control drills include the leg lowering test as above, or a slow speed/ no load deadlift using the technique I described above.

What to expect if this joint control is improved : You will be able to dictate your hip position in exercises such as the deadlift and squat. At the moment, your lack of flexibility/high tension/muscle imbalance and so on are calling the shots. Put simply, you are not in control, you don't have a choice - until you master the above.

> *Warming up 'properly' will not in itself prevent injuries - but it will reduce the likelihood of traumatic injuries, and delay the onset of chronic or use injuries.*

Appropriate Warm-Up

Warming up 'properly' will not in itself prevent injuries - but it will reduce the likelihood of traumatic injuries, and delay the onset of chronic or use injuries. The warm up commences with a general warm-up - this could be the use of exercise to raise core body temperature, blood flow and raise arousal levels e.g. stationary bike or similar. I recommend this more-so for lower body strength training, and make it optional for upper body workouts.

The next component of the warm up is the stretch, which I suggest should take a minimum of 15-30 minutes (15 for upper body and 30 for lower body). The stretch should be followed by a series of control drills for the joints and muscles to be trained in the workout. The final component of the warm

Get Buffed!™

up are the specific warm up sets for each strength training exercise. Even when doing second or third exercises for the same muscle group, if the work set reps are below say 10 reps, I like to do a warm up set - even if it is less in number of reps than the work set. I believe that when the line of movement is changed, a specific warm up set is required. The benefits of this include assessing how that line of movement feels on that day, preparing the bone and soft tissue for loading in that specific line of movement, an opportunity to rehearse technique, and to confirm equipment placement and setting.

The use of and number of warm up sets is influenced by the reps and load to be used in the first work set - the lower the reps in the first work set, the more warm up sets needed and vice versa. This is illustrated in Figure 61.

I believe that when the line of movement is changed, a specific warm up set is required.

Figure 61 - Number of warm up sets required as influenced by load and reps of the first work set. (King, I., 1998)

First Work Set Reps	Number of Warm up sets Advised	Sample Reps & Sets
15 or above	0 -1	15
10-15	1-2	15/12 or 12/10
6-10	1-3	12/10 or 12/10/8 or 10/8/6
4-6	2-4	10/8; or 10/8/6 or 10/8/6/4
1-4	3-5	10/8/6; or 10/8/6/4 or 10/8/5/3 or 10/8/6/4/2

Yes, the warm up sets should be different for 'max lift' (maximal strength) sessions. Here, the aim is to keep the volume of the warm ups sets low to avoid residual fatigue from going into the work sets. You would in essence do less reps in each warm up set, and perhaps take bigger jumps. This is shown in Figure 62.

Figure 62 - An illustration of how to lower the volume in neural training to reduce the residual fatigue. (King, I., 1998)

Work Sets & Load	Conventional Warm-up Protocol	Reduced Warm-up Protocol
4 x 120 kg	10 x 20 kg	8 x 20 kgs
3 x 130 kg	8 x 50 kg	5 x 50 kg
2 x 140 kg	6 x 80 kg	3 x 80 kg
3 x 125 kg	4 x 100 kg	1 x 100 kg

The bigger the muscle group, the more relevant a general warm up is.

Here are some more points :

- you should avoid taking fatigue from warm up into the work sets;
- in hypertrophy training, I usually do higher volume warm ups than in neural training;
- when training an injured joint, I am very particular about my warm up;
- the bigger the muscle group, the more relevant a general warm up is e.g. I recommend say cardio warm-ups prior to leg days, but don't push this on upper body days.

If you are interested in visual cues on how to perform the stretching, muscle/joint control drills and abdominal, you can get this in a video format. I have created three short videos titled *Ian King's Guide to Individual Stretching, Ian King's Guide to Control Drills*, and *Ian King's Guide to Abdominal Training*. These are available as single videos or as a three video package. For more information or to order these videos go to www.getbuffed.net, or email us at info@getbuffed.net.

Get Buffed!™

Chapter 23
Injury management and rehabilitation

Taking care of business!

When injuries do occur - and they probably will - a smart approach to them will reduce the time they take to heal fully. The following are guidelines that will assist you to be 'smarter' in how you manage and rehabilitate your injuries:

Treat it immediately : take action immediately e.g. ice etc. Don't stick your head in the sand and hope it goes away.

Seek the services of a competent injury treatment professional : seek an assessment from a competent therapist, and have them treat the cause, not just the symptom. It is important to determine the cause of the current condition. Failure to do this may mean further repetitions of this condition.

Re-gain range : through stretching.

Develop strength through range : as you re-gain the range, through appropriately selected exercises and loads.

The following are guidelines that assist you to be 'smarter' in how you manage and rehabilitate your injuries.

Assess muscle balance : (e.g. right to left / front to back) and work to eliminate any imbalances.

If you do have a significant bilateral strength difference (i.e. one side is much stronger than the other side) **avoid bilateral movements.** A bilateral movement is where you are using both limbs together — therefore a barbell exercise is a bilateral movement. When you have a strength imbalance right to left, there is a tendency to 'shift' the load to the strong side, thus increasing the imbalance. The insidious part to this it that for most observers, this is not detectable visually until the imbalance has reached ridiculous proportions. Instead, plan to use 'uni-lateral' movements. A uni-lateral movement is where you use one limb at a time. When you use uni-lateral movements, consider applying my 'Weak-Side Rules', as described below. They apply to strength and flexibility training. These 'rules' are not text-book driven - they come from real-life personal and professional experience, and are guidelines only.

Ian's Weak Side Rules

1. Strength train the **weak or injured side first** and stretch the tighter side first;
2. then **MAYBE do the strong or longer side;**
3. do **no more reps or load (strength) or time (stretching) on the strong/long sides** than the weak/tighter side could do;
4. if the **imbalance is greater than 10%** or thereabouts consider doing a lower ratio of reps/time on the strong/long side to the weak side e.g. if the weak side can only do 10 reps, do only 5 reps on the strong side (or 2 sets on the weak side to one set on the strong side); or do 10 minutes of stretching on the tight side but only 5 minutes on the long side; this is a ratio of 2:1 weak/tight side to the strong/long side; if the imbalance is greater than 25-50 %, consider doing no work on the strong/long side at all.

With front to back imbalances it is necessary to identify them as early as possible, and takes steps to correct this imbalance. These imbalances include chest vs. upper back, internal vs. external rotation of the upper arm – these are two of the most damaging upper body front to back imbalances. Correcting

Get Buffed!™

imbalances may include performing additional work on the weak side. From a long term perspective, it is important to determine the cause of the problem – and remove it from the program design. If this step is not taken then expect the muscle imbalance to stay or return – and get worse!

For your information, I include 2-4 low volume/low intensity 'control' drills at the start of EVERY workout, aimed at reducing the muscle imbalance in the muscle groups to be trained on that day. This is part of my injury prevention 'insurance' policy – and it works! I don't always show them in sample programs because they are too complex to teach. However you can see my favorite control drill routine in my video tape *Ian King's Guide To Control Drills.*

Do things to accelerate the healing process : I strongly recommend, in addition to any dietary changes to support the healing process, you consider the use of glucosamine, Omega 3 oils, and antioxidants. These have been recognised for their role in protecting and healing joint/bone related injuries. Should you not have access or know which brands to buy in these supplements, you can order the brand we use by going to www.unitoday.net/king.

The key to rehab is to avoid any aggravation as a result of training.

The use of a short-term course of anti-inflamatories or similar may also be beneficial, as may be other modalities such as ice, heat, ultra-sound, magnets. In magnets, we have found a brand called Magna Bloc make an excellent magnet for blocking of pain!

Improve your warm up : I use a number of techniques to reduce the impact of the loading in strength training. The higher the joint temperature prior to loading, the greater the lubrication available in the joint. For example, for knees, I suggest you :

- wear some type of knee sleeve throughout the workout to maintain joint temperature;
- warm up on a stationary bike or similar for 10-20 minutes prior to stretching; and
- stretch the hip and knee muscles extensively (say 20-30 minutes) between the bike and the start of the workout (I have more techniques but start with these!).

Modify if problem persists : do not do any exercise if it causes pain or discomfort to the joint (as opposed to the muscle). I don't care what anyone says about whether it is a safe or dangerous movement (e.g. leg extensions are currently politically incorrect for knee trauma) - if it doesn't hurt, it is probably OK; if it does hurt - modify. Your options in modifying exercises include :

- reduce the load
- reduce the range
- slow the speed of movement down
- use both limbs to lift, then lower only with injured side
- finally, if all else fails, delete the exercise, and select an appropriate alternative

Don't ignore the pain!

Do not do any exercise if it causes pain or discomfort to the joint.

Along the way, remember this : **if you aggravate the joint at the start of the workout, it will probably hurt for the remainder of the workout**, which means no exercises will feel comfortable. If you aggravate the joint at any stage during or subsequent to the workout, you are simply setting back the healing process. If you aggravate the joint, the muscle function often becomes neurally inhibited - which means that not only will the muscles not gain in strength or size, but the loading will be taken through the joint to a greater extent (i.e. more wear on the joint surfaces).

The key to rehab is to **avoid any aggravation** as a result of training. Always train below the level of joint pain. Failure to do this comes with a heavy penalty!

Chapter 24

Belts, wraps, straps etc.

When and how to use them!

There are a number of personal training aids available that should play a role in your training. Just how much of a role is the question. The following discusses a few of them. The aim of this chapter is not to cover every aid known to man – rather to give you an insight into how and when to use some of them. You can then apply this rationale to any other aid not covered in this book and come to a more informed conclusion.

Most of the following will increase your ability to lift load – it is important to also understand the down-sides of each.

Belts

Ten years ago almost everyone wore a belt in the gym, without question. Now that the role of a belt is better understood, there is even more confusion! I know that doesn't make sense but when I get e-mails from people saying they heard belts were bad for them and what do I think etc. you know there is some serious misinformation going around. No, belts are not bad – they just need to be understood!

Quite simply a belt increases the load that you can lift. It does so by allowing an increase in intra-abdominal pressure – like an air bag blown up in front of the lower spine, so that the load of the bar wanting to push your trunk forward and down

Ten years ago almost everyone wore a belt in the gym, without question. Now that the role of a belt is better understood, there is even more confusion!

(flexion) is countered by the resistance of this air-bag. You collapse at the spine at a higher load. The intra-abdominal pressure is raised when the muscles of the stomach are pushed out against the belt, creating an action-reaction situation.

In competitive strength sports (powerlifting and Olympic lifting) belts have a role – when you need to lift more weight, the belt has a role to play. Belts also have a role to play in bodybuilding by raising the limiting factor of the assistance muscle (e.g. failure of the lower back in the squat), therefore theoretically allowing a greater overload on the prime movers (the muscle responsible for the bulk of the work). Not all EMG studies support this. However I am sure there is some benefit to the neuro-muscular system in general from being exposed to higher loading.

Belts may allow more load, but don't improve technique.

So what is the down-side of the belt? For athletes who need to improve the ability to contract their abdominals inwards, the belts are counter-productive. An athlete may want to possess the skill of being able to recruit the abdominal muscles in a corset like manner – pulling them inwards, stabilizing the pelvis and lower back. In this case, I avoid or minimize the use of a belt.

Belts may allow more load, but don't improve technique. In fact research results of squatting with a belt suggest technical changes, which I interpret for the worse! So if the load used (because of the belt) exceeds technical ability – you have an increased risk of injury, and a reduced selective recruitment of muscle. Most people use loads in excess of their technical ability without a belt, let alone with a belt!

Some ask if it is OK to use a belt to 'protect' a back injury. I avoid absolute no's and yes's, but as a general comment, if you have a back injury, you shouldn't be doing any loading that risks lower back injury anyway! So no, I would prefer to rehab the injury and do less stressful leg exercises at the time. Using a belt will not rehab the injury. In fact the stabilizer muscles may actually be detraining with the use of the belt. Don't stick your head in the sand by using a belt and hoping the injury will go away – address the injury!

To sum up this section on belts – I don't use them very often. In the first few years of any person's strength training, there

Get Buffed!™

really is no need. The technical skill is rarely there. Then when the loads are higher, belts can be used sparingly e.g. at the peaking phases of a program. Of course this may be a little different for a competitive powerlifter, but even for them I suggest phases of no belt.

If or when you do go to use a belt, let me help you exploit them to a greater extent. If you are a person with little emotional control and want instant gratification, you will probably want to go straight to the 6" powerlifting belt. But if you have read this far I assume you have the discipline to make the short term sacrifices for the long term gain.

In the periodization of belt use, I can easily identify at least four phases :

- 4" Olympic type belt worn loosely
- 4" Olympic type belt worn tightly
- 6" powerlifting belt worn loosely
- 6" powerlifting belt worn tightly

The knee wrap neither reduces or increases risk of injury to the knee.

This is an excellent way to cycle the use of a belt, which will result in a much greater end result than going straight to the end option. There is a further variable in the age of the belt – an old belt may be less supportive – a newer belt may be more supportive. I understand that the age of the belt variable may be of greater interest to the competitive powerlifter than to the average person lifting weights.

Wraps

Wraps are elastic type bandages typically wrapped around the knees and wrists. They are a staple part of the competitive powerlifters kit. The knee wraps, like a belt, can allow a lifter to lift more. The wrist wraps unlike either the belt or the knee wraps, don't necessarily increase the load lifted. Rather they aim to reduce the strain on the joint.

There has been a lot of debate as to whether the use of the knee wraps are damaging in any way to the knee. My understanding is that the knee wrap neither reduces or increases risk of injury to the knee. The real injury risk is when they allow a load to be lifted that exceeds your technical ability – just like the belts.

And just like the belts I suggest they be used sparingly, in the heavier load phases of your program. If or when you do use knee wraps, consider this periodization, for the same reasons I gave for the periodization of the belt:

- older wraps put on loosely
- older wraps put on tightly
- newer wraps put on loosely
- newer wraps put on tightly

I did mention age of the belt as a factor, but age of the knee wraps is even more critical, as it seriously affects the elasticity of the wraps.

I recommend virtually all those using strength training to wear wrist wraps in any lift where there is compressional forces through the wrist.

I do however recommend all strength trainers use knee sleeves. These are made from material similar to diving or surfing wet-suits. They are not necessarily tight and therefore don't increase the load lifted. But they serve to increase and maintain knee joint temperature – this is vital! They should go on before the general total body warm-up and stay on until the end of the workout.

Wrist wraps are different. They are there to reduce the strain on the wrist joint. For me they are different also because I recommend virtually all those using strength training to wear wrist wraps in any lift where there is compressional forces through the wrist. This includes squats, power cleans, all pushing movements (bench, shoulder press, tricep extensions) and in some cases bicep curl (e.g. preacher bench). They have little role to play in pulling movements (e.g. chins and rows) but do serve to keep the wrist joint warm.

The variable that you should be manipulating with wrist wraps is the tension. As the load increases, so should how tight you wrap them. Of course, back them off during the rest periods!

Many commercial wrist wraps are fairly short, and this will be adequate for most trainees. But for those who are lifting more or more often, I recommend the type about 1/2 meter in length, similar to what you would expect a powerlifter to wear. They give more support, and allow a greater variation in tension.

Straps

Straps are typically used to ensure the hand grip is not lost. Bodybuilders tend to use them on pulling movements such as rows and chins, and strength sport athletes on pulling movements such as snatches, cleans, their pull variations and deadlifts. Wrist straps will allow you to use more weight, and ensure that the assistant muscle (the forearm) does not limit the load exposed to the prime mover.

The down-side is that the forearm muscles are not getting as much work. For a bodybuilder with poorly developed forearms I strongly recommend limiting the use of the straps. For a general strength athlete I would say the same – save them up for limited parts of the program where you can use them to shock the body with greater load exposure.

Wrist straps will allow you to use more weight.. The down-side is that the forearm muscles are not getting as much work.

Most Olympic lifters know not to overuse the wrist wrap as they cannot use them in competitions. Similarly most powerlifters realize that an adaptation or reliance on them could cost them as they too are not able to use them in competition.

If you are not a competitive Olympic lifter but do the cleans, snatches and their variations, know that it is OK to use the wrist straps on heavy pulls, and cleans and snatches from the hang above. In off the ground snatches and clean, try to avoid using them.

If you are not a competitive powerlifter but do the conventional (bent-knee) deadlift off the ground, use chalk as your first anti-slip option, then go to a revere grip if you find your hands slipping. If you are not sure how this is done you can check it out on the *Get Buffed!™ Video Series.* Use wrist straps as a last resort.

Bench suit

A bench suit is really a powerlifter's 'tool', allowing more load to be lifted in the bench. A general strength athlete or bodybuilder could use it to provide additional overload on their neuro-muscular system during maximal strength phases in the same way a belt can be used – but bench suits are not convenient to use. It can take up to 3 people to put them on!

Squat suits

Squats suits are similar to bench suits – they are part of a powerlifter's kit, and can take a few helpers to get on. They could be used by others to increase load and therefore affect the neuro-muscular system. Just make sure you have good spotters. Squat suits do blow! By this, I mean when the seam in the crutch comes apart all of a sudden—can be scary, especially if it happens near full-depth in the squat!

There is a soft or less elastic suit, typically worn by Olympic lifters. As an advanced non-competitive strength trainer, if you want to workout say in the deadlifts with more comfortable attire, this could be a consideration.

I like to use it with any exercise I feel myself slipping on e.g. chin ups, wide grip bench press, cleans and deadlifts, etc.

Chalk

Chalk is that white powdery stuff you see in many gyms. You can put in on your hands and it will increase the adhesion of your grip to the bar. I like to use it with any exercise in which I feel my hands slipping on e.g. chin ups, wide grip bench press, cleans and deadlifts, etc. The more important the lift, the greater attention to detail I would take in applying it.

Competitive powerlifters will also use chalk on the upper back to reduce the chances of the bar slipping down off the back.

Powder

Powder (as in baby powder or talcum) can be used to reduce the friction of the bar on the body. Competitive powerlifters use it on their thighs so that the bar will slip up. Just be careful not to get it on your hands or else the bar will slip out real quick!

Get Buffed!™

Smelling salts

Smelling salts come in various types (bottles, caps, etc.) but basically they aim to increase level of arousal. Commonly used by the strength sport athlete, they could more used more by the advanced strength trainer/bodybuilder. They may allow more load lifted, and therefore give a greater training effect. There are no real side-effects, as long as you're progressive in their use – a big sniff on the first few uses will probably cause some serious head spins!

Smelling salts come in various types (bottles, caps, etc.) but basically they aim to increase level of arousal.

Chapter 25
Recovery methods

How to accelerate recovery from training!

I have taught you the importance of the concept of recovery in the bigger picture of getting the training effect. Now it is time to get specific and learn more about recovery. The following discusses issues that you should master in your application of recovery methods.

Time

Time is one of the most powerful factors in life. Time when applied to compounding interest prompted Einstein to name it one of the wonders of the world.

You will recover from training in time. The purpose of the following recovery methods is simply to reduce the time that you have to wait before you can optimally train again.

You will recover from training in time. The purpose of the following recovery methods is simply to reduce the time that you have to wait before you can optimally train again.

However not even all the recovery methods combined can compensate or eliminate the need for time. Don't forget this. I have a little saying in training - if in doubt, don't do it. If you are not sure whether you are ready to train again - you probably aren't!

Time applies not only to number of hours or days between training session, but also in the ratio of weeks recovery to training weeks. You may be surprised as to how many recovery weeks you would benefit from taking. I recommend at least one full recovery week after each 12 week training block, and for many of you, I would suggest you consider as low a training week: recovery week ratio as 3: or 4: 1. That's right - one week off after only 3 or 4 weeks training!

The longest period of uninterrupted training that I would recommend is 12 weeks or micro-cycles (for our purposes these terms are synonymous). This would be followed by a full rest week. The minimum period of uninterrupted training I would recommend would be 3 weeks. This may be followed by a half or full recovery week.

A full recovery week would involve no specific training e.g. no strength training, but may involve non-specific alternative activity provided it was light in volume and intensity e.g. easy roller-blading, cycling etc. A half recovery week or micro-cycle involves a significant reduction in training volume, spread out throughout the week or condensed to one half, allowing a full recovery in the other half. Intensity may also be reduced in the half-recovery week.

Examples of these work/rest week ratios appear in Figure 63. Ignoring this concept is a guarantee to over-training and injury. If you feel your recovery levels are lower than ideal, use a shorter work period e.g. 3:1, 4:1 etc. Then decide whether to use a full or half recovery week in the recovery week. I find the average person should use no longer than a 6-9 week of uninterrupted training. There is no alternative after 12 weeks - take a full recovery week!

Nutrition

Diet in recovery is incredibly important. Traditionally, this is one thing that I believe bodybuilders have done well. They typically take a greater interest in their nutrition than other athletes, and take responsibility to educate themselves on this vital aspect of performance.

I won't dwell on this oft-discussed topic. But I will bring to your attention some of the aspects of nutrition that probably don't receive as much attention as does total calories and relative percentages - yet should.

I recommend at least one full recovery week after each 12 week training block.

134   Get Buffed!™

What are you really eating? : Any discussion about optimal calorie intake or percentage of protein, carbohydrates and fats is really a total waste of time - unless you are actually counting the calories and calculating the percentages! Unless have done this in writing, and over a significant period of time e.g. 4-12 weeks, any discussion of this nature is purely academic. Don't kid yourself - get out your diary, buy a calorie/nutrient counter book - and do yourself a favor. Get to really know what you are doing - and more importantly - what the result of this specific combination is.

Meal timing : The time of the day that you eat the meal is perhaps as if not more important than what you eat. A lot of debate is on-going on the subject of what is the maximal amount of protein you can assimilate per meal. Nice, but this gets a bit boring. It would be a concern if you were either overweight (more accurately over-fat) or malnourished! What I would like to see more focus go towards is the issue of optimal time between food intakes. Anyway, until commonsense prevails, and popular debate becomes focused on the real needs, I would strongly suggest you respect the time-honored tradition in bodybuilding of eating every 2-3 hours.

Any discussion about optimal calorie intake or percentage of protein, carbs and fats is really a total waste of time - unless you are actually counting the calories and calculating the percentages.

Figure 63 - Examples of Work/Recovery week/micro-cycle ratios.

Ratio	Rationale
3:1	• recommended as part of a 12 wk cycle i.e. 3+1/3+1/3+1, using half recovery weeks in week. 4 and 8 and a full recovery week in wk 12 or similar • for those with less than optimal recovery situations can also use a full recovery week after each 3 weeks
4:1	• the first method above can be used here creating a 15 wk cycle • the second method above can be used here also, using a 1x4 wk block of training or dividing the 4 weeks up into 2x2 week programs
6:1	• if training for 6 weeks continuously, you have the choice of a half recovery week or a full recovery week
8:1	• if training continuously for 8 weeks, I would lean towards the use of a full recovery week; the work period could be 2x4 wk blocks or 4x2 wk blocks
9:1	• if training continuously for 9 weeks, I again would lean towards the use of a full recovery week; this work period suits the use of 3x3 wk training blocks
12:1	• this is the longest period of continual training I would recommend and should only be used by those with superior recovery situations • your work week training blocks, if not using any recovery weeks as in the first example above, may be 6x2 wks, 4x3 wks, or 3x4 wks; only a real beginner will benefit from 2x6 wk blocks

Post training intake Part of this timing of meals is the timing of the post training intake. I strongly suggest it occurs ASAP e.g. within 10-15 minutes. Why? Even science has shown (and some time ago) the difference in ATP replenishment between no post-training intake and having a post-training intake. Training breaks the body down, erodes nutrient and substrate stores - get them back into ASAP! I consider this perhaps one of the most important meals of the day. Yet how many treat it in this manner?

What should it consist of? A post-training protein drink has been a traditional habit of bodybuilding. The academic community (especially the nutritionists), spent quite some time attempting to break down the credibility of this habit. (I suspect that it was because they didn't think of it, and they weren't required to advise on how to make a protein shake...) Science in the 80's went down the carbohydrate only path, but I question the motives. Academic support has swung back to a more balanced protein/carb mix in fluid form. Interesting... what is a protein drink....!? The research during the 80's focused on replacement of the muscle glycogen. More strength oriented research has focused on the hormonal effect. The aim of a post training intake is not only to accelerate the replacement of muscle glycogen, but also to combat/reduce the rising cortisol levels resulting from training. Elevated cortisol levels have been linked in increased catabolism.

> *The aim of a post training intake is not only to accelerate the replacement of muscle glycogen, but also to combat/ reduce the rising cortisol levels resulting from training.*

End of day meals/intakes : For those wanting to lower body fat, I strongly recommend moving the last intake for the day as far away from bedtime as you can. 3-4 hours is ideal, but at least 2-3. This increases the length of the 'fast', which in reality night time is – broken by the 'breakfast'. Using this method consistently is one of the most effective ways to lower body fat – and it is doesn't take a lot of effort!

End of day carbs : There is a well supported belief that your body doesn't assimilate carbs as effectively later in the day. In addition to the above recommendation, keep the carb content in the end of day meal low, and avoid high glycemic (fast acting) carbs later in the day.

Is there an optimal diet? : I doubt it. Why do I say this? Because diet should be like training - you should be varying it.

Even using the most simple form of variation is better than none. This might be lowering your intake on non-training days, fasting in recovery weeks or similar. The other end of the continuum is to use some form of revolving diet which is popularly prescribed by various nutrition experts.

Supplements

Are supplements necessary? No - they are not <u>necessary</u>. Do I believe they are effective? Yes. However I have to qualify this response. How your body responds to a given supplement is influenced by your genetics, your current physiology/ biochemistry, your diet, your training and so. Put simply, a supplement is more likely to have an effect where there is a deficiency, be it a deficiency created by the training, the environment or your genetic make-up.

I like to see a supplement on the market about 3 years before coming to too many conclusions.

As a coach, I like to see a supplement on the market for about 3 years before coming to too many conclusions. The power of marketing can have a great placebo effect. But after a few years, any supplements that could be described as 'unclear' get sorted out by the consumer demand and supply. If you analyzed the 'rage' supplements as per marketing dollar each year for the last 10 years, you would be stunned by how many 'almost-like-a drug' supplements have come and gone.

I see supplements as falling into the following categories of use :

Immune/health system enhancers
Muscle mass enhancers
Lower body fat enhancers
Strength/power enhancers
Anaerobic power/work capacity enhancers
Aerobic power/work capacity enhancers
Recovery enhancers
Sleep enhancers
Injury prevention/rehabilitation enhancers

Immune/health system enhancers

These supplements work to support the body's immune system. An excellent example of a supplement that we place in this category is the multi-vitamin. I believe this supplement should be the cornerstone of your supplement program. In addition to supporting the immune system and your general health, they will enhance the utilization of the nutrients in your diet and other supplements. This supplement has received mainstream support for some time, which is something that many supplements cannot lay claim to. There are a number of other supplements that I have placed in this category which are not as universally agreed upon as to their effects.

Within this category, there are two main means to achieve this goal - anabolic and anti-catabolic.

Muscle mass enhancers

These supplements contribute to increasing the non-fat weight component of the body (e.g. muscle and connective tissues). This is important for athletes who may be wanting to increase their weight (e.g. for contact sports) or (absolute) strength, as there is a correlation between muscle mass and strength potential. Within this category, there are two main means to achieve this goal - anabolic (increase muscle tissue) and anti-catabolic (prevent breakdown of muscle tissue resulting from training). A protein powder could be considered an anabolic tool, whereas the product HMB is promoted as an anti-catabolic tool.

Many of the supplements listed as lean body weight enhancers also contribute to increased strength and power.

Lower body fat enhancers

These supplements contribute to lowering the fat component of the body. In addition to those simply wanting to get lean for personal reasons, the lowering of body fat is important for athletes wanting to improve their mobility, their fluid or air resistance, or improve their strength to weight ratio (relative strength). It is possible to increase strength levels while maintaining or slightly lowering the total body weight, but this method is limited compared to the athlete who can concurrently increase body weight (absolute strength). Within this category there are two main mechanisms for achieving this goal - firstly by increasing the body temperature and/or metabolism (i.e. thermogenic e.g. ephedrine or guarana), and secondly by increasing the utilization of fat as an energy source (e.g. carnitine, caffeine). Remember, your body fat issues may require more attention than simply taking a supplement. You should at least be reviewing nutrition and lifestyle issues.

Strength/power enhancers

These supplements contribute to increased strength or power. It is important to note that increased strength does not necessarily lead to increased power, as by definition power requires that strength be applied quickly. However it is generally accepted that increased strength levels provide opportunities for increased power levels. Many of the supplements listed as enhancers of strength and power are also lean body weight enhancers.

Supplements in this category achieve enhanced anaerobic power through two main means - by increasing stores of energy available in the muscle or by buffering against elevated lactic acid in the muscle cell.

Anaerobic power/work capacity enhancers

The supplements that have been placed in this category directly enhance short term or anaerobic power and work capacity i.e. the ability to produce high level effort over a short-medium period of time (power) or repetitively (work capacity). This is relevant to sports where short to medium duration, high level expression of power are required, and range from sports where a single effort is required (e.g. weightlifting through to rowing); through to sports where multiple efforts are required (e.g. interval power sports such as most Australian team sports). The former can be described as anaerobic power, whilst the latter can be described as anaerobic work capacity. Supplements in this category achieve enhanced anaerobic power through two main means - firstly, by increasing stores of energy available in the muscle cell (e.g. creatine monohydrate) or by buffering against elevated lactic acid in the muscle cell (e.g. sodium bicarbonate).

Aerobic power/work capacity enhancers

The supplements that have been placed in this category directly enhance long term efforts or aerobic power and work capacity i.e. the ability to produce effort over a long period of time. This is relevant to sports ranging from where a continual, medium duration, high level expression of power is required (e.g. rowing) ; through to sports where a continual, longer duration, lower level of power expression is required (e.g. a marathon).

The former may be described as aerobic power, and the latter aerobic capacity. The two best known traditional nutritional supplement mechanisms for enhancing aerobic power/work capacity involve increasing the utilization of fat as an energy source, similar to the mechanisms discussed in lower body fat (e.g. caffeine); and buffering lactic acid in the blood and muscle (e.g. sodium bicarbonate).

One aspect of sleep perhaps not fully appreciated is that most of the body's daily growth hormone release occurs during sleep.

Recovery enhancers

The role of recovery in the total approach to training and competition has received more focus in the western world during the last decade. The use of nutritional supplements to accelerate recovery is a topic that has yet to receive appropriate attention however. Enhanced recovery from training and competition is relevant to all sports. The primary benefits include an increased rate of adaptation (i.e. the training effect occurs at a faster rate) and improving state of recovery prior to competition. Recovery enhancers can achieve their goals in a number of ways, including enhanced recovery of the muscle tissue, enhanced recovery of chemical substrates within the body (metabolic), and enhanced recovery of the neural system (neural). Supplements aiming to enhance recovery of the neural system have only been the subject of attention in recent time, and even then only by a small number of people.

Sleep enhancers

The main components contributing to physical preparation include training, nutrition and recovery - of which sleep is a major component. Whilst the majority of focus is given to training, and there is an increased awareness in nutrition, sleep is arguably the most neglected component of the 'training triangle'. It is during sleep that many components of recovery and regeneration occur. Sleep under normal circumstances may need no assistance, but those involved in strength training often experience situations or conditions where their sleep quality is challenged. This includes sleep disturbance caused by heavy training loads. One aspect of sleep perhaps not fully appreciated is that most of the body's daily growth hormone release occurs during sleep. It is possible that this release is negatively affected by poorer quality sleep. At this point in time, specific sleep enhancing supplements are limited in numbers, but no doubt will be added to as knowledge and focus in this area increases.

Injury prevention/rehabilitation enhancers

This category, along with the sleep enhancers, includes many new, exciting and extremely beneficial supplements - in areas traditionally neglected from the supplement perspective. Many common injury ailments of the athlete - arthritic joint pain, swelling, inflammation etc. can all be addressed through supplement methods. While not always as effective as drugs, they offer the benefit of lower toxicity. Another issue needing consideration in injury prevention is the combating of free radicals in the body. Many supplements are credited with anti-oxidant capabilities. Free radicals are molecules with unpaired electrons, and are highly reactive and potentially damaging to our cells. Free radicals are created in a number of situations, including metabolism, fat oxidation, and pollution. It is believed that participation in training increases the production of free radicals.

Many common injury ailments of the athlete - arthritic joint pain, swelling, inflammation etc. can all be addressed through supplement methods. While not always as effective as drugs, they offer the benefit of lower toxicity.

The following lists indicate which supplements I have found to perform in which categories. These lists include supplements that have been reported as being effective for a specific purpose. I have included them irrespective of whether I personally am convinced that the supplement does achieve the purpose of it's category. I feel that while some may lacks in support, we await further scientific and empirical evidence.

Immune/health system enhancers

Androstenedione
Antioxidants
Co-Enzyme Q10
DHEA
Glutamine
Iron
Melatonin
Multi-vitamin/mineral
Vitamin C
Vitamin E
Zinc

Muscle mass enhancers

Androstenedione
BCAAs
Chromium
Creatine monohydrate
DHEA
Fat supplements
Glutamine
HMB
Magnesium
Protein supplements
Vanadium (Vanadyl Sulfate)
Vitamin C

Lower body fat enhancers

Androstenedione
BCAAs
Caffeine
Carnitine
Chromium
DHEA
Ephedra (Ma Huang)
Ephedrine
Fat supplements
Glutamine

Guarana
HMB
White Willow Bark
Yohimbe

Strength/power enhancers

Androstenedione
BCAAs
Caffeine
Carbohydrate supplements
Choline
Creatine monohydrate
DHEA
Ephedra (Ma Huang)
Ephedrine
Fat supplements
Glutamine
Guarana
HMB
Magnesium
Sodium bicarbonate
Tribulus Terrestris
Tyrosine
Vitamin C

There are some perils associated with providing lists like this. I strongly suggest you see the above for what is was intended - a general guide.

Anaerobic power/work capacity enhancers

Creatine monohydrate
Caffeine
Calcium
Carbohydrate supplements
Sodium bicarbonate
Tyrosine

Aerobic power/work capacity enhancers

BCAAs
Calcium
Carnitine

Co-Enzyme Q10
Creatine monohydrate
Ephedra (Ma Huang)
Ephedrine
Fat supplements
Ginseng
Guarana
Iron
Sodium bicarbonate
Tyrosine

Recovery enhancers

Anti-oxidants
BCAAs
Carbohydrate supplements
Creatine monohydrate
Electrolyte supplements
Ginseng
Glutamine
HMB
Multi-vitamin/mineral
Protein powders
St. John's Wort
Vitamin C
Vitamin E

Sleep enhancers

Melatonin

Injury rehabilitation/prevention enhancers

Anti-oxidants
Calcium
Co-Enzyme Q10
Electrolyte supplements
Glucosamine
Glutamine
Melatonin

Multi-vitamin/mineral
Proteases
Vitamin C
Vitamin E

There are some perils associated with providing lists like this. I strongly suggest you see the above for what is was intended - a general guide. Not every supplement is going to do what was intended for every person who uses it. And as research and commercial trends change, this list is going to change. Some things don't change too much however. Check out Bill Starr's nutrition and supplement recommendations in his 1979 classic book, *The strongest shall survive : strength training for football*, (Fitness Products Ltd, Washington). Most of that information is still effective today, to his credit!

If I had to select one supplement as **the number one bodybuilding supplement** (and if you are on a limited budget you are probably interested in this) I would say creatine. Therefore I have included more information on this fantastic bodybuilding supplement.

If I had to select one supplement as the number one bodybuilding supplement I would say creatine.

What is the purpose of creatine? Creatine gained popularity in the early 1990s for its ability to boost anaerobic power. A short time later strength athletes realized the enormous strength benefits from creatine use, and then it became apparent that muscle mass development could be accelerated with creatine use. While there is limited support in science for the ergogenic benefits of creatine for the endurance athlete, we suggest that they do exist, they are just not as significant as they may be for the anaerobic or power athletes.

More recent research suggests that creatine may also be able to improve blood lipid levels and increase metabolic rate.

How long has creatine been around? Creatine was 'discovered' in 1832, and has been subject to sporadic attention until the early 1990's, when it gained popularity commercially and in scientific studies.

Which category/s does creatine fit into? Creatine is another multi-purpose supplement and we place it in the following categories :

Muscle mass enhancement
Strength/power enhancement
Anaerobic power
Aerobic power
Recovery enhancement

What is creatine derived from? Creatine is synthesized within the body from the precursor amino acids arginine, glycine, and methionine.

Is creatine formed naturally in the body? Yes. This creatine production occurs in the liver, pancreas and kidneys. This production may occur more-so when the dietary consumption of creatine is inadequate to meet the bodies needs.

The traditional approach has been to commence with a loading phase of between 20-30 gms/ day for a week, and then revert to maintenance dose of about 5-10 gms/day for about 4-6 weeks.

How is creatine proposed to work? Creatine is proposed to work in the following ways :

- **Muscle enhancement** : it is theorized that the rate of fast twitch fiber hypertrophy is accelerated in the presence of supplemental creatine; and increased strength potential provides another mechanism for hypertrophy;

- **Strength/power enhancement** : creatine draws fluid into the muscle cell, increasing cell leverage, and increases the intra-muscular stores of the energy substrate involved in muscular contraction - creatine;

- **Anaerobic power enhancement** : creatine increases the intra-muscular stores of the energy substrate involved in muscular contraction - creatine;

- **Aerobic power enhancement** : the mechanisms are unclear due to lack of support in literature, but in the least it will ensure higher levels of stored creatine when shorter, higher intensity efforts are required in the aerobic (endurance) activity;

- **Recovery enhancement** : replaces energy substrates to the worked muscle following training.

Does creatine work? There is more than adequate support for all the above with the exception of the aerobic power enhancement issue. Additionally, the effect on metabolic rate and blood lipid profile referred to in the opening paragraph are newer claims, perhaps requiring more research.

Who might benefit from using creatine? I believe that this is one of (if not the) most effective nutritional supplement available - one of the true breakthroughs in nutritional supplementation science. It's application is broad, and therefore I believe every person using strength training should consider it. And it is one of the few supplements that may give you that 'pick up' that many people are looking for - it is potentially a 'feel good' supplement (e.g. often included in a supplement stack for chronic fatigue syndrome sufferers).

What form is creatine available in? Creatine monohydrate is found mostly in powder form, but is available in capsules.

What is creatine's availability? Creatine is available over the counter in most health food stores or similar.

Considering it's effectiveness, creatine has been found to be relatively free of side-effects.

How much creatine should be taken? The traditional approach has been to commence with a loading phase of between 20-30 gms/day for a week, and then revert to maintenance dose of about 5-10 gms/day for about 4-6 weeks. This is based on approximately a 0.3 gm of creatine per kg of bodyweight during the loading period, and as low as 0.03 gm of creatine per kg of bodyweight during the maintenance phase. More advanced methods are available, taking into account the athletes bodyweight, and averaging 0.3 gms creatine/kg of bodyweight throughout the full duration of the cycle on a varied dose (ascending and/ or descending).

Should creatine be taken at any particular time of day? Dosages should be divided equally throughout the day, with some suggestion that an intake 30-60 minutes before training and another one immediately after training may increase utilization and uptake respectively. There is a lot of debate about optimal timing.

Are there any foods/supplements that creatine should or should not be taken with? There has been a popular recent trend towards consuming creatine with simple carbohydrates. The rationale is that the carbohydrates in the fruit juice will cause an 'insulin response', often described as an 'insulin spike'. Insulin is credited with enhancing the transportation of creatine into the muscle cell. Grape juice is highly recommended as having one of the highest 'insulin releasing' effects of all juices e.g. mix the creatine with three to six ounces of grape juice.

Is creatine commonly combined with any other supplements? More 'advanced' creatine products are currently being presented with other nutrients that may either increase the effectiveness of transport (e.g. insulin mimickers) or promote cellular swelling (e.g. taurine, glutamine, and glycine).

Any other user suggestions for creatine? Make sure you divide the dose rather than taking it all at once. Too much creatine in one intake is an invitation for gastro-intestinal disturbances. Multiples of 5-10gm per intake are suggested, with a strong recommendation not to exceed 10-15 gm per intake for the over 90 kg person, and to be safe, not to exceed 5-10 gm per intake for the less than 90 kg person.

So how do I know if any supplement is working for me? The only way to really know is to use it, and use it in isolation i.e. with no other supplements.

Are there any side-effects from using creatine? Considering it's effectiveness, creatine has been found to be relatively free of side-effects. The side-effects generally associated with creatine supplementation include gastro-intestinal reactions and weight gain (if you call that a side effect!). Special methods can be employed to reduce the risk of gastro-intestinal reactions.

I have heard on a lesser number of occasions athletes reporting muscle cramping, and this needs further investigation.

Is creatine an IOC banned substance? No.

Here are more further issues relating generally to supplement use :

So how do I know if any supplement is working for me? The only way to really know is to use it, and use it in isolation i.e. with no other supplements. Ideally also at a time when your life is 'usual', i.e. no unusual stresses, training is 'usual'. This is the only way to conduct your own assessment of a supplement. Provided you are objective about it, after a few weeks you should be able to come to a conclusion. Having said that, some supplement have a longer term effect e.g. an anti-oxidant, so maybe you won't feel the effect of these within a few weeks. But if the supplement is promoted as having a noticeable short-term effect, then judge it in this light. There is nothing wrong with concluding 'hey, this supplement did nothing for me'.

Should I cycle my supplements? Definitely! Ignore any manufacturers advice to the contrary. The best results to any supplement is when it 'surprises' the body. The great thing about having such a range of supplements to choose from is that when you are on a break from one, you can be using another. This doesn't mean it is bad to use more than one at a time.

Drugs

I have no intention of turning this section into a pharmaceutical guide. If you want information like that, read Dan Duchaine's *Underground Steroid Handbook* or Bill Phillips' *Anabolic Reference Guide* or similar. There is no shortage of info on how to/what to take. Nor am I going to bother with taking a moral stance on the issue. What you do is your choice. The reality is that drugs exist, they are used, and they can be very effective. But nothing is for free. Keep this last point in mind if you are considering this path. Whilst many of the bodybuilding drugs are not physiologically addictive, they are arguably emotionally addictive.

Another interesting point was the shift in perspective in viewing anabolic drugs purely as that - anabolic - through to a realization that the mechanism that many of them rely upon may well be more of an anti-catabolic role (i.e. protecting from or preventing muscle breakdown under stress). It was this realization that lead to the anti-catabolic steroid alternative search, from which supplements such as HMB were developed.

If you want mainstream balanced info on ergogenic aids read

Whilst many of the bodybuilding drugs are not physiologically addictive, they are arguably emotionally addictive.

also the writings of authors such as James E. Wright (he wrote the excellent texts *Anabolic Steroids and Sports Volumes 1 and 2* in the 70' and 80's), and Melvin H. Williams, who wrote *Beyond Training : How athletes enhance performance legally and illegally* (1989).

The bottom line from a training perspective (as opposed to a health or moral perspective) is that you need to take into account the impact of the presence or absence of drugs on your recovery ability. If you are not using drugs note you may be better off using lower volume and limiting your exposure to supra-maximal intensity methods.

Sleep

I believe that the role of sleep is the least exploited in what I describe as the training triangle - eating, sleeping and training.

Don't underestimate the importance of sleep. Most of your natural growth hormone release occurs during sleep. Most of your recovery occurs during sleep. Don't mess with it!

I believe that the role of sleep is the least exploited in what I describe as the training triangle - eating, sleeping and training. Is there lots of books about training? Definitely! Is there a lot of books about nutrition? For sure! But how many books have you read about sleep? Get the picture? (get a book on sleep and read up on it!) I believe that this un-exploited component of training will be a hip focus of the future. Why wait? Get ahead of the rest and self-educate on the topic now!

I am not interested in a debate about optimal number of hours sleep required per night. For optimal training I like 9-10 hours per night when in full training. If you can operate optimally on less, great, but you will never know if more is better until you try it.

Taking short naps during the day is great provided you are used to it, and that it doesn't interfere with you ability to sleep your usual pattern that night.

Sleep is more than just how many hours. The pattern is equally important. If you are used to getting 9 hours between 9 pm and 6 am, and one night alter it to between 11 pm and 8 am, you will probably suffer for doing so. The duration may be the same - it is the alteration in patterns relative to your Circadian rhythm that is hurting you. Minimize messing with your patterns of sleep.

There is also a theory that the hours of sleep before mid-night are worth 2 hours of sleep after midnight. I have found this to be a valid theory. Don't ignore it.

Stress and stress management

Stress is an insidious anti-recovery aspect. Insidious because many don't pick up on it. Here are some of the types of stress that I find most don't take into account or recognize the negative effect of, and therefore don't modify their training appropriately :

- work related stress (especially periods where this is elevated);
- home related stress (especially relationships or family e.g. you may have just become a parent);
- financial (almost everyone experiences this type of stress!)
- study (especially during exams);
- travel – you may be surprised that even elite level athletes and their coaches fail to respect the fatigue effects of travel, and it's interruption to normal recovery patters. If you so much as travel to go to the gym, this has an affect on your energy levels! You will really notice this is you find yourself traveling further to get to a different gym.

I guarantee that each of you could look back at a time in your life where you experienced increased stress - and didn't adjust your training accordingly.

Sounds simple doesn't it? But I guarantee that each of you could look back at a time in your life where you experienced increased stress - and didn't adjust your training accordingly. And you may have been left wondering why your training was struggling? Maybe it is happening to you right now!

The action is simple - consider any or all of the following :

- reducing the duration and volume of each workout;
- reducing the frequency of training;
- reducing the stresses;
- Increasing your use of dietary and nutritional supplements that contribute to combating stress e.g. St. John's

Wort to calm the nervous system, magnesium to relax the muscle etc.

Note that reducing the intensity is my last resort, as I place a higher premium on intensity that I do on volume.

Chapter 26
Goal setting and planning
Don't start training without it!

This section is so important it should really have come first in the book. I feel it may be even more important than the training method you use! (now that's a big wrap!) But I worked with your expectations. Commercial and social trends have educated you to believe that it may be something really 'smart' or 'advanced' or secret' that is most important - like whether you hold the DB at 88 degrees or 92 degrees. Or whether you are doing a simple knee up exercise or something much better like an exotically-named exercise - which unknown to you is exactly the same thing! So I gave you that up front to lull you into a sense of security before introducing what I believe is really more important - but of less commercial value.

Goal setting and planning may be even more important than the training method you use.

The commercial approach may be to brush over the finer details, share some 'tricks' with you, impress you, and let you go. Nice warm feeling for a day or two, but then you are scratching your head again. Reality comes back a few days later! What I am going to tell you is how to raise the likelihood of you succeeding in your training.

This is a statement you may have heard so I won't labor on it, but I've got to say it : **Failing to plan is planning to fail!**

I don't expect everyone to prepare a 16 year, quadruple quadrennial multi-year plan (although it wouldn't hurt to do so - multi-year planning is a fascinating area!). So I am going to give you the simplest and most effective planning advice - **plan each 12 week training block in advance!**

By this I mean before you start, sit down in the days or weeks before-hand and create a written plan about the following :

- what your short-term goals are;
- what method of assessment you are going to use to gain; feedback about your progress;
- how you are going to train;
- how you are going to eat;
- how you are going to sleep ;
- how you are going to live your life;
- what environment manipulations you are going to use to optimize your focus and determination.

Don't ignore the golden rules of goal setting, which include :

- *realistic and attainable*
- *measurable*
- *specific*

Your short term goals

I am not going to get carried away with a debate about the relative merits of long versus short term planning. In a 'I want it now world' (instant gratification), short-term planning will give you the light at the end of the tunnel, that will or discipline you need to delay gratification - to do the first things first, as Stephen Covey would say. To do the groundwork.

So when you are setting short-term goals (and in this case, say 12 weeks), don't ignore the golden rules of goal setting, which include :

- realistic and attainable;
- measurable;
- specific.

Assessment

Assessment is the 'measurable' component of the above. Don't panic - it doesn't have to be high-powered stuff - you wont need NASA! You can make it complex if you want, but simple will work also.

Get Buffed!™

The things you will probably want to measure will be one, some or all of the below. Basically, the things that tell you whether you are getting bigger, stronger and / or leaner. Remember - keep it simple!

Bodyfat - skin calipers are good, but not necessary. If you are going to use them, I find that a sum of a large number of sites may be more effective than the old 'one, two or three sites and put it into an equation that gives you an estimated percentage fat' method. This is nice but not my preference. If you are using a sum of skinfolds (a raw number) you know that a lower number means you got leaner! Just make sure to use the same tester for reliability.

If you don't have access to calipers or similar, don't panic. Get a tape measure, and measure the sites that reflect the fat stores e.g. waist, hips, thighs etc.

Total bodyweight - simple - use scales. I recommend this be done daily anyway, to monitor your state of recovery as well as progress.

> *I recommend this (bodyweight) be done daily anyway, to monitor your state of recovery as well as progress.*

Lean muscle mass - you can work this out by the use of extrapolated equations used in skinfold analysis, or by a simple comparison between body fat scores and total bodyweight. Simplistically interpreted, if your body fat stays the same or goes down, yet your bodyweight goes up, you can assume you have increased lean body mass (simplistically, because there is always the issue of fluid retention). As your fluid levels fluctuate with time of day, time from last meal, creatine and glucose levels, and other supplements and drugs - try to take these measurements at the same time of the day, same distance from a meal (e.g. first thing in the morning), and same nutrient/ergogenic status.

Strength - you could do a strength test, but I am happy to use the recordings from your training to assess strength changes. Compare these to previous training recordings where the variables were constant e.g. same exercise, grip, reps, rest period, prior exercise fatigue, etc.

A method that I have found to be really effective is to create a graph plotting two or more of the above and recorded over time. This can be very motivating, and ensure you are accountable for the time and effort you put into your training.

Training

Create a 12 week plan, right down to how many reps and sets. Forget the 'Weider instinctive principle'! This doesn't mean 12 weeks of training. It may be a 3 weeks on, 1 week off, times 4. Or anything really. As long as you have a plan. Want to know why most people get a result when they try a 'special' method recommended to them in the magazines etc.? Because it is a plan, and where they didn't have one previously, they are ahead - not necessarily because of the training method - but because they are now working to a plan!

And create means write it down - yes, a written 12 week training program.

Planning eating is more than what you are going to eat - it is also when. Your life should revolve around your food!

Eating

Planning your food intake is critical. Most of us have a degree of 'busy' in our lives. If it isn't bought when you do your weekly grocery shopping, if it is prepared the day before etc. - it probably won't happen.

Planning eating is more than what you are going to eat - it is also when. If you don't make arrangements in your daily schedule in advance, you may find yourself missing the meals, or running late on the meal timings. Your life should revolve around your food!

A little suggestion. Get a watch with a count-down mechanism, and as soon as you finish a meal, set it to go off in your pre-determined time frame e.g. 2 or 3 hours.

Sleeping

A need to plan sleep? You better believe it! Unless you live alone, you already have one challenge ahead of you - getting others to respect what time you want to go to sleep.

And there is always your worst enemy - yourself. Unless you make a clear and planned commitment to a specific sleep pattern, you may find the temptation of things such as TV destroy the plan before it really becomes a pattern.

Lifestyle

Your lifestyle affects recovery and therefore the training effect. Unless you live in a monastery, you may have some lifestyle habits that my be counter-productive to optimal training. These include expending energy in extra-curricular activities, stress (be it financial, relationship or work), and other bad-habits like alcohol, drugs etc.

Make a commitment at the commencement of the 12 week plan to adhere to a lifestyle that supports your training, not one that detracts from it. And then take action to make sure it happens!

Make a commitment at the commencement of the 12 week plan to adhere to a lifestyle that supports your training, not one that detracts from it.

Environment manipulations

Have you ever seen a movie and come out feeling like you wanted to take on the world? Have you ever noticed that after a major sporting event such as the Olympics, sport participation rises (at least temporarily) in the host country? Take note. The things you see, hear and feel influence your behavior (at least in the short term). If you want to optimize your training consider the following :

- hang out with people of similar goals (preferably more successful people, so they improve you);
- read material that will motivate and inspire you - yes, bodybuilding magazine are OK for this!
- place visual cues in prominent places in the house - where you see them each morning or night, to keep you focused;
- share your plans with a confidant (preferably what sociologists call a significant other - someone in your circle that influences you), and ask them to be your 'external conscience'.

Chapter 27
Training trouble-shooting
What to do when improvements cease!

$\mathbf{B}$y the time you have got to this chapter, I would like to believe that you have worked out a lot of ways to improve your current training program, and therefore are not likely to see the improvements from your training cease. At least not for some time!

As a constant reminder to you of the possible pitfalls, I have summarized what may be the top seven reasons why weight trainers progress stagnates. They include :

I believe that over-training is probably the number one reason for lack of progress.

#1 Over-training
#2 Ignoring the weakness
#3 Failing to vary muscle group allocation to training days and
      sequencing within training days
4 Creating injury potential
5 Misinterpreting 'training hard'
6 Lacking intensity
7 Lifting to impress

Here's a brief summary of these pitfalls :

1 - Over-training

I believe that over-training is probably the number one reason for lack of progress. Over-training can be caused by many factors. I'll keep it simple however and present you the three key ways to avoid over-training:

1. **Do only 10-20 work sets per workout :** for most people, most of the time, I recommend a range of sets per workout (**not** per muscle group!) of 10-20 set. That's all. You say you can do more? Great - what is it - a competition to see how many you can do, or an attempt to determine the optimal number for your progress? In fact, 5-15 sets may be an even better range.

2. **Never train continuously for longer than 12 weeks :** I feel that 12 weeks of continuous training is as far as you should take it. Then you should take a full recovery week of no strength training, but you can participate in other activities - as long as the week is not that demanding. 12 weeks is the end of the range - for most, I would recommend shorter e.g. 3,4,6,8 and 9 wks are other combinations of work weeks before rest weeks I use.

3. **Avoid assuming that all exercises or muscle groups require equal attention in volume :** have you ever see a program that gave equal attention (e.g. number of sets) to each exercise? I call this program a 'standard sets' approach - multiple sets, usually at the same load. (You are probably doing one at the moment!) Whenever I see the old '3x12' or similar (3-5x12, 3-5x10 or 3-5x8) I see a historical mistake being repeated. A blatant acceptance of tradition without any questioning or thought applied. Giving 3 or more sets to every exercise in the workout is a sure-fire guarantee of over-training.

The quickest way to improve in virtually any endeavor is to work the weakest link.

2 - Ignoring the weakness

The quickest way to improve in virtually any endeavor is to work the weakest link. If you are pursuing increase in size or strength, find the most neglected muscle group (no matter how small it is!) and work it. Most know this concept - but what most fail to do is this : when I say work it, I mean **put it first in the workout and first in the week!**

This is an exercise I do during my initial design interview with a new client. It's so simple that you may wish to give it a go. Firstly, I want you to list your muscle groups in order from weakest (that is least developed relative to the other

Get Buffed!™

muscle groups) to strongest.

Now I want you to make a second list based on your current or dominant training method. Write down the muscle groups under the training days you use, and in the order that you train them e.g. if you use a 3 day cycle, you will use three columns.

Now compare your two lists - does the order appear similar or different? If your current or dominant program is to reflect the prioritization of your weaknesses, then the muscles groups that appeared high on the list should appear either early in the training cycle (e.g. on A day) or early in each training session, or both. I bet they don't!

#3 - Failing to vary muscle group allocation to training days and sequencing within training days

From what I have told you above, the muscle group/s that receive attention first in the training week and first on the training day are the ones that will probably show the most improvement. I taught you in the above to ensure that the weak muscle groups are given this priority. But what I will teach you now is never use the same muscle group sequence endlessly. Doing so will do two things : reinforce inevitable muscle imbalances that result from any given sequence; and secondly, contribute to the neglected muscle groups stagnating.

What I will teach you now is never use the same muscle group sequence endlessly.

Here is another pen exercise for you. You may have listed in the above exercise the muscle group allocation to training days, and the sequencing of these muscle groups within each training day. Now do the same exercise for the program you did before the recent program. And do it again for the program before that, and the program before that. If you see a pattern i.e. if you seem to always be prioritizing the same muscle groups by placing them first in the week and first in the training session for most of these programs - you have found a way to create further growth - do it differently in your next program!

4 - Creating injury potential

How would you feel if I told you that most of what you do in your training program is going to cause you more damage than good? Yes, I thought so - pretty pissed off. Well, most of what I see being done is exactly that - more damage than good (even in programs designed by so-called professionals!). Damage in the form of injuries, resulting from muscle imbalances etc. When you are forced to sit out of training for a few weeks (e.g. muscle strain at best) or a few months (complete muscle tear at worst), you take little consolation in knowing that a few weeks prior you thought you were in great shape - and now the only question on your mind is how fast are you losing your hard-fought gains!

Most of what you do in your training program is going to cause you more damage than good.

There are many ways to reduce the likelihood of this happening to you. Most of this work comes from the areas of muscle balance and joint stability. Now I wouldn't expect you to become an expert in this overnight, but I will give some insights into avoiding one of the most common strength training injuries - shoulder joint pain.

This example will be based on the simple concept that the posterior shoulder strength (i.e. ability to pull back in a horizontal plane perpendicular to the body e.g. rowing movements) should be similar to the anterior shoulder strength (i.e. ability to push away in a horizontal plane perpendicular to the long axis of the trunk e.g. bench press). I call this horizontal pulling and pushing, and every exercise in this plane of movement, be it a single or double joint movement, is placed in one of these two categories.

Now count how many exercises and sets you do for pulling and pushing in each training week or micro-cycle. Are the numbers equal? If not, which dominates. If you are doing more pushing than pulling movements, you are heading towards trouble. Secondly, consider the sequence of these exercises - does the pushing or pulling appear earlier in the training week or training day? If pushing movements receive greater prioritization than pulling movements, based on their sequence within the week and within the workout, you are again heading from trouble.

#5 - Misinterpreting 'training hard'

During my first interview with a new client I will very quickly pick up on their work ethic, and their interpretation of 'hard work'. And when I hear words like 'I really work hard' or 'I can really tolerate a lot of work', I sense an immediate and easy opportunity for advancement. By teaching them **not to focus on working hard**! Confused? Let me explain.

Strength training for size and strength should be used as an anaerobic activity i.e. work set, rest, work set, rest. At the end of the workout you should only feel smashed SOME OF THE TIME, not all the time! Strength training, if used correctly, is one of the few sporting activities with significant anabolic potential. Used otherwise, it can be as catabolic as any other type of training.

The key to this is the well-known but rarely understood relationship between volume and intensity. If the total work time exceeds a certain critical point, the anabolic potential follows the intensity potential - downwards. You may as well be out on the track doing a track session. Even that has some short term anabolic properties!

If the total work time exceeds a certain critical point, the anabolic potential follows the intensity potential - downwards.

So what is that critical volume for you to avoid exceeding? Realistically, I can't predict without knowing more about you, but if you read my generalized volume guidelines in the above you will get a good idea of my perspective on this.

So instead of feeling the need to totally smash yourself every workout, consider the following tips to ensure you don't overstep the mark in a standard 3 week training cycle :

Week 1 Workouts - never miss a rep, don't lift at your limits, focus on technique quality, walk out of the gym after each workout feeling VERY fresh, under-worked.

Week 2 Workouts - work closer to your known limits, still with no intent of missing a rep; at the end of the workout you still have some reserve but you know you have just done a workout.

Week 3 Workouts - look for new PB's in the exercises you are doing, but still be realistic - missing reps may occur but don't attempt to lift a weight unless you have a strong belief you will get all the reps; at the end of the workout, you may feel a high degree of fatigue.

The above may seem conservative, but remember this - it is not about how much you can do in a workout - but rather, what amount of effort will give the greatest rate of return!

6 - Lacking intensity

In the above I have just told you to back off. Now I am going to tell you that most strength training is conducted with inadequate intensity. Contradictory? No - the above referred primarily to excessive volume. Now I am talking about inadequate intensity. What I recommend is a low number of sets, a short time in the gym - but with a high level of **focus in the effort within the set.** I believe that **intensity is more important than volume** in strength training.

> *I recommend a low number of sets, a short time in the gym - but with a high level of focus. I believe that intensity is more important than volume in strength training.*

Some of the techniques I use and recommend to raise the focus and intensity of your training session were covered in an earlier chapter.

7 - Lifting to impress

Ever been asked to spot a person, say on the bench press. You look at them, look at the weight on the bar, and shake your head. You ask them how many reps they plan on doing and they say 8. Sure! They do 1 and ½ and you upright row the remaining 6 ½!

I would say that most load selection in strength training is based upon what impact it will have on those watching, not what impact it will have on the body. Think about it - 30 seconds of glory. Perhaps as they are walking on the beach on the weekend, upon seeing someone they want to impress, they can suddenly pull the weights out of their pocket and impress in the same way. Or wear a t-shirt that says 'yesterday I benched xxxxx'. Ever wondered why so many want to tell you how much they lifted? Because taking one look at them, you could not tell!

I really don't care what weight you take out of the racks and perform a quarter rep with. If you were more serious about your body than your short term ego, you would take 75% off the load and perform the movement in a manner that had some lasting impact on your body!

Lifting heavy is great - if it is making a difference! The key is to learn how to make a difference to the body with a slow and controlled movement, then progressively add loading!

There may be many reasons for lack of progress, and I am a strong believer in the individualization of training. That is, the most accurate program design or trouble-shooting will only occur when the individual's variables are known. So I cannot say with absolute certainty that you are making any of the above 'mistakes', or that they are in fact having a negative effect on your progress. However generally speaking (and that is the best I can do in this situation - generalize), based on my experience, they probably are.

There is another alternative. You can have your training program professionally analyzed, as I have done for the following individual. I have included this example so that you may also be able to identify with some of the 'challenges' faced by the individual whose training is being analyzed – and maybe you can identify with the errors of their ways!

The training trouble-shoot that follows is based on a real person and a real report, including their original responses in their own words to my questions.

I really don't care what weight you take out of the racks. If you were more serious about your body than your short term ego, you would take 75% off the load and perform the movement in a manner that had some lasting impact on your body!

Training Trouble-shoot Questionnaire

1. *Name : Vince Zalusky.*
2. *Age : 35.*
3. *Sex : Male.*
4. *Nature of employment : Sedentary (sales, high stress at times).*
5. *Hgt : 6feet 1 inch.*
6. *Wgt : 211bs.*
7. *Bodyfat 16%.*
8. *No of years of strength training and when : 4 years between ages of 16 to 20 then on and off, started back serious half a year ago.*
9. *No of years of other training and when : Tae Kwon Do 3 years ago, trained for 5 years.*
10. *Goals : gain strength and mass and lose fat (not really ripped but tone).*
11. *Time frame to achieve goals : 6 months to 18 months.*
12. *Self-perception of response to training : I get average results, nothing great.*
13. *Self-perception of genetic gifts : average genetics.*
14. *Self-perception of recovery ability : I think with my stress from occupation, sometimes lack of sleep my recovery ability is on the lower side to average.*
15. *Self-perception of strengths/weaknesses : calves are small and stomach is a weakness (fat). Have broad shoulders for strengths.*
16. *Feedback from others re. strengths/weaknesses : The same as above.*
17. *Training methods you feel have been successful in the past : For a while three days a week worked great, and then stopped. Have tried to vary training.*
18. *Training methods that you feel have not worked in the past : I realize that I need to recover and avoid over-training.*
19. *Number of meals per day and what times of day : I try to do six meals per day with occasional meal replacement or protein with a apple or orange as a meal.*
20. *Summarize current nutrition/supplements etc. : I had success with Phosphagen Creatine 2 to 3 times per day and betagen 2 to 3 times a day. I found this to be rather expensive for my budget but it did work. I am currently using Optimum nutrition protein and their new meal replacement. I've heard mixed results about the quality but it does meet my budget. Suggestions. I tried tribulus without lots of results. I currently am*

Get Buffed!™

taking ZMAC, cod liver oil, oil, vitamin C twice per day and multi vitamin once to twice per day.

The following outlines my training program (including days, number of days per week, exercises each workout, order of exercises, sets/reps/rest periods/speed of movement/load etc).

I am currently using a program from Tudor Bompa's serious strength training book. Its for recreational bodybuilders. Before that I was hitting one body part per week. I always mix up my training speed, order of exercises, and pairing body parts. I realize that I have to get at least to 4 seconds on the eccentric and pause. The current training program leaves me rushed for time and some times a little bit whipped. I am currently very busy at work and that is playing a big factor in being tired.

Training as follows in afternoon :
Everything varies between 50 to 60 percent 1 rep max
Day 1 and Day 4
Squats / 12 reps / 3 sets, 4110, 120 lbs
Lying Leg curl 10 reps / 3 sets 4011
Leg extensions 12 reps/ 3 sets 3011
Seated leg curl 10 reps/ 3 sets 3120
Back extension 3 sets 12 reps

At night at home after 9:00 pm
Seated dumbbell curls 3 sets 12 reps/ 3 sets 3011
Laying Tricep extensions 3 sets 12 reps 3110
Reverse dumbbell curl 3 sets 12 reps
Sit ups on Swiss ball 3 sets 12 reps

Day 2 and Day 4
Standing calf raise 12/3 4110
Seated calf raise declining weight till exhaustion 70lbs 10 reps/ 60 lbs
6 reps 50lbs failure 3101 tempo
Bench press 12/3 3100
Seated rows 12/3 3110
Incline bench press 12/3 3100
Medium grip pull downs 12/3 3100

At home
Elbow against knee rotator cuff 12/3 3100
Dard 12/3 3100
90 seconds rest to 2 minutes per set.

Been on program for 3 weeks and currently taking week off. I like the workout but I feel I too busy to keep up this schedule. Occasionally when I can't make the gym I'll do hip belt squats (I really like this exercise) at home and lunges with light weight dumbbell semi stiff leg deadlifts (I've had low back surgery so I'm very careful of doing things correctly). Would doing a donkey calf raise with a hip squat be a effective version (we don't have a machine and with my low back problem I don't want anybody straddling me).

Before that I was getting my workouts of one body part a week from the Testosterone web site. I'm still unsure if I should be doing one body part per week or twice. My career is some times high stress and really busy and sometimes its not too bad. I do stretch a little before workouts and between sets (I always feel pressed for time so not enough). My pre-workout includes 5 to 15 minutes aerobics. I basically have an hour at the gym to warm up and work out.

I look forward to hearing from you. I am looking forward to the lower body video workout your coming out with soon.

Thanks Ian

Get Buffed!™

Training Trouble-shoot Report

1. Name

Vince ZALUSKY

2. Age (35 yrs)

I don't believe age should be used as an excuse, or that you should place too many limits on yourself because of your age. However, it is perhaps unwise to totally ignore the realities of age. Most importantly, because of lower hormone activity, your response to and recovery from training is affected by age, especially from the mid to late-twenties and onwards. It is silly to ignore this impact on training.

At 35 yrs of age, you need to take into account that your natural hormone levels are lower than they were in your 20's. This means less training.

3. Sex (male)

I don't believe there are too many gender issues to consider. However one that is worth discussing is the ability to train intensely. Whether this is culture or gender issue (i.e. related to testosterone), the bottom line is that many females, in my experience, will benefit from increasing their aggression during training.

4. Nature of employment (sedentary)

Again, I am not aiming to give you excuses or place limits on your possibilities. However, the more demanding employment activities have an undeniable effect on training response and recovery - the more manual your job is, the more you may need to review your training volume.

However your job, although sedentary, appears to have high levels of stress associated with it. You recognize this, but it appears to me that you have yet to modify your training volume to account for this.

What I suggest is that whatever workout you create, you create a reduced frequency and volume variation of it, so that if at any time your work stress increases, you switch immediately to the low volume option. To help you with this, you simply take the most important parts of the workout, and drop the rest. Basically you half the volume, and then can marry two workouts into one to reduce the frequency or hold the frequency with half the volume per workout.

I also pick up on your lack of sleep. If you come home wired and have trouble going to sleep, I suggest try some melatonin. I always have some of this with me by my bed at home or in my travel bag on the road, and when I know I need the sleep and it is not happening fast enough, I take 1-2 tabs.

5. Height (6'1")

Height is not a big issue, but gives an idea of your total body-weight potential - a bodyweight of 220 lbs may sound impressive - unless it is on a person standing 7 foot! The other major impact of height is on lever length. Many taller/longer limbed people struggle with strength development in compound movements e.g. bench press.

It seems to me your height is adequate for your weight, but it may be the lowering of body fat along with increased muscle size and tone you are after (simply to 'Get Buffed'! which by the way is the title of my new book to be released any time now!)

6. Weight (211 lbs)

Bodyweight gives a rough indication of training status or results, but realistically must be viewed in context with bodyfat. A heavy person is not necessarily muscular - it depends on how much body fat they are carrying. Other aspects to weight include some individuals goals (and sporting) goals are more interested in total bodyweight than bodyfat.

As I said above your weight suggests you are not totally lacking in body mass, but could do with a bit more muscle and a little less fat.

7. Bodyfat (16 %)

Bodyfat does allow one to assess how much of the total bodyweight is lean muscle weight. Bodyfat is only an issue if you want it to be - it's correlation to health is over-rated and is more of a social issue. However, some individuals aim for or their sports require lower bodyfat - in which case it does become an issue.

From what you have said you would like to lower this, and this is understandable.

8. No. of years of strength training and when

The training age (a term used to describe how many years a person has trained in any given area) gives an indication that the trainee should have developed a good conditioned response to training in general, and should be able to cope with more advanced techniques. When these years of training occurred is important e.g. you may have trained in strength training for 10 years - but that ended 5 years ago. You would also expect that the rate of return diminishes with time, but at the same time, the longer one has been training, the closer to their goals they should be.

Your training between 16-20 yrs should help you in that this would have given you some foundation. Now that you have done about ½ yr, you would have got the easy gains that any beginner gets, and will now need to ensure your training is smarter to progress.

9. No. of years of other training and when

Other training modes have an affect e.g. if a person has done a lot of cycling, you may expect that they have some above average leg development/work capacity.

Your experience in TKD will help with stretching, as I assume that as part of this you improved and spent considerable time stretching.

10. Goals

The gap between your goals and your current status will determine how happy you are with your training. Additionally, the presence or absence of goals, or the inadequate specificity of goals, gives insights into why some may fail to achieve their goals.

I have summed up your goals as a simple desire to 'get buffed' - lower body fat, raise muscle strength, tone and mass.

11. Time frame to achieve goals

Having a goal is one thing - not having a deadline or time frame may negate any benefits of having the goal in the first instance. Deadlines encourage achievement.

Your time frame of 6-18 months is realistic, but I am not sure if you have been specific enough in your goal setting. Remember to be specific is a key to successful goal setting. Be prepared to set short term achievable goals as part of the longer term, bigger picture.

12. Self-perception of response to training

What you say in a moment of honest self-reflection tells a lot about how you are responding to your training.

I commend your honesty in saying average results - now I want you to face reality - they can be better, it is a matter of working out why they are average. I am sure in your work ethic (at work) you don't like to achieve 'average results'. So don't accept this in your training!

Get Buffed!™

13. Self-perception of genetic gifts

Whilst I discourage the excuse of 'I'm not genetically gifted', it is good to know how genetically gifted you may be - and one way to determine this is to get your opinion. Genetically gifted people often err by ignoring their weaknesses, and often don't fully know what worked for them because they were bound to get a result no matter what.

Again you have been honest here, but don't limit yourself. I am rarely convinced that genetics are the limit - more often training, attitude and lifestyle.

14. Self-perception of recovery ability

Again I rely on your opinion of your recovery ability. Recovery ability will influence what is optimal in training volume, intensity and frequency.

You have been astute and recognized that work related stress is eating into your ability to recover - now we need to look at ways to modify training to suit this, and also for you to look at things in your approach to work and life that can be done better (e.g. time management, focusing only on things that really matter) so as to reduce the stress from work and reduce the time spent at work.

15. Self-perception of strengths/weaknesses

Most people know where they are weak or strong - yet rarely give adequate prioritization to their weaknesses. This is one of the quickest ways to achieve your goals. You note calves and abs as weaknesses. I looked at your program and was relieved to see that calves were done first on the day they were trained, as should any weakness be. But why are that not done first on Day 1 & 4, not day 2 & (you have typed in 4 here but I am guessing you meant 5)?

As for stomach, this is as much about lowering body fat as it is about strengthening stomach (I am assuming that you are not happy with the visual aspect of your stomach). With lowering body fat you have 2 options - lower calorie intake or raise aerobic type exercise. I don't have too much feedback on your diet but I suspect that you don't focus too much on this. Remember, as you get older, your metabolism lowers - you need to reduce total intake. As far as aerobic or fat burning activity, you don't have enough (i.e. 5-15 minutes). Maybe for a short time you need to reduce the volume of strength training and raise the volume of low level aerobic training, at least until you have the body fat down to a level that you are happy with.

As for your strength, I couldn't find any shoulder exercises in the program so I assume you are taking a rest from these due to your strengths here. This is OK temporarily, but some maintenance training of this body part may be needed.

16. Feedback from others re. strengths/weaknesses

It is often beneficial to supplement your own perceptions with the perceptions of others. Sociologists call this the 'looking glass self' - seeing yourself through other's eyes. Whilst I don't suggest you pay much attention to what other people say or think, sometimes it can be beneficial to consider.

This appears to be consistent with your own thoughts.

17. Training methods you feel have been successful in the past

You have been a walking experiment throughout your training career - sometimes you just don't realize this because you haven't sat back and reviewed the cause-effect relationships to each method of training. This analysis is made more difficult if you don't keep excellent training records.

You don't seem to be confident that any of your recent methods have given long term success. This is OK - they don't seem to have been overly effective, or at least you are not raving about them - so if nothing else you have learnt something!

Get Buffed!™

18. Training methods that you feel have not worked in the past

Why make the same mistakes again? You probably are unless you have taken the time/made the effort to analyze the effectiveness (or otherwise) of each training method you have used.

This was answered in the above.

19. Number of meals per day and what times of day

Meal frequency and timing is one of the most powerful non-training contributors to achieving your goals. I invariably recommend many small, frequent meals (e.g. every 2-3 hours) throughout the day. It is mostly the size of the meal and the type of food that may vary. Pre and post-training nutrition is also important.

Your meal frequency/total number appear good. I hope that one of these is in the form of a post training intake (taken with 10 minutes after training e.g. a protein shake).

20. Summarize current nutrition/supplements etc

What you eat is extremely critical to getting results in training. This is one area that needs consistent effort.

Creatine sounds like it worked for you but the EAS stuff was too costly. Don't bother about buying the latest 'HP' etc combinations. Just buy plain bulk creatine - it is cheap, and will do the job! If you want the same thing as the EAS HP, just take it with grape juice! Also, the new MRP's may claim to have special additives (taurine, glutamine etc) but really - you can mix up a skim milk powder shake with a few things thrown in (e.g. egg white, banana, honey etc) and buy bulk glutamine separate and you won't miss much! The MRP's are convenient to prepare but not totally necessary. They also have the taste figured out so that you want to go back to them - but placing honey or similar in your home-made shake will do just the same! The oil, multis and Vit C are excellent. Consider adding E.

21. Outline training program below (including days, number of days per week, exercises each workout, order of exercises, sets/reps/rest periods/speed of movement/load etc)

I have checked out your training program. I am going to assume that Day 2 and 4 should read Day 2 and 5. I also see what appears to be a 4/wk split e.g. Day 1 and 4 on Mon and Thur, and day 2 and 5 on Tue and Fri.

If this is correct, and you are training on a rotation shorter than a calendar week - don't. This reduces your recovery time. If you want to train 4/wk, use Mon and Thur, Tue and Fri.

I also see you are training twice a day on some days. Don't. This further erodes your already limited recovery ability. If you absolutely wanted to train 2/day, you should be doing aerobic training in one of the sessions until your body fat is down to where you want it to be.

Training 4/wk strength is OK in an OK week - provided it is low volume (this is what I believe your situation warrants). More on the volume in a minute. But what you need is to always have an alternative plan of any current program, for those weeks that your recovery is further affected by work. In these weeks you need to go to ½ volume per session or ½ frequency e.g. only 2/wk in the gym.

Now for your volume. You are averaging 15 sets per workout. Too many for you at your age and work situation. Do not exceed 10. I am interested in how you find this in a few months time. I really think this is a key point. How do you achieve this? Why do 3 sets per exercise? (I am assuming they are work sets). Do only 2. Or do less number of exercises (but you are already doing a fairly low number).

As far as duration goes. You only have 60 minutes and this is OK if you reduce volume. 10 minutes on the bike, 20 minutes stretching, 30 minutes training. And a second 20 minutes of aerobic twice a wk (later in the day). I believe you will get a far better result with 30 minutes. When I said don't exceed 10 reps, I meant that a range of 6-10 should be used. You will be surprised how effective 6 (work) sets per workout can be.

You may not have enough abdominal volume. But this doesn't have to be done with the strength workouts. (I do mine immediately upon rising). I suggest about 2 sets minimum per day, at least 4 days a week - which I think is more than you are currently doing. Do a lower abdomen first, followed by an upper or rotational one.

The sequence of your exercises is generally OK, but don't feel the need to do 2 or more exercises per muscle group. This invariably leads to either over-training or neglecting another muscle group. e.g. you have 4 leg exercises on Day 1 and 4 and only 1 hip exercise. On day 2 and 5 you have 2 chest, only 1 row, only 1 pull-down, and no shoulder.

Your programs should look something like this :

Mon	Tues	Wed	Thur	Fri	Sat
Aer-10m	Aer-10m	Aer-20m	Abs	Aer-10m	Aer-10m
Flex-20m	Flex-20m	Flex-40m	Flex-20m	Flex-20m	Flex-20m
Abs-lower	Abs-upper		Abs-lower	Abs-upper	
Legs-squat	Row		Lunge	Shoulder press	
Legs-fl/ex	Chest		Good morn	Chins	
Calf	Bicep		Shrugs	Triceps	

The above is only an example - you would change up the order in subsequent programs. You would do about 2 work sets per exercise.

Using a 3-4 wks on, 1 wk off is good for your situation.

Summary

The following summaries some of the key points raised :

- if you want to train 4/wk, train the calendar week e.g. Mon and Thur, Tue and Fri.;
- don't double-day train (i.e. don't train 2/day);
- training 4/wk strength is OK in an OK week - provided it is low volume;

- what you need is to always have an alternative plan of any current program, for those weeks that your recovery is further affected by work - of ½ volume per session or ½ frequency;
- you are averaging 15 sets per workout - too many for you at your age and work situation - use between 6-10 work sets per workout;
- 10 minutes on the bike, 20 minutes stretching, 30 minutes training;
- abdominals - do a min. of 2 sets per day, at least 4 days a week;
- don't feel the need to do 2 or more exercises per muscle group;
- use a 3-4 wks on, 1 wk off.

Get Buffed!™

Chapter 28
A 12 week training program
The Ian King way!

I have included this sample 12 week training program for a number of reasons. Firstly it is a real, live example of how I manipulate all the variables to come up with a program. Secondly, it gives you a ready-made program to use. Remember this program is a generalized program – not modified to suit your individual needs. So there may be need to make some adjustments. Also realize that it is only a 12 week program – it may give you an alternative but it shouldn't be relied on for more than – at most – 12 weeks of each year!

Remember this program is a generalized program.

It is a 4 day a week split routine, using the calendar week. It might look something like this :

Sun	Mon	Tue	Wed	Thu	Fri	Sat
	A	B		C	D	

There are 4 stages to the program, using linear periodization. For the average strength trainer these stages would be 3 weeks each. The less experienced may use 4 weeks per stage, the more experienced 2 weeks.

During the workout I expect you will record each and every rep, load, speed and rest period. In other words, get yourself a training diary and use it! Remember – it is not what you do in the workout on the day that matters – it is how much better you did today compared with last time you did the same workout – and no, I don't know anyone who has an adequate memory to clearly remember every rep, set, speed, rest period and load from the previous workout! Stop kidding yourself and just use a recording diary!

Now if you want to make sure you are executing the movements in the way I intended, there is a great supporting option for you - I have created a video series of the same name to support the program from the *Get Buffed!*™ book!

The program you are about to be exposed to in this book provides all the information that many will need – reps, sets, speed, rest period, guidance in loading, exercise description and so on. But there's one thing the book cannot show you – and that is a visual demonstration of how to do the exercises! This is what *Get Buffed!*™ the video will do!

The *Get Buffed!*™ video does more than show you how to do it – it has me showing you in person how I wants you to do it! You get coached by the 'master' coach! The *Get Buffed!*™ video shows every exercise in each of the 16 different workouts that make up the 12-week program. It shows you how to do them, and discusses additional issues including load selection and smart little tricks and techniques to enhance the result.

This video program consists of two video tapes, with Stage 1 (Wks 1-3) and Stage 2 (Wks 4-6) on Tape 1; and Stage 3 (Wks 7-9) and Stage 4 (Wks 10-12) on Tape 2. Each workout is separated by a header indicating the start of that workout e.g. Stage 3, Workout C. The videos are packaged in a firm plastic case with an impressive front cover and spine – aimed to look smart on your training library shelf!

Would you like to be sure you are executing this program in the way I intended? Then there is no better way than to have me personally show you on video tape.

Here is what some of our viewers have said :

"The body of knowledge you've provided through these tapes, and the accompanying Get Buffed book is invaluable. Appreciate the clear, straight

forward style, and the absence of bells, whistles and BS."

Dan Barrett

"Ian, here is a story you will enjoy! I was so sore on Sunday, I decided to rest and not do my quad dominant leg workout until Monday. (this workout happens to be phase 2 of Get Buffed 12 week routine) So since I wasn't going to the gym I popped in video on abs and as I told you before I was blown away! After watching the ab video I thought since I am squatting next I will learn how to squat your way! So on Monday, I did my workout (which this phase consists mostly of squats!) and let me tell you squatting your way was different at first and I had to go somewhat lighter but I liked it....until today! MY QUADS ARE KILLING ME!! I can barely walk! It is unbelievable! I think I have fairly decent quad development but I can't help but wonder where I would be if I had learned from you years ago!

Thanks for pain - and subsequent growth!"

Matt Slaymaker

The *Get Buffed!*™ *Video Series* can be ordered on-line by going to **www.getbuffed.net** or emailing us at info@getbuffed.net.

General Notes for all the Workouts

Prior to the lower body workouts I expect the following :
1. 10-20 minutes of light aerobic type activity e.g. stationary bike;
2. 20-40 minutes of lower body stretching;
3. 5-10 minutes of abdominal exercises (this can be done at the end of the workout in the last 2 stages);
4. 3-5 minutes of control/stability drills for the knees and hips.

Prior to the upper body workouts I expect the following :
1. Optional 5-20 minutes of light aerobic type activity e.g. stationary bike;
2. 15-30 minutes of upper body stretching;
3. 5-10 minutes of abdominal exercises (this can be done at the end of the workout in the last 2 stages);
4. 3-5 minutes of control/stability drills for the shoulders and upper arm.

Here are some **codes** that you will see used in the program :

Load and reps and rest
BW = bodyweight; EXT = external load; ECC = eccentric overload
AMRAP or AMRP= as many reps as possible
RP or R/Per = rest period; ALT = alternate with another exercise
Body relative to bar or equipment
B = back or behind; F = front or to the front
Grips
WG = medium grip; MG = medium grip; CG = close grip; RG = reverse grip
Stances
WS = wide stance; MS = medium stance; NS = narrow stance
Bar Position/Lines of Movement
HB = lower bar high up on chest in the bench press (to neck); sit the bar high on back in the squat
MB = lower the bar to the middle of the chest in the bench; sit the bar in a medium position on the back in the squat
LB = lower the bar low on the chest in the bench; sit the bar in a low position on the back in the squat
Foot Positions
FA = feet up in the air (e.g. in bench press); FB = feet on bench; FD = feet   down on the ground
Weight or Body Position relative to the support base
OG = plates start on the ground; OB = plates start on blocks; SOB = you stand on a block
Equipment
EZ = ezy curl bar; DB = dumbbell

Get Buffed!™

Notes for Stage 1 (Wks 1-3)

The workouts in Stage 1 involve a lot of different exercises, mainly only one set per exercise, in an unconventional order (pre-fatigue sequence). I have prioritized the lower body over the upper body and the vertical pushing and pulling over horizontal pushing and pulling. Take minimal rest between sets, and where there is a warm up set or more than one work set, alternate with the opposite muscle group in a super-set fashion (upper body only).

- don't intentionally go to failure on any of the exercises in the first workout. Each subsequent workout go closer to this failure, so that by the last workout you take it to the limit;
- do only 1 warm-up set and 1 work set in the first workout; if you feel you need to add a second work set on any of the exercises in later workouts, do so – but I doubt it;
- use this workout once every 4-7 days, depending on your recovery ability;
- take only 30-60 sec rest between each exercise;
- do this workout for only 2-4 wks; you will know when it is time to move on; this type of training has a lot of benefits if used sparingly i.e. you need to move back into more loading after a while;
- weak side rule : always work the weak side first. Do not do more weight or reps on the strong side than the weak side can handle. If the imbalance is between say 10-20%, look to do an extra set on the weak side. If the imbalance is between say 20-50%, consider doing only a total of 25% of the reps on the strong side compared to the weak side. If the imbalance is greater than 50%, do not do any reps on the strong side until the imbalance is reduced.

If you can walk and clean your teeth pain free at the peak of delayed muscle soreness (about 2 days later) on this program (especially in week 1), something's not right! (yes, even with taking it easy as per my 3 week cycle intensity instructions!) This is one workout that should accelerate your muscle size immediately, and give you significant boost to your strength upon return to more loaded methods.

You mightn't enjoy the stigma of struggling with next to nil loading, but you will enjoy the results.

Stage 1 : Weeks 1-3

Workout A

Exercise	W/up sets	Work sets	Speed	R/Per (minutes)
Calf combo (single)				
1. Standing, bw only	nil	10-20	321	nil
2. Single leg press	nil	10-20	321	nil
3. Seated	nil	10-20	321	nil
4. Toe ups	nil	10-20	321	nil
5. Ankle bouncing	nil	20-100	*	nil
6. Static balance	nil	1 min		nil
Leg flex	1x12-15	1x12-15	1 1/2's @311	1/2-1
Leg extension	as above			1/2-1
Single leg partial squat	nil	1x20-50	311	1/2-1
Single leg squat (back foot on bench)	nil	1x10	515	1/2-1
Ski squats	nil	5x10-40s holds		1/2-1
Single leg hack squats	nil	8-12	302	1/2-1
Single leg leg press	nil	1x10	3x3	1/2-1
Squats	nil	1x6-8	814	1/2-1

Exercises for A Day, Stage 1

Calf combo

This is how to do the calf combo :

Single leg bodyweight standing calf press to failure, @ 321. No rest. Then to :
Same leg, single leg bodyweight bent forward calf press to failure, @ 321. No rest. Then to :
Same leg, single leg calf press on incline leg press machine, @ 321. No rest. Then to :
Same leg, single leg calf press on seated calf press machine, @ 321. No rest. Then to :
Same leg, single leg toe up (dorsi flexion - can do this on the lying leg curl machine) to failure @311. No rest. Then to:
Same leg, single leg hopping for between 60-120 reps, without any heel contact on ground. Height of hop is not that important for now - just get the volume in - the more the better. No rest. Then to :
Same leg, single leg balance for 30 sec to 1 min (eyes closed if you find this easy). Now you can rest for a minute or two, and then do other leg.

Use a full range of movement and a controlled speed : when you are no longer able to maintain either, move to the next exercise. If you are really keen, you can always go for a second multi-set, but I would prefer you wait until the next day or two before determining your calves tolerance to this program.

Leg Flexion and Extension

The first two exercises are the leg flexion (curl) and leg extension. Provided your gym hasn't over-reacted to the 'latest news' about the evils of open-chain kinetic exercises and so on, there will still be a leg flexion and extension machine in the gym. I like this exercise for this type of routine. I don't use isolated exercises a lot - say about 25% of total training time in general.

I want the flexion done before the extension, to counter any muscle imbalance in favor of the quads. Use one leg at a time on both. This is not only an opportunity to isolate the action of knee extension and flexion, but also to isolate the limbs. (I know - another criticism is the alleged non-specificity knee extension/flexion. Who cares. You are simply using a pre-fatigue method) If the gym is not too crowded do one set of the leg curl followed immediately by one set of the leg extension ON THE SAME LEG. If the gym is busy, do both legs (individually) on the flexion, then do both legs (again individually) on the extension. Start with the weakest leg first. If you don't know which one that is at the start, you will by the end of the workout! (see weak side rule)

Use the 1 and 1/3's rep technique. On the flexion, raise the heel to the butt in 3 sec, pause for 1 sec, lower the heel 1/3 of the range out, pause for 1 second. Return the heel to the butt taking 1 second, pause for 1 sec, lower the weight all the way down taking 3 seconds. This is one rep.

Leg extension is done in a similar fashion - extend fully taking 3 seconds, pause for 1 second, lower 1/3 of the range, pause for 1 second, return to full extension in 1 sec, pause for 1 second, lower completely taking 3 seconds.

In both use a load that causes you to lose the ability to complete the range you started with, between 12-15 reps. Do one warm-up set using normal speed, then do one work set as described.

Single leg partial squat

Stand on the edge of a low block (e.g. 1/3 to ½ the height of a normal bench height). Have the weak leg on the box and the strong leg off the edge of the box. Bend at the knee of the weak side, lowering down (2-3 seconds) until the sole of your feet almost brushes the floor. Keep sole parallel to ground. Pause for 1 second and return to full extension in about 1-2 seconds. At the 10th rep, pause at the bottom position for 10 seconds. You must not rest the non-supporting leg on the ground at any stage during the set. Hands on hips. Then continue reps until you get to 20. Repeat the 10 second pause. Can you go on? If yes, remember, what you start you must finish - this exercise must be done in multiples of 10, with a 10 second pause in bottom position at the completion of every 10 reps. If you get to 50 reps, look to raise the height of the block. Preferably don't hold on to anything during the set - the challenge of balance will add to the fatigue. However you may wish to do this near a wall or squat stand just in case. You don't need to do a warm up set - get straight into the work set. And be careful when you get off the block at the end of the set.....!

Single leg squat with back foot on bench

Some know this as a Bulgarian squat - with a difference. Face away from a normal height bench, and place your rear leg up on the bench. You can check your distance by having a relatively vertical shin throughout the movement. Place your hands on your head, and keep your chest and trunk vertical throughout. Lower the body down by bending the knee of the lead leg until the knee of the back leg is almost on the ground.

We are going to use a speed of 515 - 5 sec lower, 1 second pause top and bottom, and 5 second lift. If you can do more than 10 reps, you can hold dumbbells in your hand. I don't expect this to be necessary initially. Keep the knee aligned over the feet during the lower and the lift. You don't need to do a warm up set - get straight into the work set.

Ski squats

You may have seen a recreational ski enthusiast do this one, but don't get too comfortable. You might get a big surprise here. Place your feet shoulder width apart about 2 feet out from the wall, and lean your back against the wall. Bend your knees to a half squat position. This is position one. After a specified time, lower down to position two, about 2 inches lower. After the specified time, lower another 2 inches down to position three. You should be about thigh parallel by now. Use another 2 lower positions, with position five being about as far as you can bend at the knees. How long is the specified time? Start with somewhere between 10-20 seconds per position, adding 5 seconds per workout. The 5 positions done with no rest between them constitutes a set. Just one set on day one remember. If you are finding this too easy? Do it on one leg at a time.

Single leg hack squats

This is another one for those gyms whose hack squats survived the purge. If you have no hack squat, you can do a one legged standing squat, holding the other leg out in front. With the hack squat, hold the non-working leg out with your heel just off the ground at all times. Start with no weight on the machine other than the machine itself, and don't expect to be able to do full range initially. Maybe start with a limited range, and look to progress in range from workout to workout, as well as reps or weight. Look for 8-12 reps. If you are struggling, not able to do full range, work with a standard 302 speed. If you are doing it easy, do 1 and 1/3's. Ensure neutral knee alignment.

Single leg on leg press

Using one leg at a time, stop three times during the eccentric (lowering) phase, for 3 seconds each time. Look to vary the stopping angle. Explode up during the concentric (lifting) phase, but avoid full lockout in extension - stop short of full extension. Don't get carried away with load on day 1 - start with 50-100 lbs, doing 8-10 reps.

Squat

At last the moment you have been waiting for - normalcy, an exercise you know. Your pleasure may be short lived, as you face fatigue from a near non-existent loading. It takes a brave person to keep going. Not only because of the physical pain, but also because of the emotional trauma of sweating and shaking under minimal load in this squat. But remember, you are doing this for the training effect, not the visual effect!

Place the bar as high as is comfortable on the neck, take a narrower than shoulder width stance, and allow only a slight external rotation of the feet. Immediately prior to commencing the descent, bend your knees slightly, suck in the lower abdomen, and squeeze your cheeks. This will 'set' your pelvis in a slightly posteriorly rotated position. As you lower, keep the hips in line with the spine - which means maintain this hip position.

Don't misinterpret this - you can flex forward at the hips, just don't change the hip/spine relationship. Squat as deeply as you can without exceeding forty-five degree trunk flexion relative to vertical. Keep your knees equal distance apart during the lift. Immediately prior to the ascent, focus on squeezing the cheeks tight and hold them tight during the concentric phase. The aim here is to prevent anterior rotation of the pelvis during the initial phase of the ascent. This is a tough technique to master, but it is worth it.

Take 8 sec to go down, no pause, 4 sec to come up. Do 6-8 reps.

Workout B

Exercise	W/up sets	Work sets	Speed	R/Per (minutes)
Forearm extension and flexion – bar	nil	20+20+20 strip set	311	nil
Incline DB Bicep curl tri-set :				
1. hammer grip	1x10	1x10	422	10s
2. palm up	1x10	1x10	422	10s
3. palm up and elbows out at top	1x10	1x10	422	10s
Tricep Press-down tri-set :				
1. close prone grip	1x10	1x10	422	10s
2. med prone grip	1x10	1x10	422	10s
3. med supine grip	1x10	1x10	422	10s
DB Pullover (1 DB in each hand)	nil	1x10-12	1 ½'s	s/set
Front DB Raise (Palms in)	as above	as above	as above	
Lat pull-down (WG/limited range) i.e. hardest half only	nil	1x10-15	421	s/set
Lat DB Raise (limited range) i.e. hardest half only	as above	as above	as above	
Lat pull-down (MG/F)	nil	21	311	1/2-1
DB Shoulder press (seated)	as above	as above	as above	
Chin up (RG)	nil	1x4-8	613	s/set
Shoulder press (bar/WG)	as above	as above	as above	

Exercises for B Day, Stage 1

Forearm extension and flexion

Kneel on the ground and hold the bar with a medium grip. Rest the forearms on a prone bench, with the hands just off the side. The bar should be parallel to the long axis of the bench. You will have grip with the palms facing upwards (supine) for flexion and downwards (prone) for extension. Note the relatively slow speeds - this will reduce the amount of load required (you may be stunned by how light you need to go, especially in the extension!) Use a full range for both, and in flexion, allow the bar to roll to the end of the fingers (as far as you can go without losing it!). You may want to do a light warm up set, or even just do 2 work sets instead.

Incline DB Bicep Curl Tri-set

The aim of these tri-set is to do all three exercises with minimal rest between (i.e. no more than 10-15 seconds). On the incline bench, keep the elbows still and behind the body. The first set is down with a hammer grip, which is palm inwards. The second is with a palm up grip, and the third is with the same grip but as you raise towards the top allow the elbows to drift outwards, reversing this in the lowering. Note the slow speed as per the forearms. Only do warm-up set if you feel you need to, and note the potential for using lighter DB's in each subsequent exercise in the tri-set (as they go from strong to weak positions, and as fatigue sets in).

The Tricep Press-down Tri-set

Uses the same principles as above, with the three grips being described below.

DB Pullover (1 DB in each hand)

Lay on a bench with your head at one end. Have the arms go over the end of the bench. The unique aspects of this exercise include the use of 1 DB in each hand, and the use of a 1 and ½ speed or rep method. In this case, lower the DB's down as far as you can stretch, pause, raise them 1/3 of the way up, pause, lower them down all the way, pause, and then lift them back up to the starting position, which should be short of vertical. This is one rep. Aim to keep the DB's even during the exercise, but not touching. If this movement has a habit of aggravating the joint, start off with less range and ease into the range with each set.

Front DB Raise

Stand with a DB in each hand, arms straight, palms in. Raise the DB's up directly in front of you with straight hands until they are just above shoulder height. Pause here and then lower them down just below shoulder height. Pause here and then raise them back to just above shoulder height. Pause, then lower them down all the way. This is one rep. Avoid leaning back at the waist during the movement.

Lat pull-down - WG/B - limited range

This is a lat pull-down to the base of the neck behind the head - with a difference - only allow the bar to raise to the top of the head before pulling it back down, and try to keep the elbows under the wrists. Aim to minimize the movement of the shoulder blades. Note the long pauses at each end of the movement.

Lateral DB - limited raise

Stand with a DB in each hand. Raise the DB's to the side until they are just above parallel to the ground, or just above shoulder height, pause for 2 seconds, lower the DB's back down half the way, pause, and return to the top position. This is the range, and remember the longer pauses.

Lat pulldown - MG/F

Sit in the lat pull-down and take a shoulder width prone, grip. The first seven reps are to be done in a range from the chest to the eyes, the next seven reps to be done with full range, and the next seven reps to be done between the eyes and the top stretch position. Remember to pause each time you change direction.

Seated DB Shoulder press

This is a similar concept to the above - the first seven reps from the bottom of the movement to the eye level, the next seven reps full range, and the last seven reps from eye level to the top of the extension.

Chin Up - RG

Take a supine, shoulder width grip, and hang fully from the bar (i.e. no touching the ground - tuck up the legs behind and cross them around the ankles if needed). Now take 3 seconds to reach the top, with the chin well and truly above the bar. Pause for 1 second and take 6 seconds to lower down. Don't attempt a rep that you are not confident of getting, and don't count an incomplete rep.

Shoulder press - WG/Bar/seated

The same speed as above - 3 seconds to lift, 6 seconds to lower. Always go down to the same point on the bottom of the neck, and pause there.

Workout C

Exercise	W/up sets	Work sets	Speed	R/Per (minutes)
DB shrug combo				
1. Behind body	10	10	321	nil
2. To side of body	10	10	321	nil
3. To front of body	10	10	321	nil
Leg abduct	1x12-15	1x12-15	323	1/2-1
Leg adduction	as above			1/2-1
Single leg hip/thigh extensions	nil	1x15+	322	1/2-1
Single leg back extension	nil	1x5-15	322	1/2-1
Single leg stiff leg deadlift	nil	5-15	313	1/2-1
Single leg good morning	nil	5-15	313	1/2-1
King Deadlift	nil	5-15	312	1/2-1
Bent knee deadlift	nil	1x6-8	316	1/2-1

Exercises for C Day, Stage 1

Trap Combo

The trap combo with DB's goes like this :

1. Standing, DB's behind body (actually behind your butt) palms facing backwards, shrug shoulders, (1 x 10, 321). No rest; then
2. Standing, DB's beside body, palms facing thighs, shrug shoulders (1 x 10, 321). No rest; then -
3. Standing, DB's in front of body, palms facing body, shrug shoulders (1 x 10, 321).

In all these exercises, ensure the following technical cues :

1. keep the arms straight at all time i.e. no elbow bending;
2. keep chin in, head still;
3. shrug straight upwards, not up and forwards;
4. terminate the movement if you can no longer maintain the full range you used in the earlier rep.

Use a second set of the above tri-set only after you have determined the body's response to this whole workout i.e. not on the first workout! Basically, if one set can make you grow, don't use any more. Only add more if the response fails to occur.

Leg Abduction and Adduction

The first two exercises are the leg abduction (taking leg away) and leg adduction (bring leg in). You can do these either on a dedicated machine, or low pulley cable, or even lying on your side on the ground with ankle weights. Sure, you might think these are useless, female exercises. Remember, one of the aims of this routine is to isolate, learn to recruit, and then prefatigue the smaller muscles. I would not ask you again to do these exercises for 12 months. But think about it - where are you going to get the best results? By doing things you don't normally do! (don't expect high level fatigue from these exercises - but when you don't want to sit down 2 days later because of the soreness in your gluts, you will understand how these seemingly harmless exercises fitted into the bigger picture of ripping your cheek muscles apart).

I want the abduction done before the adduction, to allow priority to be given to gluteal recruitment. Superset the two exercises, using a 323 speed (not the longer pause at each end. In both use a load that causes you to lose the ability to complete the range you started with, between 12-15 reps.

Single Leg Hip/thigh Extension

This exercise has been getting a lot of attention lately - it is the one that Louie Simmons sells a machine to perform on. You ly on your tummy, and extend one leg (in this case one leg at a time) from just off the floor to in line with the trunk, focusing on squeezing the gluts (I know, the hamstrings involved big time, but I want glut focus throughout this workout - you will appreciate this when you blow out of the 'hole' i.e. the bottom position of a big squat a few months later)

You don't need a special machine to do this exercise, although it is handy. In the absence of a machine, you can attach ankle weights, or even just the weight of your leg. I am using this as a pre-fatigue and a learning movement, so you again don't need high level 'can't walk' now loading. Done 1 legged, you won't need too much external resistance. Lift the leg in 2 seconds, hold for 2 seconds, lower for 3 seconds. If using the weight of your leg, you may need to take the reps high e.g. over 20. With ankle weights or a device, work to about 15 reps before looking to increase the load.

If you are using bodyweight or ankle weights, don't worry about a warm up. If using the device, do one warm up set with minimal loading, 15 reps. Make sure you don't externally rotate the leg too much during the concentric (lifting) phase i.e. keep the foot pointing to the ground and the heel pointing to the ceiling.

Single Leg Back Extension

Some know this as a hyper extension. Whatever - get on a

normal bench or a purpose made bench - have your hips and legs supported, face down, with your trunk hanging off the end. You will go from head nearly on the ground to where the upper body is in line with the legs. Provided you are up to it, have only 1 leg hooked under the foot holders (or if using a standard prone bench, have your partner hold down only 1 leg). You may have been thinking up to this point how easy this routine - well, the honeymoon is over - you are about to face reality!

Lift the trunk/upper body in 2 seconds, hold for 2 seconds, lower for 3 seconds

If you cannot do at least 5 reps at the speed indicated, go back to 2 legs together.

Remember the weak side rule, and start with the weaker leg (again, if you don't know which one that is in this movement, you will know shortly!) You don't need to do a warm up set - get straight into the work set.

Single leg standing stiff leg deadlift

Let the fun begin! Stand on one leg - have the other foot off the ground, but kept roughly parallel with the leg doing the supporting. Bend the knee slightly, but that knee angle should not change during the exercise (get a partner to watch for this, as it will be tempting to do so!). Now bend at the waist, allowing the back to round and reach slowly towards the floor. If your range allows, touch the floor with the fingertips and return to the starting position. Use a speed of 3 seconds down, 1 sec pause at the ends, and 3 seconds up.

You may struggle with balance, but persist - you will be developing the muscles in the sole of the foot! The first time you do this you may find you are touching down with the non-supporting foot regularly to avoid falling over. This is ok, but in later workouts, try to minimize this. When you have mastered this exercise, and touching of the ground by the non-supporting leg means terminate the set - this is your challenge. Don't be surprised if you can only do 5 reps on day 1! Look to increase the reps from workout to workout. Hold light DB's in your hand ONLY when you get to 10 reps at the speed indicated. No warm up set necessary. Remember the weak side rule.

Single leg Good Morning

This is exactly the same as above except I want you to start with a broomstick or 10 kg bar on your shoulders ala the Good Morning Exercise. I have simply shifted the external resistance, and affected the joint angles at which the load will be experienced. Hold onto the broomstick/bar with your hands in the normal fashion. Apply the speed, reps and load guidelines of the above exercise. Again, don't panic if 5 reps is your starting situation, and respect the weak side rule.

King Deadlift

This is a single leg bent knee deadlift - one of my very own creations! Stand on one leg (starting with the weak side) and bend the other leg up until the lower leg is parallel to the ground. Hands on hips or by side. The aim is to bend the knee of the supporting leg until the knee of the non-supporting leg is brushing the ground. In reality, you may have to settle for a shorter range (you'll understand why I say this as soon as you do this workout). If this is the case - and I expect it will be - look to increase the range from workout to workout.

You are allowed to flex (bend) forward at the waist as much as you want, and doing so will increase the gluteal involvement. Keep the working knee aligned neutrally throughout the movement. Take 3 seconds to lower, 1 second pause each end and 2 seconds to lift. No warm up set needed. When you can do more than 15-20 reps FULL RANGE look to hold DB's in the hands - this I suspect is a long way off!

This is one of my favorites, and after you see the benefits, you will probably have similar appreciation.

Deadlift

Again - the moment you have been waiting for - normalcy. Starting from the bottom position, weight rested on the ground, take 6 seconds to lift the weight to a standing position. Lower in 3 seconds.

This is how I generally recommend you deadlift :

Start Position :

1. feet shoulder width apart;
2. bar on shins;
3. shoulders vertically over the bar;
4. back flat, pelvis and head aligned with spine;
5. scapula retracted and depressed.

Get Set : (immediately prior to take-off)

1. extend legs slightly to take up slack (tension on the bar);
2. suck tummy thin (ensuring pelvis neutral with spine, not arched or rounded);
3. squeeze cheeks (to assist in above, and add focus to the point that this is where I want the drive to come from);
4. raise tension in upper back, where scapula position is to be held.

Take off (first pull = from ground to just above knees)

1. extend the legs, imaging pushing legs through the ground using gluts as prime mover;
2. as legs extend, trunk angle does not change (stays at same angle as in start) i.e. hips do not raise faster than shoulders - evenly slightly!);
3. upper back maintained in a flat position (scapula retracted/ depressed);
4. bar stays in contact with skin at all times;
5. drive with legs - back is a stabilizer!

Second Pull (from just above knees to standing)

1. now you stand up, forcing hips through with drive from gluteals;

2. bar stays in contact with skin at all times;
3. finish in upright position (no need to hyperextend trunk or roll shoulders!);
4. if upper back position held throughout, shoulders will be down and back in finish position automatically.

Lowering

1. unlike most exercises (including the squat) the eccentric phase of the deadlift is not a mirror reverse of the concentric phase;
2. as a general comment, unless I see the specific need, I do not place as much importance on the lowering of the deadlift as I would in other lifts, such as the squat.

Focus on using the gluts out of the bottom position. If you are experiencing lower back pain or excessive fatigue, you are using a technique different to what I recommend - I want all the work in the gluts and the legs. The back is mainly a stabilizer.

Do 6-8 reps. If the 20 kg bar or similar blows you away by this stage of the program (and don't be surprised if it did), you wont need a warm up set. If you are capable of 60 or more kilograms in the work set, look to use a warm up set, but you don't need to be as strict with the speed in this set.

Stage 1 : Weeks 1-3

Workout D

Exercise	W/up sets	Work sets	Speed	R/Per (minutes)
Forearm extension & flexion (DB)	nil	1-2x10-15	422	super-set
Standing bar bicep curl tri-set :				
1. wide supine grip	1x10	1x10	422	10s
2. close supine grip	1x10	1x10	422	10s
3. Med. prone grip	1x10	1x10	422	10s
Lying tricep bar tri-set :				
1. supine grip, to fore-head	1x10	1x10	422	10s
2. supine grip, to chin	1x10	1x10	422	10s
3. prone grip, to chin	1x10	1x10	422	10s
Prone DB flye	nil	1x10-12	1 ½'s	s/set
Supine DB flye	as above	as above	as above	
Prone DB row (limited range/ i.e. hardest half only)	nil	1x10-15	421	s/set
Decline DB press (limited range i.e. hardest half only)	as above	as above	as above	
Seated row (supine/MG)	nil	21	311	s/set
Incline DB Press	as above	as above	as above	
Seated row (prone/WG)	nil	1x4-8	613	s/set
Bench press (bar/WG/HB/FA – or cambered bar)	as above	as above	as above	

Exercises for D Day, Stage 1

Forearm extension and flexion

As per the earlier workout, but using DB's. The DB's will allow you more freedom in movement, and isolate arm to do equal work.

Standing bar Bicep Curl Tri-set

This is similar to the earlier program in that it is done with no rest between exercises. The grip positions are self-explanatory.

The Tricep Press-down Tri-set

Lay on a bench with the head half off the end of the bench. Grip the EZ or straight bar with the grip required for each exercise in this tri-set. The start position should be with the arm straight but off vertical, towards the end. This will keep tension on the muscle at all times. Make sure the elbow doesn't move forward/backwards or in and out during this tri-set.

Prone DB Flye

Lay face down on a bench with a DB in each hand. Keeping the elbow slightly bent extend the arms out at right angles to the body. Don't allow the elbow angle to change during the movement. Pause at the top, then lower down 1/3 of the way. Pause again, lift back up to the top, pause again, and lower all the way down. This is one rep. Minimize the movement of the head or the involvement of the upper traps.

Supine DB Flye :

Similar to the above but lying on your back (supine). Start with your hands above you and then lower them at right angles to the body. Keep the elbows slightly bent and don't allow this elbow angle to change during the movement. Pause at the bottom, then raise the DB's up 1/3 of the way. Pause again, lower back up down to the bottom, pause again, and lift all the way up. This is one rep.

Prone DB row - limited range

Lay face down on a normal height bench, with a DB in each hand, palms facing inwards. Use the range from the top of the pull to half way down. Note the pause at each end.

Decline DB press - limited raise

Use a decline of about 30-45 degrees. Use the range from the bottom position to half way up. Note the pause at each end.

Seated Row - supine medium grip

Sit on the seated row and take a shoulder width underhand (supine) grip. The first seven reps are to be done in a range from the chest to the half way out, the next seven reps to be done with full range, and the next seven reps to be done between half way out and the fully stretched position. Remember to pause each time you change direction. I like to keep the trunk, hips and head in a straight line, slightly behind a vertical position (i.e. very slightly leaning back), and still throughout the movement.

Incline DB press

This is a similar concept to the above - the first seven reps from the bottom of the movement to half way up, the next seven reps full range, and the last seven reps from half way up to the top of the extension.

Seated row - prone wide grip

Take an overhand (prone), out-side shoulder width grip. Note the point made above about trunk angle during seated rowing. Take 3 seconds to reach pull up to the body, pause for 1 second and take 6 seconds to lower out to full stretch. Don't attempt a rep that you are not confident of getting right up to the body, and don't count an incomplete rep.

Bench press - WG/Bar/HB/FA

Lay on the bench press. Raise your feet up, bend the knees and cross the ankles. Take a wide grip on the bar, and lower the bar to the bottom of the neck/top of the sternum. The same speed as above - 6 seconds to lower, 2 seconds to lift. Always go down to the same point on the base of the neck each time, and pause there.

Notes for Stage 2 (Wks 4-6)

The workouts in stage 2 involve a lesser number of exercises, and the number of sets per exercise has increased. The workouts are now being done in a more conventional order – bigger muscle group exercises to smaller muscle group exercises. The rest period between sets has also been increased.

- don't intentionally go to failure on any of the exercises in the first workout. Each subsequent workout go closer to this failure, so that by the last workout you take it to the limit;
- use this workout once every 4-7 days, depending on your recovery ability;
- do this workout for only 2-4 wks; you will know when it is time to move on; this type of training has a lot of benefit if used sparingly i.e. you need to move back into more loading.

You can still expect some muscle soreness during this stage, and you will also notice your strength start to increase. Do not compromise the technique you have developed in stage 1 for load in this phase.

Stage 2 : Weeks 4-6

Workout A

Exercise	W/up sets	Work sets	Speed	R/Per (minutes)
Squat	1x10@40% 1x8 @60@ 1x6 @ 80@	2x6-8	311	2-3
(high bar, medium stance, close grip)				
Squat (high bar, medium stance)	nil	1x10-12	311	2
Breathing Squats	nil	1x20	311	2
OR				
Continual controlled jump squat	nil	1x15-20	20*	2
Static lunge	1x6@50%	1-2x10-12/leg	311	2
Single leg squat	nil	1xAMRP	301	1
Calf press (on leg press)	15	15+15+15	311	strip set

NB The warm-up set loads are expressed as a %age of the first work-set load.

Exercises for A Day, Stage 2

Squat - high bar, medium stance

What a relief! Back to the old favorite. Place the bar as high on your neck as comfortable. Grip the bar with your hands as close to the shoulders as comfortable, and ensure that your elbows are pointing directly downwards to the ground. Use a foot stance that is shoulder width, and have your feet either straight or slightly externally rotated.

Following a progressive warm-up of a set of 10 (approx. 30% of first work set), a set of 8 (approx. 60% of 1st WS) and a set of 6 (approx. 80%), select a work set load that creates a high degree of fatigue yet allows excellent technique for 6-8 reps. Repeat a second work set 2-3 minutes later with a load up 2.5-5% on the first work set. Use a 3 sec eccentric, a 1 second pause either end, and a controlled explosive concentric (I say controlled because until you master the hip control during the ascent you cannot afford to accelerate it). Sit down between sets.

Now lower the weight on the bar to a load that allows 10-12. This will probably be somewhere between your second and third warm up sets. The only change here is increase the time of the pause at the bottom and the top to 2 seconds. Avoid going to failure in any of the work sets in week 1. Look then to add load each subsequent repeat workout, with the only possibility of failure in the final workout.

The next exercise will be a choice between two. For those with lower levels of hypertrophy, poorer squat technique, and / or reasons why they shouldn't be jumping under load (e.g. arthritis, lower back injuries), I recommend the second option - the breathing squats. For those whose hypertrophy is well advanced, wish to try something different, don't mind developing explosive power, and don't have any physical contraindications to impact - try the continual controlled jump squat.

Breathing squat

This golden-oldie is a variation of doing 20 continual reps. When your great-grandfather was doing this exercise (after reading about it in the magazine 'Ironman' when this magazine was owned by the Peary and Mabel Rader), he may have been doing it to 'expand his rib cage'. I don't know how much science has come out in support of that claim but there has been a significant amount of study that shows the unique benefits of performing intermittent reps (such breathing squats). They include :

- more reps can be performed at the same weight;
- reduced starving of oxygen to the working muscle, allowing increased activity of and therefore training effects upon (including hypertrophy) of FT muscle fiber.

Use a 3 sec lower, a 1 sec pause in the bottom position, and during the first 10 reps, a 1 second pause at the top. Between reps 11-15, use a 2 sec pause at the top (breathing twice) and during reps 16-20, a 3 second pause at the top (breathing 3 times).

Make sure you have a spotter as you might find your legs getting wobbly (and if the leg fatigue is not high enough, the multiple breathing could spin you out). And on completion of the set, don't walk anywhere that doesn't have something vertical to lean upon - or you might find yourself horizontal.

Continual controlled jump squat

Lower the bar weight to about the weight of your first warm-up set (for some this may be the bar only!). Control the lowering in about 2 seconds and pause for 1 at the bottom - then jump in the air as high as you can. Upon landing, decelerate the descent but don't stop it abruptly. Just fight to stay in control as you lower and repeat the cycle described. Look for 15-20 reps.

If doing the jump squat, hold the bar tight on your back as you don't want it to 'shift during flight', to take a line from the air flight industry!

Static lunge

Place the bar on your back or dumbbells in your hand, and take a long step out. The horizontal length of this step will be determined by the shin of the lead leg during the lowering. Keep it fairly vertical. Not because I support some bogus story about the knee should not exceed the vertical line of the toes - rather because I find this is a superior position for loading the appropriate musculature.

The bottom position should be one where the knee of the rear leg is almost brushing the ground. The top position should be just short of end of range. Complete all the reps on this first side (which of course you will know to be your weak side) before going with the other leg. Yes, you can take a short rest between legs - no more than 30 seconds though.

Take 3 seconds to lower the weight, pause of 1 at each end and lift with controlled explosiveness. Not as many complex directions in this exercise as in the squat, but keep the trunk upright. After a 50% of WS warm-up of 6 reps per leg, look for a load that creates significant fatigue (note - not failure, and definitely no technique breakdown in wk 1) between 10-12 reps per leg. Only 1 work-set per leg the first workout you do. If later you feel more volume is necessary (which I doubt) you can add a second work set to each leg. If there is a significant difference between strength or size right to left, you may chose to repeat only the smaller or weaker side.

Single leg squat

You know I wouldn't want you to miss those unilateral movements! So here we go - stand on 1 leg beside the squat rack or similar. Place the other leg out so that the heel stays just off the ground at all times. Bend the support knee and go down as far as you can whilst keeping your foot flat on the ground. 3 seconds down, no pause, controlled explosive up. Initially I suspect your range will be limited but as you get better at it over time, aim to increase range as well (and maybe even more importantly) as reps. Using your bodyweight only, I expect somewhere between 5-10 reps on day one, and look to use DB's in one hand if you exceed 15 reps. If this is the case, I have to wonder what you were doing during the earlier part of the workout?! Use the squat rack to hold on to for balance if needed (and you probably will need to) but don't get sucked into the temptation of using it to pull yourself up. Remember this is a leg day!

Calf press

If you have an on-going muscle imbalance (size or strength) between calves, do this single legged. If not, do two legs together. Work to fatigue around 15 reps, strip to a weight that allows about 15 reps, and strip again (3 sets in total, no rest).

Stage 2 : Weeks 4-6

Workout B

Exercise	W/up sets	Work sets	Speed	R/Per (minutes)
Chin up (WG/overhand)	1x10@ 40% 1x 8 @ 60% 1x 6 @ 80%	2x6-8	311	alt with sh pr (full recovery)
Shoulder press (Front/seated/mg)	as above	as above	as above	alt with chins
Chin up (RG)	1x8@LPD	1xAMRP	311	alt with sh press
Shoulder press (DB/seated)	as above	1x10-12	311	alt with chin
Lat pull-down (WG/B)	nil	1x15-20	311	alt with sh press
Shoulder press (WG/Bar/seated)	nil	1x15-20	311	alt with lat pd
Bicep curl (prone grip/MG)	1x10@60%	1-2x10	311	alt with tri
Lying tricep extension (to forehead)	as above	as above		alt with bi

NB The warm-up set loads are expressed as a %age of the first work-set load.

Stage 2 : Weeks 4-6

Workout C

Exercise	W/up sets	Work sets	Speed	R/Per (minutes)
Deadlift	1x10@40% 1x8 @60@ 1x6 @ 80@	2x6-8	311	2-3 m
(off ground, wide grip)				
as above	nil	1x10	311	2
Snatch pull (wide grip)	1x6@60%	1x6	10*	2-3
OR				
Deadlift (off ground, wide grip)	nil	1x15-20	311	2-3
Romanian Deadlift (chest up, flat back)	1x6@50%	1x8-10	311	2
Good Morning (2 legs)	1x6@50%	1x8-10	311	1-2
King deadlift	nil	1xAMRP	301	1
Bar shrugs (mg/front)	10	10+10+10	311	strip set

NB The warm-up set loads are expressed as a %age of the first work-set load.

Exercises for C Day, Stage 2

The Snatch Pull

The snatch pull is a wide grip deadlift to above the knees, and then accelerating to the toes and simultaneously shrugging your shoulders in the top position. If you struggle with the wider grip, use a medium, just outside shoulders grip (clean pull). Basically the technique is as per the deadlift except for the more aggressive acceleration in the second pull. Look for a warm up set of about 60% WS at 6 reps, and a work set at of 6. The criteria for load selection in addition to trunk/hip/scapula technique, is the height and speed of the pull (on toes and traps). Avoid any elbow flexion until the last moment, at which time allow the bar to rise if the acceleration has been significant.

Romanian Deadlift

In plainer terms this is a flat back version of the stiff legged deadlift. With the bar on your back, take a shoulder width stance and slightly bend the knees. The knee angle is now not to change during the lift. Flex or lower forward from the waist, keeping your chest up and hip/spine flat i.e. aligned. Only flex forward as far as you can PRIOR to any rounding of the spine or posterior rotation of the hip. For most, this will not be very far!

You can also accentuate the hamstring involvement by pushing the bum back and allowing your weight to drift to your heels during the lowering. During the lift, squeeze the gluts. This increases the hamstring involvement, which is the aim.

Use a 3 sec lower, a l sec pause in the bottom position, and a 1 second lift. A warm up set of 60% WS @ 6 reps, and a work set of 8-10 reps. Look out for uneven weight distribution - if one hamstring in sorer the next day than the other, this is what may be occurring.

Good Morning

I am really breaking my own rules using this exercise name - I usually prefer that the name at least describes the movement! Anyway - bar on back, knees slightly bent, shoulder width stance - pretty much as per the Romanian Deadlift in that the knee angle is not to change. The big difference is that on this occasion I want you to lower the head down as far as it will go by rounding over in the spine. Keep a good grip of the bar as you approach the bottom position. I stress - on this occasion I want range over load - get that head down to your knees, even if it means using the bar only! Same warm up/work set and speed as the Romanian Deadlift, but perhaps with a little less weight.

Bar shrugs

Use a load in the front bar shrug with a medium grip that causes fatigue around 10 reps, strip the weight, go again with a weight that causes fatigue around 10 reps, and go again (3 sets, no rest).

Stage 2 : Weeks 4-6

Workout D

Exercise	W/up sets	Work sets	Speed	R/Per (minutes)
Incline Bench press	1x10@40% 1x8 @60@ 1x6 @ 80@	2x6-8	311	alt with bo row
Bent over row (MG)	as above	as above	as above	alt with b/press
Decline bench press (Bar or DB's)	1x10@6-%	1x10-12	311	alt with s/row
Seated row (supine/MG)	as above	as above	as above	alt with decl
Bench press (WG/HB/FB)	nil	1x15-20	311	alt with s/row
Seated row (WG/ prone grip)	nil	1x15-20	311	alt with bench
Dips	1x10@bw bench dips	1-2x10@bw or ext load	311	alt with bi curl
Seated hammer DB curl	as above	as above		alt with dips

NB The warm-up set loads are expressed as a %age of the first work-set load.

Notes for Stage 3 (Wks 7-9)

The workouts in stage 3 involve even less exercises, but with a further increase of sets per exercise. The priority of lower body over upper body has been reversed, as has the priority of vertical pushing and pulling over horizontal pushing and pulling.

You may also note that the hip dominant and quad dominant priorities have also been reversed.

For many this will be the first time you will have given equal attention to what I call hip dominant exercises as you have to quad dominant exercises. To clarify these terms I consider the deadlift and squat to be the head of their respective family trees. So it will be interesting to see how you respond to this approach.

If you haven't already seen or experienced the benefit of this approach I will take 30 seconds to underline the potential benefits. The obvious benefits are the development of hip and back musculature and strength in a balanced manner with the front muscles group, the quads. But there is a little, lesser known but no less important benefit from doing exercises such as the deadlift and it's variations - and this is the stresses it presents to the muscles of the upper back.

One of the 'diseases' of the average bodybuilding approach as I see it is the development of imbalances between the anterior and posterior muscles of the upper trunk and extremities. Put simply, the pushing and pulling muscles (not that sort of pulling!) e.g. the pecs in bench and the upper back in rowing. The result for many after years of training is an imbalance in this horizontal plane that may produce the following :

- a visual appearance of being hunched over or rounded in the upper back;
- a less than optimally developed upper back;
- an apparent cease to gains in chest strength;
- an increase in the incidence of neck, shoulder, elbow and forearm injuries.

Quite a benefit - not! Why does this occur? Apart from the obvious - one's attention is focused more on what one sees when you look in the mirror - that is, the front of the body. It is often only when you find yourself in the change room at the local men's clothing store that you have the benefit of seeing the posterior aspect (your back) etc. via the opposing positioned mirrors. But wait there's more (as the salesperson might say)!

How much can you bench? How much can you row? Are they equal? Invariably, the answer is no, that you can bench more. So automatically you are applying unbalanced load stimulus to these opposing muscle groups. How can you expect balance? This is where the deadlift and related lifts come in. They provide a loading stimulus which is usually equal to or sometimes even more than the load presented in benching. This goes a big way to ensuring muscle balance. This benefit is optimized of course if there is focus on scapula retraction and depression (holding the shoulder blades down and back) during the deadlift.

Posturally, this is a feature that distinguishes most weightlifters and powerlifters from most bodybuilders.

The rest periods are now more approaching for training heading into 'neural territory'. Consider these points :

- don't intentionally go to failure on any of the exercises in the first workout. Each subsequent workout go closer to this failure, so that by the last workout you take it to the limit;
- use this workout once every 4-7 days, depending on your recovery ability;
- do this workout for only 2-4 wks; you will know when it is time to move on; this type of training has a lot of benefit if used sparingly i.e. you need to move back into more loading.

In this stage I expect that you will add new levels of strength to your recently developed new levels of muscular development. This program is based around the highly effective load alteration method for neural (strength) enhancement that I learned from East European weightlifting methods in the early 1990's. It uses a form of neural dis-inhibition, but at the end of the day I expect you will be more interested in how to do it rather than why it works. Do not compromise the technique you have developed in stage 1 for load in this phase.

The issue of rest weeks needs also be discussed here. That is, the ratio of work to rest weeks. I usually recommend no longer than 12 weeks of continuous training before taking a full rest week. There are some who don't even bother with rest weeks - it comes back to recovery factors including age, lifestyle, nutrition, supplements, drugs etc. I want to make it very clear - it is not a matter of how much training you can do - rather how much is optimal. Most contemporary sports training methods have been influenced by programs where the state provided the 'vitamins'. It is simple - if you are going to do those training methods, you will need the same 'vitamin program'. If you are not using these drugs, or not using the same dosages, you will burn out unless you modify the program accordingly.

For the average drug free-got a job/go to school person, I recommend consider using a recovery week after 2 stages (6-8 wks i.e. 2x3-4 wk blocks). For the older trainee or those whose recovery ability is stressed by work/lifestyle etc., I recommend using a recovery week after every 3-4 wks of training. How do you know which option to use? Easy - think back over your previous training programs. If for example, you recall burning out and 'getting weaker' after only 3 wks training, you either need to lower the training load or use a recovery week after 3 wks, or both.

So before you start with this third stage, ask yourself the above questions and resolve this issue. Most err on the adventurous side (e.g. 'I don't need a rest week now') and learn the hard way, when their results diminish at some stage during the next block of training. Making this mistake is not a problem - failing to learn from it is though. And considering many of you have been making the same mistakes for the duration of your training career, is their much hope of the voice of reason dominating?

Get Buffed!™

Workout A

Exercise	W/up sets	Work sets	Speed	R/Per (minutes)
Bench press (MG/MB/FD)	1x10@40% 1x8 @60@ 1x5 @ 80@	1x5 1x1 1x5 1x1 1x10-20	211	alt with row
Seated row (Triangle grip)	as above	as above	as above	alt with bench
Close grip bench (6-8")	1x10@60%	1-2x6-8	211	2-3 m

NB The warm-up set loads are expressed as a %age of the first work-set load.

Stage 3 : Weeks 7-9

Workout B

Exercise	W/up sets	Work sets	Speed	R/Per (minutes)
Deadlift	1x10@40%	1x5	311	3-4
	1x8 @60@	1x1		
	1x5 @ 80@	1x5		
		1x1		
(conventional bent knee, MG)				
Off-block Deadlifts nil		1x5	211	3
(bar start position just under knees)				
Clean pull	1x5@75%	1x 5	10*	2-3
OR				
Conventional deadlift nil		1x10-20	311	2-3
Speed shrugs	1x6 @75%	1x6-8	10*	2-3
(from the above the knees)				
OR				
MG stiff legged deadlift				
	1x5@75%	1x8-10	301	2-3
Hurdle or box jumps	1x10	1x10	*	2-3
OR				
King deadlift	nil	1xAMRP	301	2
Optional bar shrugs	8	1-2x6-8	211	1-2

NB The warm-up set loads are expressed as a %age of the first work-set load.

Exercises for B Day, Stage 3

Deadlift off Blocks

This is a limited range deadlift, allowing you to expose to supra-maximal loading (that is relative to your off-ground strength). Use a load somewhere in the vicinity of 20-30 % greater than you would for a full range set of the same number of reps. The box height should be such that with the weight plates on each box, the bar height in the start is just under the knees, or from the 'hang below' position. Do 5 reps, each rep recommencing from a resting start. For those interested in increasing their explosive power, focus on accelerating (or at least trying to do so) during the second pull i.e. from above the knees to lockout. You may find the start position of this exercise unusual, in which case be conservative in your load selection until you come to terms with it.

Clean Pull or High Rep Deadlift Set

I have used 'forks in the road' in the early programs, by showing programs that potentially create the different training effects of power or hypertrophy.

In this case, go to the clean pull for power and the high rep set for hypertrophy.

Clean Pull : we used the snatch pull (wide grip) in the previous phase. The clean pull is the same width grip as the deadlift above - grip comfortably outside knees. Again, this supports an increase in load. Reduce the load to about or just below the weight of the first work set of 5 reps deadlifts. The aim of this lift is to go slow in the first pull (to just above the knees) and then to accelerate to the toes as fast as possible, minimizing role of elbow flexors, and finishing on the toes with upper traps fully contracted. At the end of the first pull (bar just above shoulders) you should have the same trunk angle as in the start position off the ground. Place a premium on the acceleration of the second pull.

High rep deadlift set : as with the high rep squat set, this set presents an incredible window of opportunity to perform a greater amount of work than usual, due to the sequencing of this set AFTER the maximal loading. You are looking for a weight that will allow between 10-20 reps at your 'normal' speed, and as a guide you will be looking at about a weight somewhere between your second last and last warm up set. Whatever you use, you will be able to do more reps at this stage of the workout than if you had attempted the same weight as your first work set (due to increased neural firing/ reduced inhibition). Again, cease the rep if the technique breaks down. You also have the alternative of performing this set continuously or using intermittent short pauses. For those that wish to totally deplete their fiber pool, this high rep set is an excellent compliment to the earlier lower rep sets, giving you the 'best of both worlds'.

Speed shrugs or MG Stiff Legged Deadlift

Another fork in the road - speed shrugs again for those primarily interested in explosive power; the MG stiff legged deadlift for those more interested in hypertrophy.

Speed shrugs: reduce loading to about the weight of the second warm up set. Take a medium grip, and stand up with the bar. Keeping a flat back, lower the bar down to just above the knees (known in 'lifting as the 'hang above' position) and immediately accelerate upwards, aiming to finish as high on the toes and with as forceful a contraction of the upper traps as possible. Excellent lift for upper back, traps, and calves!

Remember - this is for speed and maximal contraction of calves and upper traps

Look for 6 reps in the warm-up (with a load of about 75% of that you expect to use in the work set) and a work set of about 6 -8 reps. If speed or pull height decrease, terminate set.

MG Stiff Legged Deadlift : take a medium grip (about shoulder width) and commence in a standing position. Lower the bar down by bending at the hips, not at the knees. In the start, the knees should be slightly bent and remain exactly at joint angle during the lift. The WG chest up stiff legged deadlift (or Romanian Deadlift) was used in earlier phases. The grip and technique of the MG Stiff Legged Deadlift also supports increase in load.

Look for 5 reps in the warm-up (with a load of about 75% of what you expect to use in the work set) and a work set of about 8 - 10 reps.

Hurdle jumps or King deadlifts

The final fork in the road - for power, do the hurdle jumps; for hypertrophy, the King deadlifts.

Hurdle jumps : if you have hurdles excellent. If not, use objects like benches to jump over. The aim is to use a height of hurdle or box (or other object) that challenges you whilst maintaining a quick and short eccentric contraction upon landing, and an extremely short ground contact time.

Use a warm-up set of 10 ground contacts, and where possible and appropriate, raise the jump height to challenge you in the work set of 10 ground contacts. Remember - the emphasis should be on the speed of the ground, not the height of the box. And if you have any lower limb injury that is not suited to jumping, DON'T DO THIS OPTION!

King deadlifts : the technique for these has been well documented in previous pages. If you want a further challenge, consider either or both of the following options :

- place DB's in each hand;
- stand on the edge of a low block or box, so that the working side range can be increased over that which is available when standing on the floor.

Stage 3 : Weeks 7-9

Workout C

Exercise	W/up sets	Work sets	Speed	R/Per (minutes)
Chin up (Neutral grip)	1x10@40% 1x8 @60@ 1x5 @ 80@	1x5 1x1 1x5 1x1 1x10-20	211	alt with shou press
Shoulder press (seated MG/bar/behind)	as above	as above	as above	alt with chin up
Bicep curl (EZ on preacher bench)	1x10@60%	1-2x6-8	211	2-3

NB The warm-up set loads are expressed as a %age of the first work-set load.

Stage 3 : Weeks 7-9

Workout D

Exercise	W/up sets	Work sets	Speed	R/Per (minutes)
Squat	1x10@40%	1x5	301 or 201	4-5
	1x8 @60@	1x1		
	1x5 @ 80@	1x5		
		1x1		
(med bar, med stance, med grip)				
Quarter Squats	nil	1x5	201 or 20*	4-5
Explosive Squat	nil	1x 4-8	20*	4-5
OR				
High rep squat set (MS/MB/MG)	nil	1x10-20	301	3-4
Intermittent limited range jump squat				
	nil	1x6-10	10*	2-3
OR				
Dynamic Lunge	1x5/leg@50%	1x10/leg	10*	
In-depth jump	1x10	1x10	*	2-3
OR				
Single leg squat	nil	1xAMRP	301	2-3
Optional calf press (standing)	12	1-2x8-12	211	1-2

NB The warm-up set loads are expressed as a %age of the first work-set load.

Exercises for D Day, Stage 3

Quarter squat

This is a limited range squat, allowing you to expose to supra-maximal loading. Use a load somewhere in the vicinity of 20-30 % greater than you would for a full range set of the same number of reps. Do 5 reps. For those interested in increasing their explosive power, focus on accelerating (or at least trying to do so) during the concentric phase, such that you end up on your toes. If in doubt as to how far to go down, be conservative in the first rep, and progress in depth in subsequent reps. If you go beyond your sticking point, you may not come back up, so be careful here. For safety have a spotter/s and / or safety rack.

Explosive Squat or High Rep Set

We have come to a fork in the road - those primarily interested in developing explosive power go the explosive squat, and those wanting primarily to increase muscle size go the high rep set of squats.

Explosive Squat : reduce the load to about the weight of the first work set of 5 reps. Aim to perform these reps with maximal acceleration in the concentric phase. This is more about trying to lift fast than actually looking fast, but at least the final stages of the concentric phase should gain some speed, ideally allowing you to finish on your toes. Look for 4-8 reps, but stop if or when you lose the speed or the technique breaks down.

High rep squat set : this set presents an incredible window of opportunity to perform a greater amount of work than usual, due to the sequencing of this set AFTER the maximal loading. You are looking for a weight that will allow between 10-20 reps at 301 speed, and as a guide you will be looking at about a weight somewhere between your second last and last warm up set. Whatever you use, you will be able to do more reps at this stage of the workout than if you had attempted the same weight as your first work set (due to increased neural firing/

reduced inhibition). Again, cease the rep if the technique breaks down. You also have the alternative of performing this set continuously or using intermittent short pauses.

Jump squats or dynamic lunges

Another fork in the road - jump squats again for those primarily interested in explosive power; the dynamic lunge for those more interested in hypertrophy.

Jump squat : reduce loading to about the weight of the first work set. Use a short and as quick as possible eccentric (lowering) phase, and shift to the concentric phase with as little delay as possible. Jump for maximal height, and land with bent knees, absorbing the shock. Pause, reset mentally, and repeat. Remember - this is for speed and height. Look for between 6-10 reps, but again if speed or jump height decrease, terminate set.

Dynamic lunge : use a load somewhere between the first and second work-set. With the bar on the shoulders and feet side by side, step out with the weak side leg first, landing with a foot position that keeps the knee of that leg between the heel and toe at all times during the last stage of the eccentric and first stage of the concentric phases. Go down as moderate speed and drive back up with maximal speed. A little trick for those with significant right to left leg imbalances - do 2 reps on the weak side to every rep on the strong side. Do a total of 20 reps (if equal, i.e. 10/leg; if imbalance exists, that may be 14 on weak side, 7 on strong).

In-depth jumps or single leg squats

The final fork in the road - for power, do the in-depth jump; for hypertrophy, the single leg squats.

In-depth jump : stand on a box about half the height of a standard prone bench. Have a prone bench or equivalent about 1 meter in front. Step off the low box leading with one leg, land on the ground with 2 feet, and jump to the higher box/bench with a short as ground contact time and as limited a knee bend as possible. To know if the jump heights are appropriate, you can assess your ground contact time, but you may benefit from another persons feedback on this (e.g. a coach). Look for 10 reps, one to 2 sets.

One-leg squat : the technique for this is outlined in the previous quad dominant workout. This is an option excellent for those with leg imbalances. If the imbalance is so great, you may chose not to do any on the stronger/larger size. For variety, or if your bodyweight for whatever reason is too much for your leg strength, you can always do a one-legged leg press or hack squat. If using bodyweight, do as many reps as possible at about 311. If using leg press or similar, look for between 10-20 reps at the same speed.

Get Buffed!™

Notes for Stage 4 (Wks 10-12)

The workouts in stage 4 specialize in the cores lifts, using longer rest periods and lower reps – classic neural training.

The options in the earlier workouts have been in exercises - dependant upon your specific goals. The options in this stage will be reps. If you aren't too advanced, you may not respond optimally to the very low reps, so I would prefer those to take the 'high road' or in this case the higher rep options.

I have used the beginner/intermediate/advanced definitions for the three rep options I have presented. I won't get drawn into providing definitions for each - I believe you will know which combination will work for you. Except those with less experience - which means if you are in your first 2 years of training take the first option! As for the rest, if you are realistic, you will learn the hard way.

It might seem ridiculous that I show a difference of 1 rep between methods. Don't underestimate the power of 1 rep. 1 rep is 20% of 5 reps - is this a significant number? My experience has taught me that there is no value taking reps lower than one's technical skill or neural firing ability. As a simple guideline, use a load that you can feel in total control of from a muscular control perspective. Simply having the balls or the stupidity to dive-bomb the eccentric phase and bounce back up like a crumbled mass is of limited value to getting bigger and stronger - but it will make your chiropractor happy!

The method I have provided is a wave-loading method. To get the best result in this method takes some emotional control - I don't believe the first wave should be performed at optimal load. But the second can be. Can you wait that long? I have found that if you over-dose on the first wave, the second wave is performed at the same or lower loads. And this is not the goal - the goal is to use a slightly heavier load in the sets of the second wave when compared to the respective set in the first wave. If this is not possible, I believe you have failed to achieve the intent of wave loading, which can provide significant neural dis-inhibition - in street language, you should be much stronger in the second wave!

Another significant difference with this program that I want to bring to your attention is the use of lower volume warm up sets. Unlike the habits of most weight trainers, I recommend an extensive warm up set protocol. I find the following benefits with doing this:

- reduces wear on the joints by increasing joint temperature and lubrication;
- increases neural awareness so that the body is firing in time for the first work set;
- the volume involved may present some pre-fatigue (although this is not aimed for), which in a hypertrophy phase I believe is desirable;
- if the reps in the last warm up set are equal to or greater than the reps in the first work set, it contributes to your confidence that you can achieve the reps required in the first warm up set.

But in a neural phase I want to ensure no residual fatigue from the warm up sets into the work sets, so I lower the volume. Not so much in the number of warm up sets or the jumps from one warm up set to the next - I have still shown a jump in the warm up sets of no more than 20% (although for a powerlifting in a competition warm up I might use bigger jumps). Instead, I have reduced the volume by reducing the number of reps in each warm up set, to the point that the reps in the last warm up set are lower than the reps in the first work set.

On rest periods. For those who like to sit around and recover, you will enjoy this - I want between 4-10 minutes between sets. For those who are a little more hyperactive, I can understand your frustration - but tell someone who cares - sit down! The challenge with longer work sets include these :

- don't get lost in conversation - at least a minute before you are going to go again, focus on the task ahead, use your visualizing technique, begin to lower you arousal level;
- don't get too cold. At risk of being accused of being too obvious (*"we all know how to do that..."* - yeah, but do you do it....) use the towel on the shoulders to maintain body temperature. I also like to have the knees covered in lower body days for this reason;

- manipulating your level of arousal. A few minutes into your sitting your arousal levels are very low. You need to get them up to peak in time for the next set. How long this takes depends on your ability to control your emotions (the use of ammonia smelling salts will be valuable here - check out the powerlifting suppliers catalogues).

If you were ever going to use knee wraps, belts and even squat suits now would be the time. I am not suggesting you need to (unless you are a competitive lifter, in which case you had better use them, if only to get used to them!)

To give you a feel of how to periodize squat assisting equipment, I provide the following example : (note, example only, and more for a competitive lifter than anyone else!)

Wks 1-3   No belt
           No knee wraps, but a knee sleeve
           No squat suit

Wks 4-6   4" belt
           No knee wraps, but a knee sleeve
           No squat suit

Wks 7-9   6" belt, not tight
           Knee wraps, pulled loosely
           Squat suit half way up

Wks 10-12 6" belt, tight
           Knee wraps, tight
           Squat suit, on fully

NB these time frames can be turned into longer periods, but the message is there.

Stage 4 : Weeks 10-12

Workout A

Exercise	W/up sets	Work sets	Speed	R/Per (minutes)

Beginner Rep combination

Exercise	W/up sets	Work sets	Speed	R/Per
Bench press	1x10@20%	1x5	211	alt
	1x8 @40%	1x4		with
	1x5 @60%	1x3		bi
	1x3 @80%	1x5		curl
		1x10-20		

(med bar, low bar, feet down, can use powerlifting arch)

Exercise	W/up sets	Work sets	Speed	R/Per
Bicep curl (standing, EZ bar)	as above	as above	as above	alt with bench

Intermediate Rep combination

Exercise	W/up sets	Work sets	Speed	R/Per
Bench press	1x10@20%	1x4	211	alt
	1x6 @40%	1x3		with
	1x4 @60%	1x2		bi
	1x2 @80%	1x4	Eccentric (500)	
		1x10-20		

(med bar, low bar, feet down, can use powerlifting arch)

Exercise	W/up sets	Work sets	Speed	R/Per
Bicep curl (standing, EZ bar)	as above	as above	as above	alt with bench

Advanced Rep combination

Exercise	W/up sets	Work sets	Speed	R/Per
Bench press	1x8@20%	1x3	211	
	1x5 @40%	1x2		
	1x3 @60%	1x1		
	1x1 @80%	1x3 Eccentric (500)		
		1x10-20		

(med bar, low bar, feet down, can use powerlifting arch)

Exercise	W/up sets	Work sets	Speed	R/Per
Bicep curl (standing, EZ bar)	as above	as above	as above	alt with bench

NB The warm-up set loads are expressed as a %age of the first work-set load.

Exercises for A Day, Stage 4

With the upper body training in this final stage of the four stages, I have retained two exercises, unlike the lower body, where I have gone back to one. With two exercises, my volume limits (aiming to keep it to 10 or less work sets) meant I could not use the 2 wave method as used in the lower body. The first wave is used, and you can go closer to your max in this case.

When doing the bench press in this phase, consider using the arch technique used by powerlifters. It involves setting up an arch in the spine prior to taking the load, and maintaining this arch throughout the lift. Ideally there is not head, butt or feet movement.

The aim of this arch is to allow you to lift more. It works by

- reducing the range of movement;
- increasing the rigidity of the base;
- increasing the involvement of the lats;
- avoiding gravity - creating an arc movement.

If you are going to use the arch, make sure you warm the spine for this position. Come out of it slowly, and do cat stretches after each set or at the end of the workout to counter the hyperextension.

I strongly recommend using wrist wraps during heavy benching.

Stage 4 : Weeks 10-12

Workout B

Exercise	W/up sets	Work sets	Speed	R/Per (minutes)
		Beginner Rep combination		
Deadlift	1x10@20%	1x5	201	4-6
	1x8 @40%	1x4		
	1x5 @60%	1x3		
	1x3 @80%	1x5		
		1x4		
		1x3		
		1x10-15		

(med grip, off ground)

Exercise	W/up sets	Work sets	Speed	R/Per (minutes)
		Intermediate Rep combination		
Deadlift	1x10@20%	1x4	201	5-7
	1x6 @40%	1x3		
	1x4 @60%	1x2		
	1x2 @80%	1x4		
		1x3		
		1x2		
		1x4 Eccentric or ¼ squat		
		1x10-15		

(med grip, off ground)

Exercise	W/up sets	Work sets	Speed	R/Per (minutes)
		Advanced Rep combination		
Deadlift	1x8@20%	1x3	201	6-10
	1x5 @40%	1x2		
	1x3 @60%	1x1		
	1x1 @80%	1x3		
		1x2		
		1x1		
Deadlift	nil	2x3, step load, 211		4-8m

(off blocks i.e. higher start position)

Exercise	W/up sets	Work sets	Speed	R/Per (minutes)
Deadlift	nil	1x10	311	3-6m

(med grip, off ground)

NB The warm-up set loads are expressed as a %age of the first work-set load.

Exercises for B Day, Stage 4

This workout is going to center around the deadlift. I realize that there may be a number of you that have other preferences. For example, if you wanted to focus more specifically on power and were competent in the power clean, you could use it (or it's variations such as the clean pull) instead.

That's the easy part. The harder part is for those whose lower back situation is such that they shy away from heavy deadlifts. I understand this. However there are not many other hip dominant exercises I would recommend for use with such low reps. Perhaps the only alternative may be to do an alternative leg exercise, a variation to the squat e.g. front squats, leg press or whatever.

However if this was the case it would be a repeat of the quad dominant training performed in the earlier program. If you do go down this road, I would suggest a lower volume and higher reps on this day. See the alternative program towards the end.

The reps and sets are similar to the squat routine presented earlier. Remember - to optimize wave loading, you need to be conservative in the first wave.

What about straps? Straps can be used in the deadlift to negate grip strength limitations. The disadvantage of straps is the reduction of work that the forearms get to do. I do recommend minimizing straps, but at this end of a program I appreciate that some of you may want to use them. What I would consider prior to this is developing the reverse grip option used by competitive powerlifters - for the deadlift; and the power clean, the hook grip - as used by Olympic lifters. However the straps are there as a fall back. Of course if you are doing clean pulls or snatches as an alternative to deadlifts, you will need straps.

The squat and deadlift (and clean etc) are lifts that really do require feedback from anther party. If you can still see yourself in the mirror during the set you aren't lifting enough. Maximal loading should push your blood pressure up so much you don't remember anything during the set, let alone be able to see yourself!

For the more advanced I have included a deadlift off blocks (i. e. the weight plates sit on the blocks, raising the starting height). The aim is to expose to greater loading than you may otherwise be able to do. I have suggested 2 sets of 3 and provided you were conservative in the first work set, look to step-load (go up a bit in load in the second work set). This exercise is best left to those with more training experience.

In the event you are going to use the power clean I am providing some refreshers :

- the starting position is similar to the deadlift -bar on shins, shoulder vertically over the bar, hip/spine/head aligned;
- the movement during the 'first pull' (from start to just above knees) is also similar - bar stays on skin, at the end of the first pull (just above knees) shoulders should still be vertically above bar, hip/spine/head aligned etc;
- which means that the hips are not to be raised faster than the shoulders;
- now this is where the two lifts diverge : the second pull (from above the knees to the 'rack' position) in the power clean is explosive. There are many ways to teach this pull, but basically the bar is to stay close to the body, and the arm involvement to be minimized (as a teaching rule, the elbows don't bend during the lift!);
- the movement finishes with the bar resting on the anterior deltoids, elbows up and out;
- the foot stance in this catch or rack position will be a bit wider than the stance you started with if you do the jumping action associated with the second pull; if you do go to this wider stance, return to the pull stance (your starting stance) before lowering the bar.

Deadlift- off ground, medium

This is the same deadlift technique that I described in an earlier article. The challenge here is to maintain your form within some degree of your capabilities. Yes, I know - some of the best deadlifters (read people who can lift the most weight in a deadlift) have some of the worst technique i.e. rounded back. This is of no concern to you. If you want to optimize the way you look and your function - retain a focus on technique. As far as stress to the lower back, there is going to be some. But if this is excessive, it is more a function of technique break-down than anything else.

NB

- The warm-up set loads are expressed as a %age of the first work-set load;
- the power clean can be substituted for the deadlift;
- the following workout is an option for those who chose not to perform heavy deadlifts.

The non-deadlift option

Exercise	W/up sets	Work sets	Speed	R/Per (minutes)
Squat variation (or alternative)	1x10@30% 1x8 @60% 1x6 @80%	2x5-6 1x10-12 1x15-20	301	3-4
Secondary hip dominant exercise	1x10	2x8-10	311	3

(such as mg stiff leg d/lift or good morning or back extensions

Stage 4 : Weeks 10-12

Workout C

Exercise	W/up sets	Work sets	Speed	R/Per (minutes)
	Beginner Rep combination			
Chin up	1x10@20%	1x5	211	alt
	1x8 @40%	1x4		with
	1x5 @60%	1x3		close
	1x3 @80%	1x5		grip
		1x10-20		
bench				
(med overhand grip)				
Close grip bench	as above	as above	as above	alt
(shoulder width grip)				with
				chin
	Intermediate Rep combination			
Chin up	1x10@20%	1x4	211	alt
	1x6 @40%	1x3		with
	1x4 @60%	1x2		cgbp
	1x2 @80%	1x4 Eccentric (500)		
		1x10-20		
(med overhand grip)				
Close grip bench	as above	as above	as above	alt
(shoulder width grip)				with
				chin
	Advanced Rep combination			
Chin up	1x8@20%	1x3	211	alt
	1x5 @40%	1x2		with
	1x3 @60%	1x1		cgbp
	1x1 @80%	1x3 Eccentric (500)		
		1x10-20	211	
(med overhand grip)				
Close grip bench	as above	as above	as above	alt
(shoulder width grip)				with
				chin

NB The warm-up set loads are expressed as a %age of the first work-set load.

Exercises for C Day, Stage 4

Chin ups

Should you use straps in these chins? I tend to use them for the eccentrics and high-rep back off set only.

You will be needing (hopefully) to add external loading. This can be done quite simply with a rope and belt, from the waist.

Close Grip Bench Press

The grip is about shoulder width, feet down on the ground. Get a spotter!

Stage 4 : Weeks 10-12

Workout D

Exercise	W/up sets	Work sets	Speed	R/Per (minutes)
		Beginner Rep combination		
Squat	1x10@20%	1x5	201	4-6m
	1x8 @40%	1x4		
	1x5 @60%	1x3		
	1x3 @80%	1x5		
		1x4		
		1x3		
		1x10		
		1x10-20		

(low bar, med stance, med grip)

Exercise	W/up sets	Work sets	Speed	R/Per (minutes)
		Intermediate Rep combination		
Squat	1x10@20%	1x4	201	5-7m
	1x6 @40%	1x3		
	1x4 @60%	1x2		
	1x2 @80%	1x4		
		1x3		
		1x2		
		1x4 ¼ squat		
		1x10-20		

(low bar, med stance, med grip)

Exercise	W/up sets	Work sets	Speed	R/Per (minutes)
		Advanced Rep combination		
Squat	1x8@20%	1x3	201	6-10m
	1x5 @40%	1x2		
	1x3 @60%	1x1		
	1x1 @80%	1x3		
		1x2		
		1x1		
		1x3 Eccent. (400) or ¼ squat		
		1x10		
		1x20		

(low bar, med stance, med grip)

NB The warm-up set loads are expressed as a %age of the first work-set load.

Get Buffed!™

Exercises for D Day, Stage 4

Squat - low bar, medium stance, wide grip

In this stage we are going to use the same width stance as the previous stage (i.e. shoulder width, toes slightly pointed out). The main difference will be the lowering of the bar further down the back to what I call the low bar position - this is not necessarily the most comfortable position, but it will decrease the length from the hips to bar. The shortening of this lever increases your load ability. You can also take your hand grip wider if you need. All of this will result in more forward flexion (lean) of the trunk. Use a lower speed that optimizes your use of elastic energy UNDER the loads involved - and this is the key - theoretically the faster the eccentric the greater the strength potential - but when you have to do a 180 degrees U-turn with maximal loading in the squat, a degree of control during the eccentric phase is advisable! No pause, and come straight back up.

There may be a temptation to throw technique focus out the window - don't. I appreciate that there may be some degradation of the immaculate technique you developed at lower loading, but fight to bring some (or ideally most) of this selective muscle recruitment into the squat in this phase.

There is only one variation of the squat to consider and that is the eccentric or quarter squat. Not everyone has the skills or facilities (e.g. spotters) to do eccentric loading. For those, I recommend going with the quarter squat. The quarter squat was described in the previous stage, and the safety and loading guidelines all apply.

Another alternative is the eccentric load hooks that can be attached to the bar at the top of each rep and drop off when the bar is lowered.

Now for those who are going to do the eccentric squat. You really need to be very experienced. You need excellent spotters, and I discourage the use of 2 only (i.e. one each side) - they will kill you! (read lift unevenly). Go with at least 3 spotters and have the center spotter (standing behind you) call the shots (tell the side spotters when to come in) and take the most load. I stress - you need to be experienced to do this (both the lift and the spotting!!) The loading should be 20-40 % greater than your 1RM, dependant upon your skill and state of freshness. Take about 4 seconds to lower the weight Remember, with an eccentric - if you cannot lower the load under control at every joint angle - don't do it - terminate. And the spotters should know this so they can get early warning signs of fatigue.

Chapter 29
Questions and Answers
On a variety of topics!

I have included these questions and answers because I believe the information contained may be of interest to you the reader.

On body parts - Training methods for....

Q. *I have made great progress using the "Swiss Ball" to build my lower abdominals, an area that, until just recently, was a major weak point in my overall progress in the weight room. Now it seems because of the overemphasis on the Swiss Ball Reverse Crunch in my abdominal routine over the last 6 months I have the exact condition that this type of training was supposed to "correct". My lower abdominals bulge out "like a pouch." My postural alignment has never been better. And the added strength to this previously weak body part feels great! My body fat is around 10.5% so this "pouch" isn't all fat. Could very heavy squatting exacerbate this condition? Any suggestions on a remedy?*

Tom

A. I am about to give you my interpretation of this so-called "pouch". But before I do I say that I suspect from what you say that you have mis-interpreted the role of the 'lower abdominal'. The way I see it the role of the 'lower abdominals' (and here I refer to the transverse and oblique abdominal muscles) is to stabilize the pelvis for when the bigger and more powerful muscles such as the rectus and hip flexor mus-

> *The way I see it the role of the 'lower abdominals' is to stabilize the pelvis.*

cles contract. These lower abdominals aim to maintain a 'neutral' pelvis position. Your first goal in training the lower abdominals should be firstly, to learn how to selectively recruit them (i.e. without recruiting all other abdominal muscles) and secondly to develop their ability to stabilize the pelvis under load. Now most of the exercises to achieve both these goals should be either static (isometric) and or controlled through a limited range - because, in most cases, anything more would exceed your ability to stabilize the pelvis!

What I fear you have done (and most do this!) is overload the 'lower abdominals' such that they have not been able to maintain the neutral pelvis position. The outcome of this approach is that the hip flexors get more of a workout than anything else.

Which leads me to my theory on THE POUCH! If your pelvis is anteriorly rotated as its neutral position, you will look as if you have this 'pouch'. This is usually caused by tight, short hip flexors, which dominate the muscles of posterior pelvis rotation (lower abdominals, gluteals). This gives the appearance of an extended abdomen. Yes, heavy squatting (because of it ability to shorten the quads and hip flexors) can contribute to this condition.

The solution - stretch the hip/thigh muscles and strengthen the abdominal muscles to create a more vertical pelvis!

The solution - stretch the hip/thigh muscles and strengthen the abdominal muscles to create a more vertical pelvis!

Q. Despite doing sit-ups every day, my abs look pathetic. To be specific, they have got no definition and after a big meal, I look like a snake that swallowed a bowling ball. Can you recommend a good ab program?

A. Let's clear this issue immediately - doing sit-ups in themselves is not going to guarantee 'great abs'! Until you lower the body fat in general, you may never have the definition you desire. When you do see people with great abdominal definition, it tells you more about their body fat levels than the condition of their abdominals. As for looking like you have swallowed a bowling ball following a big meal - simple - don't make a habit of having big meals. Smaller more frequent meals may be more beneficial - especially to support your goal of lowering your body fat....

Get Buffed!™

A Day

Exercise Name	Sets x Reps	Speed of Movement	Rest Period	Description of Exercise
Thin tummy	10 x 5-10 sec contractions.	5-10 sec isometric holds	nil	Ly on your back, knees bent, feet flat on floor. Place your fingers on either side of your lower tummy just under the line of your pants. Now 'suck' the tummy thin as you can at the bottom. Hold this for 5 sec. Initially you may have to hold your breath, but aim to be able to breath normally.
Lateral leg lowers	1x10-20	303	nil	Ly on your back, arms out flat on floor at 90 degrees. Legs together in the air - lower them together at 90 degrees to the body until they are nearly touching the ground. Then return to the top and lower to the other side etc.
Toes to sky	1 x 10	5-10 sec isometric holds	nil	Ly on your back with both legs in the air at 90 degrees to the body. Keeping the legs at this angle i.e. vertical, lift the pelvis off the ground marginally. Hold this position for 5 seconds.
V-sit leg cycles	1 x 10-30	303	Nil	Sit on the ground with trunk at 45 degrees to ground, upper thighs at 45 degrees to ground, knees bent. Bring one knee towards the chest, whilst taking other leg out to ground. The swap legs action. Trunk stays still at 45 degrees to ground.

B Day

Exercise Name	Sets x Reps	Speed of Movement	Rest Period	Description of Exercise
Slow up and slow down	1 x 10-15	515	nil	Ly on your back on the ground, knees bent so that feet are flat on the ground. Initially place arms out in front so that they remain parallel to ground throughout. Take 5 seconds to sit-up, moving at a constant speed i.e. no jerking or acceleration (if you can't do this, cheat up and focus only on the lowering phase). Now take the same time to lower back down to the starting position. The range is full i.e. sit up as much as you can.
Controlled Russian Twists	1 x 10-20	303	nil	Sit on the ground with trunk at 45 degrees to ground, upper thighs at 45 degrees to ground, knees bent, feet off the ground. Place your palms together, arms straight, at 90 degrees from trunk. Lower rotate trunk (not twist from waist, not shoulders) until your hands touch or nearly touch the ground on one side. Repeat to other side etc.
Reverse curl downs	1 x 10	101,202,303, 404 etc	nil	Sit on the ground with your knees bent, feet flat. Starting in the full sit-up position, lower down a few inches for 1 sec, take the same time to return to top. Now lower down for 2 seconds, going a few inches further, return to top in same time. Extend this until the 10 sec lower results in you nearly lying back fully, but of course not resting on the ground.
Touch toes	1 x 10-20	303	nil	Ly on your back, legs straight up in the air at 90 degrees to body. Have your hands outstretched and together, towards your toes. Raise your upper body until your hands touch your toes, lower down.

Now for that abdominal program : if you want to do abs every day, I support the concept of alternating muscle groups, in an attempt to avoid training the same abdominal muscles on subsequent days. I say attempt, because despite our beliefs that different exercises work different abdominal muscles, I suspect that they do not quite work to this degree of isolation. In other words, who really knows which abdominal muscles in any individual are really doing the work! Moving on…

Try the above 'A / B rolled' program. That means do A program one day, B program the next, A the next etc. I have kept the volume low, and no equipment is required.

Q: Despite performing all the various exercises, rep/set ranges, etc., I can't seem to develop thickness anywhere on my body. I have really wide upper body and good quad width, but when turning sideways, I don't have any thickness to my physique. The only place where I've gotten some good results are my glutes from doing squats and dead-lifts, but my hams are lagging. Any variations, etc. you can offer to help would be appreciated.

Who really knows which abdominal muscles in any individual are really doing the work!

A: When you train your legs (i.e. your leg day), do you do hamstrings first or last? By simply changing the sequence, do-ing hamstrings first, you will get an amazing superior result. As far as thickness goes, I believe that most lifters in their first few years don't possess this 'thickness'. It comes with time spend training - years. How does this apply to you?

Q: I tried every version of the hammer curl and my biceps are still extremely thin from the front. What do you suggest to thicken them besides changing my genetic make-up?

A: There is more to training than the exercise selection. What I want you to do is to be able to answer this question - which rep brackets do your biceps respond best to? If you don't know, you may benefit from finding out. From my experi-ence, you may find the higher reps initially will give you the best response. If this is the case, this is a starting point. The next step for you to establish is volume. Do your biceps re-spond best to low or high volume workouts? Try both. Do workouts that include only 2 sets of biceps, right up to work-outs that involve up to 12 sets. When you know the answer to these two questions, you are on your way to bigger arms. Of course there is more ideas you can try, but you have enough homework - come back to me in 21 days with the results and we can go on from there.

Q: I have a problem. My left arm is about half an inch behind my right arm. The worst part is that this lack of size is coming completely from my left biceps. What would you prescribe for this problem? Thanks a lot.

T Johnson

A. I was wondering how you could tell this size difference was caused solely by the bicep? Anyway - size imbalances left to right are extremely common, and the circumference difference you quote is fairly normal or just a bit above average. You may benefit from applying the 'King Weak-Side Rule' in full.

Consider the following until the imbalance has been eliminated or satisfactorily reduced :

1. do biceps before triceps;
2. do only unilateral bicep work (i.e. one arm at a time or independent e.g. dumbbells);
3. initially do only left side bicep i.e. do not right arm bicep work ;
4. when you do return to right side bicep work, never do more reps or weight on this side than the other side was capable ;
5. when you do initially return to doing both side, do 2 sets on the left to 1 set on the right;
6. exploit the full options of bicep exercises .

Size imbalances left to right are extremely common. You may benefit from applying the 'King Weak-Side Rule' in full.

Q: My problem is with training my abs and obliques. When doing twisting crunches, I use a decline bench with twenty five pound plate on my chest. It seems I'm training my hip flexors more than my midsection. What are some exercises I can do to work on my midsection more than hip flexors? I don't have any fancy equipment like an ab bench or a ball.

A: Hip flexors are usually reduced in their contribution by two simple things :

1. don't anchor them (as you were) under anything;
2. bend the knees to 90 degrees or more.

Any abdominal exercise that integrates these two variables will increase the role of the 'mid-section'. You don't need any fancy benches, and the inclusion of the Swiss ball in the 90's training equipment list is more for fashionable compliance that need.

I am interested in knowing however - do you not want to work the hip flexors because that is doing something to you that you don't like, or because you heard or read that training them is 'bad'?

Q: I base my training around full body exercises such as squats (high bar, full range) and deadlifts. I also cycle in Olympic style lifts for at least three out of every 12 weeks. I've read from various sources that doing an exercise like the squat or power clean activates the abdominals better than a specific abdominal exercise. And if you can handle a decent amount of weight on these lifts, your abs are certainly not weak.

> *The squat and clean and the like certainly do activate the abdominals, but I would not say 'better' than a specific abdominal exercise.*

It has been suggested that training mainly with the aforementioned exercises would require no additional, specific abdominal work. Is this a wise suggestion? Or would I be holding myself back neglecting the abs?

Thank you for your time,

Nick

A: The squat and clean and the like certainly do activate the abdominals, but I would not say 'better' than a specific abdominal exercise. Most specific abdominal exercises allow you to focus on a specific abdominal action e.g. activate the corset-like abdominal muscles to pull inwards. I believe that during a loaded full body exercise the abdominals are working to aid the movement, and one of the things that may occur naturally is for the abdominals to push outwards, rather than inwards. In pushing outwards, they potentially increase the intra-abdominal pressure. This is especially so when a belt is used. Pulling the abdominal muscles inwards during these lifts is something that needs to be taught.

Does the ability to lift heavy in exercises such as the squat and clean prove that your abs are not weak? Depends on your definitions. They are certainly not limiting the movement, but when tested in other functions, I doubt that there will be much correlation between load lifted in the major exercises and any specific abdominal test.

Do you need to do other abdominal exercises? I am not convinced that doing other specific abdominal exercises is going to directly enhance your squat and clean strength. But what doing other specific abdominal exercises may do for you is contest the muscle imbalances that squats and clean cause (e.g. shortened hip flexors), and therefore the specific abdominal exercises may indirectly contribute by reducing the risk of use injuries such as aggravated spinal nerves in the lumbar region.

From this viewpoint, you would be holding yourself back by ignoring other specific abdominal exercises.

Q. Your calf program in issue #39 of the T-magazine (www.t-mag. com) Questions of Power was kick ass! I couldn't walk for a week! Got any programs for the show-off muscles, like abs and biceps?

I don't want you to self-combust so I will give you them one at a time, starting with abs. There are two programs below. Do A on day 1, and do B the next day you feel it would be wise to go there again!

The specific abdominal exercises may indirectly contribute by reducing the risk of use injuries such as aggravated spinal nerves in the lumbar region.

Abdominal Routine A

Exercise Name	Description	Sets x Reps	Speed	Rest
Slow speed sit up	on back, knees bent to 90 degrees feet flat on floor hands remain parallel to ground (constant velocity, up & down) go from full lying to full sit-up	1 x 10-15	515	nil
Toes to sky	On back, arms out at 90 degrees, on floor legs in air, lift pelvis off ground, hold for 5 sec then lower	1 x 10-15	5 sec holds	nil
Knees in air, crunch	On back, knees and hip at 90 degrees Curl up as far as you can	1 x 10-15	313	nil
Modified v-sit	Lye on back, legs out straight bending knees, lift up legs and trunk and meet them together 90 degrees to ground	1 x 10-15	515	nil
Legs in air-touch toes	Lye on back, arms and legs in air 90 degrees to the ground Curl up trunk as far as you can, looking to touch your toes	1 x 10-15	313	nil

NB Repeat 1 more circuit (if you can).

Abdominal Routine B

Exercise Name	Description	Sets x Reps	Speed	Rest
Fast sit-up+twist	on back, knees bent to 90 degrees feet flat on floor hands remain parallel to ground (constant velocity, up & down) go from full lying to full sit-up	1 x 10-15	10*	nil
Wrist to knee from full lying position	On back, legs out, touch both hand to forehead sit up and lift opposite leg, have them meet perpendicular to the ground	1 x 10-15	10*	nil
Bar rollouts	Knees on ground, hands placed on a bar on the ground under shoulders Slide the bar out until you are nearly flat out on the ground, and return	1 x 10-15	201	nil
Full v-sit	Lye on back, legs out straight keeping legs straight, lift up legs and flex trunk and meet them together 90 degrees to ground	1 x 10-15	10*	nil
Legs in air-touch toes	Lye on back, arms and legs in air 90 degrees to the ground Curl up trunk as far as you can, looking to touch your toes	1 x 10-15	10*	nil

NB Repeat circuit 1-2 more time (if you can).

Get Buffed!™

On equipment...

Q: Very much appreciated your comments on deadlifts. What is your opinion on the use of a trap bar? I like it because my arms are at my sides rather than having my shoulders rolled forward.

Rosemary

A: The trap bar is a nice tool. It allows a shrug in what you could say is a more posturally correct position. For powerlifters and Olympic lifters, however, I would caution. Don't spend too much time on this device as you will need the strength in the position of the bar in front of body. However an excellent supplementary device, and great for bodybuilding.

Q: I was reading your Question of Power column (in www.t-mag.com) when I saw something that made me confused. You were responding to someone's question regarding the use of leg machines. As I understood it, you were saying as long as machines like the leg press, hack squat, and Smith machines were not the core of your leg program they were okay to use. In reading other people's work, I've had the idea that these machines were not good to use because of the stresses they put on your spine and knee. The spine because the back is held in a straighten position and the knee, especially Smith machines, because you are locked in a fixed position. I've also heard that the "pattern overload" caused by these machines are responsible for serious injuries. I hope you would be able to clarify when it is appropriate to use these machines and if you agree with others when they advise to stay away from them. I would also appreciate your opinion of the leg extension. Again I've read that it is bad for the knee and not an effective way to build strength or mass. I'm really excited that you are writing for Testosterone and hope that you will contribute more articles.

Sincerely,

Josh

A: If this is what others are saying, I don't share the same opinion (and as this is third hand I don't assume that this is what they are saying). I think this information is a typical over-reaction in the short term to new understandings about the possible downsides of machine exercise. I often wonder if

The trap bar is a nice tool. For powerlifters and Olympic lifters, however, I would caution. Don't spend too much time on this device.

some of this is motivated by the desire to gain attention, be controversial. To have information to suggest that the mechanics of these devices are whatever is one thing - to relate them in a causal manner to injury is simplistic and inadequate.

Leg extensions are an even greater example of the classic over-reaction in the short term to bad publicity. In the 80's therapists claimed that squats were bad because they loaded the knee excessively and leg extensions were good. In the 90's they did a 180 degree flip and gave leg extensions the black clothes and squats ('as long as you don't do all the way down!') the white clothes. Talk about the herd mentality!

Sure a greater understanding of the mechanics of the leg extension revealed greater than previously appreciated loading on the patella-femoral joint and so on. That doesn't mean it is bad! Or that you need to throw the machine out of the gym (if I hadn't actually seen gyms where this has occurred I probably wouldn't have believed it!)

Leg extensions are an even greater example of the classic over-reaction in the short term to bad publicity.

The leg extension, just like machine leg exercises, has it's role in the total arsenal of options. Don't feel obliged to agree with the consensus opinion, irrespective of what self-proclaimed experts have said. Make your own mind up!

Q: *I trust your expertise in the fields of bodybuilding and strength training and wanted to ask for your opinion on rib cage expansion exercises/stretches such as the Rader Chest Pull. I recently read about them and how some people manage to put an inch on their chest and increase their posture by doing these exercises, and wanted to know if these were safe to do and if they actually are effective. Thanks a lot!*

Mike

A: There is not a lot of scientific support for this concept, with most stating that the rib cage will be predetermined genetically etc. However, not being one who likes to hear the word 'can't' or 'never', I encourage you to give it a go.

This concept has been around since at least the era when strength training was called the 'iron game' by all. The pullover was the favorite exercise for this so-called rib expansion. Another popular combination was a set of 20 reps 'breathing squats' super-setted with a set of bar pullovers. Such sweet memories. Followed of course, but the mandatory vomiting!

Let me know how you go. You should get some training effect, even if not the rib cage expansion. I certainly did when I used these methods back in the early 80's!

Q: Can a person develop strength and mass with resistance cables/ chest expander type equipment like the lifeline gym?

A: Anything is possible. If the resistance offered is in excess of your prior experience, there is a possibility for an adaptation. The limit will be that there may be a point at which you stop adapting, when the resistance offered no longer presents the stimulus needed for further gains. As long as you know the limitations of the device you shouldn't be disappointed.

Q. You're a big advocate of the deadlift. What do you think of doing them with one of those diamond- shaped trap bars? This is more conformable on my back, but is it doing any good?

A. You are right - I am a big advocate of the deadlift. It has great application to sport due to biomechanical specificity to the start position in sprinting. Done my way it teaches leg and hip extension in the absence of trunk angle change. And provides a rare opportunity to strengthen the scapula retractors with loads equal to bench pressing. The trap bar simple changes the center of mass in the deadlift, taking it closer to the center of the body. This is not bad or good. It just shifts it along the continuum of lower body exercises closer to the squat. It will allow execution with a more vertical trunk, decreasing the stretch on the hip extensors and thereby shifting more load back on the quads. If you were a sprinter wanting to improve your start position strength, I would say the conventional deadlift bar would be more specific, biomechanically at least. But if you were taught by me to deadlift using the conventional method, you would have probably not have any back soreness. When I teach it my way, back soreness is clear indicator that the technique is not what I want it to be. When we get it right, any back soreness disappears. It becomes a leg exercise in a forward flexed position, using the back primarily

I am a big advocate of the deadlift. It has great application to sport due to biomechanical specificity to the start position in sprinting.

as a stabilizer. The most common causes of back pain in the deadlift are hips rising faster to shoulder during the first pull (trunk angle changing), and anterior rotation of the pelvis also during this first pull (which is from the ground to just above the knees).

On Exercises...

Q: In individuals who's rear end tucks under them below parallel in a squat (pelvic tilt), what are the possible deficits, and what are the best ways to correct them? It seems to many squatters fail to notice they do this, and they do nothing to correct it.

Is the side bend with a dumbbell in your mind an effective exercise for the abdominals/obliques? If not, what would be your best recommendations?

How can one acquire a list of books you have published?

Thank you,
Chris

A: I am not as concerned by this 'rear tucking under in the squat' as many appear to be. It think it is an over-rated concern. The downsides of this technique may be greater load through the posterior lumbar, a reduced involvement of the gluteal in the concentric phase, and the increased likelihood of the hips rising faster than the shoulders. This are some of the possibilities. It is like reading the possible side effects of ana-bolics. They don't necessarily always happen. Don't be too concerned by 'those not correcting it'. Try watching a number of Olympic lifters in the bottom position of the snatch - you might see one or more of them doing a similar thing.

> *I am not as concerned by this 'rear tucking under in the squat' as many appear to be. It think it is an over-rated concern.*

The side bend with a DB is a nice exercise, but just what mus-cles are being recruited in each abdominal exercise is mostly a matter of whose EMG study you chose to believe in. The number exercise I want any person to master for their abdomi-nal is what I call 'thin tummy', which is developing the ability to make the waist as thin as possible using the muscles at the lower end of the abdominals.

Q. I have a few questions about the deadlift.

1. Is it possible to do too many pulling exercises such that one could develop an imbalance (I guess the opposite of someone who did too much benching and no heavy pulls)? I don't flat bench hardly at all, it bugs my shoulder and doesn't ever feel comfortable. I do incline presses and a lot of overhead/ shoulder presses. I love heavy pulls of all kinds - weighted pull-ups and 1 arm db rows are my favorites.

2. When doing the deadlift, is there a way to keep the bar from removing the skin from my shins and knees or is that something you get use to?

3. When lowering the bar you said it is not just the reverse of lifting the bar. Please explain the proper way to lower the bar.
Thanks in advance for your help.

Fred

A: I have answered your questions in the order you asked them :

1.   Maybe, but I haven't seen it yet! Remember it is not just the volume of pulling that matters. It is the quality of the pulling. The retracted, isometric position of the scapula that can be achieved in the deadlift is rarely trained in many of the rowing movements. Therefore I don't see them as being as valuable e.g. 3 reps of a rowing movement may equal 1 correctly performed rep of a deadlift, as far as posterior/anterior shoulder balance is concerned.

Use a bar with enough knurling for grip, but not the roughest knurling available. The range in knurling is that significant.

2.   Two things - use a bar with enough knurling for grip, but not the roughest knurling available. The range in knurling is that significant. Check out all the bars in the gym and go with the one with the middle-of-the-range knurling roughness. Secondly, wear track suit pants when deadlifting. If you insist on using shorts or similar, lightly sprinkle talcum powder on your legs (but not on the grip section of the knurling or your hands!) The good news is, when you legs do bleed, you know the bar is close to the body.. . . .

3.   Unless you specifically want the training effects of the eccentric, I tend to lower the bar by bending forward at both the hips and knees until the bar passes the knees, then either dropping it or letting it go with limited control. This is a competitive lifting training influence, and you ideally need rubber plates and a wooden platform for this. I would be a little more controlled with steel plates. In brief, however, this is one lift where I concentrate on the concentric phase a lot more than on the eccentric.

Get Buffed!™

Q: I'm having difficulty increasing my bench press. I've decreased my warm up reps, stopped gradually increasing weight, and tried numerous forced reps and negatives but final set still has not increased. Any suggestions?

A: Yes - stop benching. Go away from it for a while. I know what you are thinking - you will need therapy if you do that! So I will give you the bench pressing program for those who don't want to end up at Bench Pressers Anonymous, yet still want to gain. It is simple, and still allows you to bench in some format :

4 wks of flat bench camber benching followed by one week of either light or no benching
4 wks of incline bench press followed by one week of either light or no benching
Now you can come home to flat benching. Within 2 weeks of 'coming home' I expect you to be challenging your old PB. But along the way, I want to see some progression in rep and load selection.

Q: I've been lifting for about a year. I'm 6'3 210 lbs with about 6% body fat. I'm trying to get my bench press up. I max out at about 285 lbs and I'm trying to get 315 lbs by this summer for football season. What do you suggest any special exercises? My friends told me push ups will help and also using dumbbells because they force u to use all the muscle fibers. Is this true? What can I do? Please reply. Thank you

> *The power clean is a complex lift with a higher degree of risk than a bicep curl. However risk and return are inversely related.*

A: Forget pushups. They suffer the fate of constant resistance. DB's are nice, but stop looking for a magic exercise. Concern yourself more with your plan - how you intend sequencing the exercise selection, load, reps and speed. Some call it periodization but don't feel the need to comply with the word police. No exercise is going to work if it is over-used.

Q: I was wondering what you think of the Power clean. I have gotten good gains from it, but I've been told it is dangerous.

A: Walking down the street is dangerous. Just depends on how you do it. Walking on the footpath has a higher degree of safety than walking in the middle of the road. The power clean is a complex lift with a higher degree of risk than a bicep curl. However risk and return are inversely related. The power clean may also has a lot more to offer (at least to a power athlete) than a bicep curl. Anyone who tells says as a generalization that it is a dangerous lift may as well be saying they don't know enough about the lift to feel comfortable with it.

I want to say this however - the way I have seen the power clean performed by the majority of people makes me cringe and look the other way.

The power clean is an excellent exercise for a lot of reasons. If you are getting good gains from it, why throw it out? If you have any concerns about the danger aspects, do your research on how your technique compares with accepted models of performance. You could do this by participating in a course offered by either the US Weightlifting Federation or the National Strength and Conditioning Association, or by seeking guidance by a coach accredited with either organization.

The way I have seen the power clean performed by the majority of people makes me cringe and look the other way.

Q: My question is on pull ups. (I like doing these heavy, with added weight.) I have a little difficulty at the top of the movement. Is there any assistance exercises I can do to get that extra 2-4 inches I seem to have the most difficulty with at the top? Also does my having short arms going to affect my performance? (I have a piss poor reach.)

Richard

A: I suspect the main reason you struggle at the top is your history of technique in this drill i.e. in your early days of doing this exercise, did you place importance on getting your chin right above the bar, or were you a bit slack in this regard? One way to get into trouble in this regard is to chin on a bar that has no center horizontal bar, such as the chin bars that came with the Universal multi-station machines of the 80's. If you are in this situation, make sure to string some tape between the two ends to give you feedback about chin placement over bar.

There are few techniques that I could suggest to improve this ability :
1. reduce the external load i.e. use bodyweight only, and really exaggerate the height of the pull i.e. take your head

Get Buffed!™

as far over the bar as possible;

2. in this method, use an extended pause in the top position e.g. 2-3 sec hold at top;
3. when doing eccentric load reps (i.e. lowering a load in excess of your concentric ability), ensure you start right at the top and focus on controlling the movement down;
4. improving your bicep strength through isolated bicep exercise will assist you pulling ability in the chins.

I don't see your arm length as being a limiting factor.

Q: I need your help! The integrity of all natural trainers across the world depends on this!

Let me explain. Recently, one of my friends came across 200 dbols. He has never juiced before, but he figures if he got 'em, he'll take 'em.

Currently his 1RM on the bench is about 265 lbs. My 1RM is about 285 lbs. He issued me the following challenge: On July 15th we will have a bench off. Whoever benches more for 1 rep wins. If he wins, I have to hit the juice (which isn't that bad, I've been looking for an excuse), and when I win his brother will juice (another guy who is dying for an excuse, but doesn't have the balls to just do it). My friends plan is to get up to a 275 lb max, by may, and then start his modest 3-4 week cycle.

> When doing eccentric load reps ensure you start right at the top and focus on controlling the movement down.

Currently, my bench routine consists of 5 sets of Incline Barbell Press:
135 x 10
185 x 8
215 x 6
235 x 5
205 x 8

(I am not exactly sure of the exact tempo I use, but it is a controlled descent, followed by an explosive ascent) (I usually do incline bench for 4 consecutive workouts, then I do flat for the 5th workout, then back to incline) I then do decline dumbbell presses (3 sets 80, 90, 95 for 6-10 reps) Followed by slow flat dumbbell flyes (4 second negative, 10 second concentric)

My workout splits are: Chest & Shoulders, Back & Traps, Legs, Arms

I remember when T-Rone first came out, they promised that they would be happy to devise programs for its readers.

Well here I am, asking for a program to increase my bench as much as possible within the next 3 months. Thanks in advance for any advice you give.

Hoping to stay natural,
Pete A.

A: Increasing your bench won't be difficult. For starters, if you are going to be tested on a 1 RM, you had better get your reps under 6 in training!! And if the test is a flat bench test, you are going to have to spend more time on the flat bench.

The following is a 12 week program aiming to peak for a 1 RM test on the flat bench. I have used what I consider variables that I consider applicable to an intermediate trainer. It involves two upper body workouts per week (A and B).

Remember - start with conservative load selection in the first week of each 3 wk cycle, and add a few kgs each week.

If you are going to be tested on a 1 RM, you had better get your reps under 6 in training!!

Wks 1-3

Work out	Exercises	Position	Warm up	Work sets	Speed	Rest Period	Comments
A	Chin up	supine grip	1x10 1x8 1x6	1x6 1x1 1x6 1x1 1x10-20	311	alternate with shoulder press, using full recovery	
	Shoulder press	wide grip	as above	as above	as above	as above	
	Reverse grip bicep curl	bar standing	1x10	2x6-8	311	alternate with tri exercise	
	Overhead bar tricep extension		as above	as above	as above	as above	
B	Incline bench press-30 degrees	wide grip	1x10 1x8 1x6	1x6 1x1 1x6 1x1 1x10-20	311	alternate with bent over row, using full recovery	
	Bent over row	wide grip	as above	as above	as above	as above	
	Lying tricep extension		1x10	2x6-8	311	alternate with bicep exercise	
	Hammer grip dumbbell curls	seated	as above	as above	as above	as above	

Work out	Exercises	Position	Warm up	Work sets	Speed	Rest Period	Comments
A	Flat bench press	medium grip / feet on ground / to mid chest	1x10 1x8 1x5	1x5 1x1 1x5 1x1 1x10-20	211 211 211 211 311	alternate with seated row, using full recovery	
	Seated row	medium grip	as above	as above	as above	as above	
		EZ bar / med grip	1x8	2x4-6	211	2 min	
B	Chin up	neutral grip	1x10 1x8 1x5	1x5 1x1 1x5 1x1 1x10-20	211 211 211 211 311	alternate with shoulder grip, using full recovery	
	Shoulder press	med grip	as above	as above	as above	as above	
	Close grip bench press	shoulder width grip	1x8	2x4-6	211	2 mins	

Work out	Exercises	Position	Warm up	Work sets	Speed	Rest Period	Comments
A	Flat bench press	wide grip / feet on ground / to mid chest	1x10 1x8 1x6	1x4 1x4 1x4 1x6-10 1x10-20	211 211 500 311	alternate with bicep curl, using full recovery	go slightly heavier in second set of 4; then add 20% for the 500 or eccentric set
	Preacher bench bicep curl	EZ bar / med grip	as above	as above	as above	as above	
B	Chin up	prone grip / wide grip	1x10 1x8 1x6	1x4 1x4 1x4 1x6-10 1x10-20	211 211 500 311	alternate with close grip bench press, using full recovery	go slightly heavier in second set of 4; then add 20% for the 500 or eccentric set
	Dips		as above	as above	as above	as above	

Work out	Exercises	Position	Warm up	Work sets	Speed	Rest Period	Comments
A	Flat bench press	medium grip / feet on ground / to low chest / use power-lifting compet-ition arch	1x10 1x8 1x6 1x4	1x3 1x2 1x1 1x3 1x2 1x1 1x3 1x10-20	211 211 211 211 211 211 400 211	5-10 min	go slightly heavier in sec-ond 3/2/1 wave than corre-sponding first wave - which means that you should not go to max in first wave
B	Chin up	prone grip, just out-side shoul-ders	as above	as above	as above	as above	as above

Q: What's the correct way of doing Barbell Rows? Can you prescribe a kick ass routine for the Back?

A: I don't believe there is a correct way of doing the barbell row. The first decision to make is do you want to do an iso-lated scapula retraction exercise (a strict technique where there is no change in trunk angle) or do you want to use a 'cheat' movement which will introduce the spinal erectors to the movement and allow a greater load to be used. I lean to-wards the stricter movement for the majority of the time.

The other variable to consider are the width of grip (wide or medium), type of grip (supine or pronated) and line of pull (to neck, chest or abdomen). Which means you have a lot of op-tions. At least 24 so far!

I lean towards the stricter movement for the majority of the time.

The following is an example of how I would periodize the bent over row to exploit most options :

Wks 1-3
Prone Fly   W/up @ 1x6   1x10+1x10+1x10 @321   1m
Seated row   Palms facing to the roof
                      W/up @ 1x6   1x21 *
DB Row   W/up @ 1x8   1x12 @ 1 ½'s
Bent over row   Wide prone grip / to chest
                      W/up @ 1x10/1x8 2x6 @ 814
* 1x7@ hardest half + 1x7@full range + 1x7@ hardest half

Bent over row	Med prone grip / to chest			
	W/up@ 1x10/1x8	2x6-8	311	2-3m
Bent over row	Med supine grip / to tummy			
		1x10-12	311	
Bent over row	Wide prone grip / to chest			
		1x15-20	311	

Wk 7-9

Bent over row	Med prone grip / to tummy			
	Wup@1x10/1x8/1x5	1x5	211	3-4m
		1x1		
		1x5		
		1x1		
		1x10-20		

Wk 10-12

Bent over row	Med supine grip / to tummy			
	Wup@1x10/1x8/1x6	1x4	201	4-5m
		1x3		
		1x1		
		1x3 eccentric		
		1x10-20		

Weight on the back leg means the leg muscles are being strengthened in this joint angle. If you wanted the lead leg to do all the work, keep your weight on the front leg.

Q: I have been doing split squats (knee positioned back is extended and front knee stops directly over ankle). I have read that there should be little or no weight on the back leg during this exercise, but I feel great tension in my back leg throughout the movement. Am I doing something incorrectly?

A: There are no rules. Weight on the back leg means the leg muscles are being strengthened in this joint angle. This is good! However, if you wanted the lead leg to do all the work, yes, keep your weight on the front leg. Don't panic - if your muscles are hurting and you can feel them working, it can't be bad!

On injury prevention and rehabilitation in strength training....

Q. My question is about knee pain. Last Friday I did legs, including squats (below parallel, with good form) and Cybex leg presses (also deep, but slow and controlled). I don't think I'm bouncing at the low point. Sometimes my knees crack a bit, but it's nothing extreme or painful at all. Over the weekend my left knee got a little stiff, and this week at work some pain developed distal to the patella. This Friday I didn't work legs because my knee was pretty bad, swollen and painful. I've never experienced this before, and I've squatted for a few years.

After researching on-line I've self-diagnosed this condition as chondromalacia patellae or softening of the cartilage under the kneecap. Is this correct? And more importantly, do I have to give up squatting? With your collective years of experience in weight training you guys must've seen this before. What do you think?

Thanks,
Robert

A. The cracking in your knee can be described as crepitus, the noise that results from two roughened surfaces rubbing together. The addition of loading intensifies this noise. You say you have a history of 'cracking' at the knees, but this is not normally associated with knee pain. This is not uncommon, although I prefer to use special warm up techniques to reduce this friction related noise. Any form of cracking or crepitus is an early warning sign of joint surface roughness, and it is not uncommon for this to eventually to 'blow up' (i.e. joint swelling). The swelling is a protective mechanism which causes the stiffness.

> *The cracking in your knee can be described as crepitus. I prefer to use special warm up techniques to reduce this friction related noise.*

You were smart in not working legs again whilst the knee was still swollen. As for chondromalacia patellae, maybe it is, maybe it isn't. Here is what I recommend you do.

1. **Treat the current condition (not the symptom)** : you can and should do things to accelerate the healing process, including icing the joint for 20 minutes daily until the heat dissipates. Then you will need to regain range through stretching. The use of a short-term course of

anti-inflammatories or similar may be beneficial. Seek the services of a competent therapist in treating the knee.

2. **Determine and treat the cause :** good on you for checking out the possible causes, but don't expect to be able to successfully self-diagnose yourself. Again, seek an assessment from a competent therapist. It is important to determine the cause of the current condition. Failure to do this may mean further repetitions of this condition. One cause I think you should investigate is the tension in your iliotibial band. Releasing the tension in this (and other muscles of the knee and hip) may eliminate the majority of non-specific knee pain. Make sure you look into this.

3. **Improve your warm up :** in addition to any tight muscles, you do appear to have some degree of roughening of the joint surfaces. I use a number of techniques to reduce the impact of this. The higher the joint temperature upon loading, the greater the lubrication available in the joint. I suggest you : i. wear some type of knee sleeve throughout the workout to maintain joint temperature; ii. warm up on a stationary bike or similar for 10-20 minutes prior to stretching; and iii. Stretch the hip and knee muscles extensively (say 20 mins) between the bike and the start of the workout. (I have more techniques but start with these)

One cause I think you should investigate is the tension in your iliotibial band. Releasing the tension in this may eliminate the majority of non-specific knee pain.

4. **Modify if problem persists :** your condition is not likely related to the exercises you did, and therefore I doubt you will need to avoid these in the long run. However if the short term, ensure that you reduce the load, slow the movement down, and if it does cause discomfort, consider reducing the range of temporarily using an alternative exercise. I find leg presses generally cause less knee pain than squats (and I speak from experience on that!).

Q. I am coming off a layoff due to injury and would like to get my hard-earned muscle and strength back ASAP and greatly exceed my previous gains. What kind of split should I use? I am 75% concerned with strength and power and 25% concerned with growth.

A. Coming back from a layoff with the goal of not only achieving but exceeding previous levels is common and commendable. But what is also common but not so recommendable is the rush to apply loading or neural training. What I stress is that the expression of strength is a combination of factors - including metabolic, mechanical, neural and psychological. This must all be rebuilt. What I often see occurring is a rush back into loading without developing all the contributing factors. Many times this results in disappointment, altered technique, frustration, and even injury.

Relax! The previous gains will return! Re-traveling the same road is easier than the first trip! As a rough rule of thumb, I suggest that the time to return to previous levels is approximately half of the time taken off e.g. if you have had 3 months off, you may be back to your old levels in 1 ½ months. And further, there is a school of thought that the detraining that occurred during the layoff is actually conducive to pushing past prior limits.

It is how you get back there that is critical. Conventional methods of program design suggest metabolic (hypertrophy) training periodized through to neural training. There are of course 'faster methods' as you have suggested, which combine neural and metabolic training (e.g. med rep sets alternated with low rep sets; low rep sets followed by higher rep sets). However the longer the layoff (e.g. more than 1-2 months), the less inclined I would be to use these methods at least in the early stages (the first few weeks) of your comeback. They do not allow adequate development of muscle tissue and technique prior to exposure to loading.

Conventional methods of program design suggest metabolic (hypertrophy) training periodized through to neural training.

Q. I was hoping that you could help me out with a serious problem that I am having. Several years ago I dislocated my hip in an accident and underwent reconstructive surgery where the doctors pretty well rearranged everything. During the course of the surgery I had all of the muscles of my upper leg removed from my pelvis and re-attached afterwards. After finally regaining my mobility with the use of a cane, I began to exercise to regain my muscle strength.

My quads and hamstrings are now back to about 100% but my abductors and adductors are, well.......screwed!!! It seems as though I don't even have enough strength there to even begin to get their strength back in order to stabilize my walking and finally get rid of my cane.

I began to train seriously about 6 months ago and all of my body parts are coming along nicely, now I would like to ditch the cane if at all possible. I have tried all of the inner and outer thigh machines to no avail. My left leg (the good one) would end up doing all of the work and my right leg cannot move an ounce of weight.

I was wondering if you could suggest something to help me overcome this problem? I was also wondering if perhaps a cycle of steroids or something might help me to get past the initial stage?

Any advice that you could give would be greatly appreciated. Keep up the good work with Testosterone, it's an excellent publication and I love the T-Shirt that I got from your store!

Thanks,
Mobily Impaired

A. Firstly, I ask is it really the adductors/adductors that are what stands between you losing that cane? I can imagine that someone had told you this, and I am not saying it is right or wrong. Just make sure that it is valid before you go down that right. Having said that, you have a serious challenge in completing your rehab, but I suspect from what I have read that you have the determination. With regard to muscle function (or strength expression), muscles fail to fire for two main reasons : they are detached, or they are experiencing neural inhibition. No amount of training will rectify improve muscle function if these conditions exist. I strongly suggest you seek competent advice in eliminating these two, especially neural inhibition. Another factor contributing to 'weakness' can be addressed through massage. Immobilized, inactive soft muscles can have their rehab accelerated by massage.

> *With regard to muscle function, muscles fail to fire for two main reasons : they are detached, or they are experiencing neural inhibition.*

In brief what I am suggesting is a therapist with a leaning towards 'hands-on' treatment - massage and stretching. As far as steroid go, I don't think that they will be the magic touch you are hoping for. Get function back in the weakened muscle first, address the right-left imbalance second, and then consider your options. Anti-inflammatory agents such as glucosamine may be of greater benefit initially.

All the best with your rehab.

Q: *I'd like to start off by saying that I'm a big fan of your work and that while using some of the workouts and techniques over the last 6 months, I've managed to put on a considerable amount of mass.*

I'm a 16 (almost 17) year old wrestler and about a month ago I sprained my shoulder, got deep contusions in my elbow, severely strained the tendons in my trapezius and got a small fracture in my collar bone during a wrestling match in which my opponent decided to use an illegal throw.

While recovering from my injuries, I've seen the muscle that I've accumulated over the last few months start to wither away, especially in my shoulders while my fat levels are starting to go up again.

My doctor said that I'm OK to start lifting again slowly, but every time I start to any type of upper body lifts, I just feel extremely weak (less than a quarter of my pre-injury weights) and I can hear and feel a clicking sound from my left shoulder whenever I do a shoulder press.

What can I do to start to regain some of my former strength? Also what kind of diet should I follow while I'm still not at a 100%. I tried to continue with my 6 meal-3000 cal diet while not going all out in the weight room but I noticed a significant body-fat increase (I'd guess that I'm up to somewhere around a 23% or higher body fat % now).

Thanx for any help you can give me. I just want be strong enough to beat that bitch's ass next year.

John

A: First of all, you shouldn't be doing any two armed (bilateral) movements for the upper body - at least until your arm and shoulder strength (right to left) are balanced. To take it a step further, coming back from shoulder injury, you probably shouldn't be doing any conventional movements until you have ensured that the shoulder is stabilized. Primarily I refer to the control of the scapula, which I see to being the 'key to the health' of the shoulder. Inadequate control of the scapula (which is common post-trauma) I find to be highly correlated with shoulder and elbow injuries resulting from lifting.

Spend 1-2 weeks performing control drills for your shoulder, with particular focus paid to scapula control (e.g. retraction and depression). You may wish to locate a therapist that understands this concept and can prescribe and supervise these

Coming back from shoulder injury, you probably shouldn't be doing any conventional movements until you have ensured that the shoulder is stabilized.

rehab drills.

Once you have established satisfactory control of the shoulder, look to return to conventional strength exercises, selecting initially uni-lateral movements. You need to apply my 'weak side rule' (see above) and perform the movements with a slow and controlled speed.

Only when the pain is absent and the strength (right to left) is equal, can you return to bilateral movements.

In conclusion, don't worry about your strength levels initially - focus exclusively on control and the quality of the movement. As for your diet, cut back whilst your energy expenditure is low.

Q: I have herniated L4-L5 disks. I'm currently doing physical therapy, but it's not working. The doctor said that if it doesn't work after 3 weeks, I would have to have surgery to relieve the pain on the nerve. If I have to have the surgery, I wouldn't have it for about 2 months. What type of training program do you recommend up until I have the surgery, and then after I have am healed after the surgery. Thanks for any help.

A: Are you sure you have a herniated disc? Get more than 1 opinion - get 3. Surgery is an option, but not one I would rush into. For two reasons. Firstly, nothing's for free - and I am not talking about your contribution to your orthopedics' next holiday. Surgery often creates a new problem. And secondly, surgery often treats the symptom, not the cause. Which means that after the surgery is over, and the problem theoretically should have gone away, it often hasn't.

I recommend looking at every non-invasive method option prior to agreeing to surgery. If I was in your shoes (and I have been for the very same medical condition), I would be looking very hard for a different solution. I know you didn't ask for ways to avoid surgery, but I am going to tell you anyway - exhaustively explore the relationship between the length and tension of the hip flexors and quads and your lower back.

What type of training leading up to surgery? You will know what hurts and what doesn't. At a guess loading through the spine (e.g. overhead shoulder presses and similar) will be out.

Loading in trunk flexion and extension will also be out (e.g. deadlifts, good morning, back extensions). Machines exercises may be a wise choice in this situation. Also be mindful of any exercise that creates soreness or tightness in the hip flexors/quads. If my theory is correct, increased tension/decreased length in these muscles will lead to aggravation of your back condition.

Same rules apply post-surgery. I strongly advise you prioritize the hip stabilizers - e.g. lower abdominals and gluteals. You should also have a post-surgery rehab progression planned out. Once you achieve certain pre-determined milestones in capability and absence of pain, you can progress to the next level of difficulty.

Q: I had cancer surgery a couple of years ago which included a neck dissection (removal of the lymph nodes between the neck and shoulder). This area of the upper back (left side only) is still not up to par. Can you suggest a routine to add mass to this area? Also, due to the radiation (I think) I get cramps in my neck when fatigued. Is there any routine, or supplement that may help this? I am otherwise healthy and am lifting my old poundages.

A: After only reading the first sentence the following though struck me - have you regained your full range at the neck. Often after surgery or immobilization the trainee does appreciate the need to regain at least pre-trauma range. Range is one of my first rehab goals. Without range, I believe, function is impaired. In the absence of function, expect less mass and strength.

Range is one of my first rehab goals. Without range, I believe, function is impaired. In the absence of function, expect less mass and strength.

So when I read the next sentence when you say your neck cramps when fatigued, it supported my initial thought. Another cause for neck cramps is imbalance in the anterior/posterior upper torso muscles (e.g. chest shorter/stronger than upper back). In my experience (including personal experience!) this condition can also affect nerve transmission to neck.

What routines would I suggest? A solid stretching program for the neck and chest. A minimum of 5 minutes per side for the neck, at least twice a week; and at least 10 minutes on the chest alone, again at least twice a week. You may be happily surprised by this. Unfortunately you are unlikely to be able to ask any anyone else about their experiences with this approach - the upper traps are one of the most neglected upper body muscles as far as stretching goes.

Q: I seem to be getting pain in my left shoulder when doing chest flyes, or incline benches. I've been to a 'muscle manipulator' in Melbourne and they appear to fix the problem until it reappears 1-2 months later. Do you think I need to be doing extensive rotator cuff exercises / stretching during every workout or do I have to see an Active Release Technique professional? (If so do you know of any in Melbourne?)

And what would you recommend would be the best exercises?

Jim S.

A. Your first job is to find out why your shoulder is hurting. In the interim, apply a simple rehab golden rule - don't aggravate the problem!

Stretching and stabilizer exercises should be part of EVERY pre-strength training warm.

You have two choices - you can actively seek to rehab the injury, or you can side-step it, using only exercises and ranges/loads that do not aggravate it - and let time heal it. In reality, the latter, whilst not what I would necessarily recommend, would be more effective than most methods employed in physical therapy!

Most shoulder pain is caused by muscle imbalance, but there may be more to it. Get around to a number of therapists until you have a diagnosis that you believe to be on track. To find out whether there are any ART trained therapists in Melbourne, try contacting Dr Leahy's office.

Should you be stretching and doing rotator cuff exercises because of the shoulder injury? Definitely not. You should be doing them all the time! Had you been doing this you may not have the injury! Stretching and stabilizer exercises should be part of EVERY pre-strength training warm-up.

Get Buffed!™

On nutrition and supplements....

Q. You written that you like creatine, but that most people take it wrong. You don't like the traditional loading and maintaining protocols. What do you recommend?

As I wrote in my book *Creatine : A Guide for Athletes and Coaches* (written in 1997 and co-authored with Darren Haworth), most manufacturers put the standard protocol on their label instructions : 20 grams a day for 5 days, 5 grams a day for 6 weeks. If you check the earlier research on creation, this protocol was what I call the second (historically) of the two research protocols. The manufacturers were copying the majority of the early research protocols. There were so many studies done using this protocol because the scientists, as they are often inclined to do, were copying their colleagues, ensuring peer conformity. Was the research protocol working? Mostly, but what about the subjects - typical smashing-smashing strength athletes. Not likely. One published survey did catch my eye. The author, referring to use in professional rugby league players in Australia, supported my observations - the traditional methods had two main flaws. Firstly, the incidence of gastro-intestinal disturbance was too high and the incidence of no benefit was also too high.

The 'loading' dosage of 20 gms a day from day one may be too high for some, particularly the GI sensitive. I prefer to start with a lower dose.

If you have been around long enough to remember, the early scientific studies on anabolics - you know, the ones that concluded they didn't improve strength or size - were invariably based on 5 grams a day. Not really a reflection of the real world was it, even back in the 60's and 70's. You could learn a lot from the way that whole issue was handled by the researchers and the medical profession. Getting my point. The dosage was inadequate to be significant.

As for the 'loading' dosage of 20 gms a day from day one, I believe that is too high for some, particularly the GI sensitive. I prefer to start with a lower dose to allow familiarity. Of course you can argue that impact is lost, but my first concern is to minimize time on the can!

As for the 'maintenance' dose (5 mgs/day) - it is too low for most over 75 kgs. The fluid held for the 7 day loading phase is lost. It is critical to retain this fluid in the cell - because :

1. its presence increases cell leverage and therefore strength - which in turn allows greater tissue breakdown; and
2. this cell environment has been linked to a greater rate of fast twitch fiber growth.

You need to hold this fluid for a period long enough for adaptations to occur e.g. 6-8 wks. So to overcome the two flaws in the traditional approach, we developed a beginners 'smarter loading protocol' for creatine, based on ascending and descending dosages (see tables).

Advantages

- it significantly reduces the incidence of gastro because the athlete starts on such a (relatively) low dose that they have a chance to become accustomed to the substance; as they raise the dosage on a weekly basis they have an opportunity to anticipate whether a further elevation in dose will likely cause them discomfort; if this is the case they know not to elevate the dose further;

You need to hold this fluid for a period long enough for adaptations to occur e.g. 6-8 wks.

- the cycle is a long cycle, allowing the athlete to retain the cell volumizing effect for a longer period of time; this provides a greater opportunity to gain the benefits associated with this e.g. cell leverage (stronger), increased fiber diameter (increased rate of hypertrophy) etc.;
- the dosages are adjusted to bodyweight, which increases the likelihood of the athlete receiving the desired benefits; this is not the case when the athlete uses the Traditional Method; you will see higher dosages in this cycle than in the Traditional Method.

Disadvantages

- in some cases the athlete does not experience some of the gains related to creatine use (e.g. increased bodyweight in particular) until during the third week. The third week is usually closer to the optimal dosage via our formula;
- this is a much more expensive method than the Traditional Method

Get Buffed!™

Table 1 - Beginners Method Example A (for an athlete weighing approx. 85 kgs).

Wk No.	Daily Dosage (grams)
1	10
2	20
3	30
4	40
5	40
6	30
7	20
8	10
Average daily dose	**25 gms**

Table 2 - Beginners Method Example B (for an athlete weighing approx. 115 kgs).

Wk No.	Daily Dosage (grams)
1	20
2	30
3	40
4	50
5	50
6	40
7	30
8	20
Average daily dose	**35 gms**

Summary

We believe that this is a much more effective method for the beginner than the Traditional Method. We have rarely seen any gastro-intestinal disturbances, and have seen a 100% desired response to the creatine supplement, which one cannot guarantee with the Traditional Method.

Questions could be raised about the effective of using the high dose for so long with regards to efficacy (i.e. do the benefits equate to or correlate with the dosages in the second block of four weeks?). This is an argument for moving on to the Intermediate Method after one to three Beginner's Method cycles, as outlined in the book.

Q. I am interested in knowing which supplements you use and recommend? Thank you,

David P.

A. Generally speaking I use a brand called Usana for health and Biotest products for performance enhancing. Usana have the best multi-vitamin/mineral I have found, called the 'Essentials'. They are so powerful you could describe it as being ergogenic! Only a few companies can compete with them on label dosages, and Usana lose these few because they manufacture in house, to FDA regulations (GMP) and guarantee potency of each pill. In addition to selling the highest quality vitamin range around, they also have one of the best fat metabolizes I have seen (Lean Formula with Z). I like it because it is effective without being too harsh. Biotest produce the best tasting protein powder on the market! They are an ethical company that produce high quality products you can trust, which if you knew what I knew about this industry, you would value! They are continually looking for the latest developments and bring these to the market. You can order Usana nutritionals at www.unitoday.net/king and Biotest products at www.t-mag.com.

Biotest produce the best tasting protein powder on the market!

On sport - strength and other training for....

Q. I am a 190 lb. 6'1" 15 year old sophomore in high school. I play starting halfback and defensive end at my high school. I am looking for a workout that will increase my leg strength a lot, so I can run right over people just like "the Bus" and Natrone Means. I currently incline leg press 405 lbs. 5 times for 3 sets, going as far down as possible.

I would also greatly appreciate it if you give me some good advice on which exercises I can do to increase the strength of the muscles I use for blocking and getting past offensive linemen. I am currently bench pressing 200 lbs. at 5 reps for 3 sets.

Thank you,

Big Al

A. You obviously take your training seriously, which is great. You have quoted your incline leg press as a measure of your current leg strength levels. Does this mean that this is the focal exercise of your lower body program? If it is, what I suggest is that you look for perhaps more functional exercises, and exercises that contribute in a broader manner to the hip/thigh and leg extension involved in your game.

> *The deadlift is what I consider to be the 'king' of hip dominant exercises. The squat is what I call the 'king' of the quad dominant exercises.*

The main hip exercise categories that I like to see a running/ jumping athlete cover include what I call 'hip dominant' and 'quad dominant' exercises. These two groups may appear similar, but I recommend they gain equal attention in your training. The main difference is that due to the greater trunk flexion in the hip dominant exercises, the gluteals and hamstrings are given a better workout than they might be in quad dominant exercises.

The leg press is a 'quad' dominant exercise. What exercise are you doing in an equivalent loading and volume to cover the hip dominant category? Probably none. The deadlift is what I consider to be the 'king' of hip dominant exercises. The squat on the other hand is what I call the 'king' of the quad dominant exercises. Most exercises are variations of these two basic lifts. So you may need to add some 'hip dominant' exercises.

Earlier I suggested you look for exercises with more 'function'.

The leg press is a great exercise, but I would prefer a up-coming athlete such as yourself develop the skills of what may be a potentially more beneficial exercise such as the squat. More beneficial because the adaptations to squatting may transfer to your on-field performances to a greater extent than leg pressing. What I do stress however is to ensure that you seek the services of a competent and qualified strength coach to teach you safe and effective techniques for all these lifts.

If you train legs twice a week, the following may serve as a guide for long term development :

And don't neglect on-field resisted speed drills (e.g. towing) to complement your all-round explosive power and speed development.

Exercise Category and Day	Stage 1 : Aim = to use exercises that develop strength in contributing joint/ muscle segments	Stage 2 Aim = to develop technique, muscle size and strength in key exercises	Stage 3 : Aim = to develop maximum strength in key exercise	Stage 4: Aim = to develop explosive power and or reactive strength in key exercises
Leg Day 1 - Quad Dominant Workout	Example exercises : leg extension/curl, leg press, split squats, bench steps, calf press	Example exercises : squat, and squat variations including hack squat, dynamic lunges	Example exercises : squat, squat and more squat!	Example exercises :Explosive squats, depth jumps or similar
Leg Day 2 - Hip Dominant Workout	Example : good morning, stiff leg deadlift, back extension, shrugs, leg abduction / adduction	Example exercises : deadlift, and deadlift variations, explosive shrugs	Example exercises : deadlift, and introductory Olympic lifts such as clean pulls and power cleans from the hang above	Example exercises : exercises such as the power clean (from various positions) should dominate here; hurdle jumps etc.

Q: What are your thoughts on incorporating Olympic lifting in an athletic oriented routine? Also, any tips on increasing fore-arm and grip strength?

Thanks
Armstrong

A Olympic lifts are great for athletic oriented programs. The only criticisms I have is that they are often over-rated. They are not the panacea for power - not all sports benefit from them. There are also other options.

Get Buffed!™

I also fear many are under-prepared for their use. Develop of upper back, lower back, leg strength etc. is needed for optimal technique. I am tired of watching a chiropractors dream come true. For some, there is surely a safer way to do upright rows and reverse bicep curls!

On forearm and grip strength - step one - don't use wrist straps!

Q: What is the best way to increase my vertical plyometrics, jump squats, weight training, Olympic weight training or a combination of all?

Thanx
Dave

A: If you wanted the text-book approach you would summarize the studies on this question - and there is no shortage of them! I would say that the although there is no complete agreement in research, the majority would lean towards a mixture of methods as being superior.

That information is nice, but you may want to be treated as an individual, not as a generalization. Without knowing many of your individual factors, I will apply the training age (experience) variable. In the early stages of training, most gain will probably come from simply rehearsing the movement i.e. the vertical jump, or the sporting activities that include this action.

In the early stages of training, most gain will probably come from simply rehearsing the movement i.e. the vertical jump, or the sporting activities that include this action.

After a while (maybe a year or so), these gains will diminish to the point of nil, and this is when another methods needs to be added. My experience and research leads me to believe that the next appropriate training method to add are general strength exercises. Some one to two years later, I look to add maximal strength movements and introduce the technical development of power exercises such as the power clean.

Once the power exercises are mastered technically, I load these also. (of course not all of them are of high technical complexity e.g. the jump squat is fairly simple). Along the way I would also expose to low level jump simulation drills such as depth jumps and hurdle jumps. (note low level being the key)

When the strength levels are high enough to allow me to add light external loading to these jumping drills, I do so. This is when you can see the highest gains, especially when using advanced techniques such as wave loading in the jumping drills.

If you look back a few years you will find an article I wrote for a US publication on this exact topic in 'Performance Conditioning for Volleyball'. (www.performancecondition.com/ volleyball).

Q: I practice Filipino Stickfighting as a martial art. Could you recommend some exercises that would increase my rotational waist movement, both backhand, and forehand? I currently swing heavier sticks, and even pipes in training. I am looking for total body power like a hammer thrower, Mark McGuire, or a discus thrower. Not just putting a barbell on my shoulder and twisting, ineffectively moving ACROSS gravity like most trainers recommend.

Tom

A: Specific strength such as this is often most effectively trained using non-traditional movements, such as over and under loaded imitation of the specific sporting movement - which you are already doing. The West German researcher Schmidtbliecher makes a good point in relation to this specific loaded movements. They are specific, but the variations in the movement (e.g. the greater load) alter the specificity slightly. Be mindful when using specific but loaded movements to keep the volume of this type of training low, so as to avoid an adaptation in technique and acceleration to the 'specific exercise'. This adaptation may be detrimental to the execution of the actual sporting movement.

I must say that I am not totally familiar with this type of martial art, but if you are looking for a another loaded movement with apparent specificity, try the following :

hook surgical tubing (exercise tubing) up to each end of a bar or broomstick. Sit down (more like lean back) on a high bench with weight still on the feet, knees bent. The tubing should be anchored at a point that is at the same height as the bar or broomstick, behind the body. When you rotate one way, you will be stretching one side of the tubing. When you rotate the other way, you will be stretching the other side of the tubing. Whilst tubing has some limitations as a form of resistance, until a machine using conventional loading is available to do this exercise (try the high pulley machine?), it may do. Also, check out the medicine ball with handles. They may be suitable for rotational movements also.

Q: I enjoy the performance aspect of lifting more than the looks, but it is nice to look OK. That being said, could you give some advice for an athlete who wants to get to a certain level of muscularity and then concentrate solely on strength and athletic performance while participating in their chosen sport? I know it is tough. I grapple and do striking training Tuesday, Thursday, and Saturday. I plan on lifting m, w, f, utilizing a Louie Simmons -like program but with the addition of one or two Olympic lifts. First though, I want to body build for a while to get rid of some fat and gain some muscle. I am coming back from an injury soon and I haven't lifted much in the past year. Should I lift 4 days a week, do GVT, or some other program for the hypertrophy work? Keep in mind I might be aided by some anabolics soon, maybe not. Any advice on frequency, volume for each phase, etc.... would be greatly appreciated.

Best regards, Craig

A: If you want both the looks and functional strength, stick predominantly to the core lifts e.g. the power and Olympic lifts, with some peripheral bodybuilding thrown it. The only difference is that it will take longer to be evident from a visual perspective. If you take the bodybuilding-type training only approach, you will look like Tarzan very quickly - but probably perform like Jane.

Take the forearms for example. Some of the best forearms I have seen have been on Olympic and Power lifters.

Some of the best forearms I have seen have been on Olympic and power lifters.

My suggestion would be to do the core lifts for technique initially, and then do additional bodybuilder exercises and reps for hypertrophy. Training frequency is recovery dependant. If you are growing on 4 workouts per week, great. If not, cut back to three etc. Don't get too wrapped up in which method to use - pick 4 of them, use each for 3-4 weeks. That will give you a great program of 12 weeks or so. Periodize these from the higher reps to the lower rep methods. My thoughts on volume are that you would want to be on some great stuff to recover and continuously develop strength/size if using more than 10-15 sets per workout.

Q: I am a 25 year-old male who loves to sprint. My best time is around 10.78 accutrac. I weigh 152 lb. and stand 5'10. I have recently started my track season and disappointingly didn't put on the muscle mass I wanted to during my off season. Is it possible for me to still put on muscle mass and train for the 100 meter dash at the same time? I only run twice a week because I feel that's all I can recover from. As Charlie Francis used to say: "If you're not going to improve, don't show up!"

How might I periodize my training (I can train any day of the week) and what types of exercises should I emphasize in my routine to improve my sprinting performance? Any advice you could give would be greatly appreciated! Thanx.

A: I am not surprised you didn't put on muscle mass in your last off-season. After it is all over (i.e. the off-season), where you were allegedly trying to put on muscle mass, you are still asking if it is OK to do so! I am going to be blunt, but I believe this is a case of needing to be cruel to be kind. Many sprinters (and other athletes with fear about bodyweight) claim to be trying to add muscle mass but 'just don't seem to be able to do it'. The limit is sometimes not a physical one, but in my experience, a psychological one. Until you belief it is OK, or better still, that your performance will be enhanced by a greater level of muscle mass, it probably will not happen. Sort this issue out in your head first!

Sprinting twice a week may be OK, but you could also consider the model actually used by Francis.

Sprinting twice a week may be OK, but you could also consider the model actually used by Francis (as I interpreted it from his writings), where they would run with intensity one day, and then do a lower intensity session the next day e.g. drills.

I have provided a GENERALIZED periodization model for you, showing the integration of speed and strength training. Note it is a generalized model! With regards to specific exercise, if you want to follow the lead of Charlie Francis, he appeared to favor major muscle group exercises e.g. squat, deadlift, power clean, bench press, lat pulls etc.

Get Buffed!™

General Preparation Phase (2-3 months)

	Sunday	Monday	Tuesday	Wednes	Thursday	Friday	Saturday
AM		STR-LB	STR-UB		STR-LB	STR-UB	
PM	rest	SPE-20 min starts	SPE-20 min drill	Recovery Method e.g. Stretch or massage			Recovery Activity e.g. Swim, bike or jog - 20 mins

Specific Preparation Phase (2-3 months)

	Sunday	Monday	Tuesday	Wednes	Thursday	Friday	Saturday
AM		STR-LB		STR-UB		STR-LB	
PM	rest	SPE-starts & accel	Rec Method	SPE-max velocity	Recovery Activity	SPE-speed endurance	Recovery Method

Competitive Phase (2-3 months)

	Sunday	Monday	Tuesday	Wednes	Thursday	Friday	Saturday
AM		SPE-starts, accel	SPE-technique/ drill	Recovery methods	SPE-max velocity and speed endurance	SPE-technique/ drill	Recovery methods
PM	rest		STR-LB			STR-UB	.

Q: I'm looking forward to your all your advice in the future. I play lots of softball is there a way to train around 3 games a week and a full time job that would give you the most benefits. Most guys stop lifting during the season saying it makes you too tight. I'm 41 yrs old. Is a circuit program the way to go? Thanks.

Mike

A: There is always a way. The guys who get too tight from lifting during games - do they do a good pre-season program, or are they just starting up during the game season? Do they stretch their upper body? Do they avoid new exercises during the game-season? When they did the strength training upon which they have based their opinion (assuming it is their opinion and not someone else's!), did they keep the workout short (e.g. 20 minutes) and the volume low (e.g. <10 sets)? This will give you some idea why they struggle mixing strength training and playing!

Circuit training is 'non-invasive'. That's a polite way of saying it probably wont cause you too much soreness, but after a while it probably wont do you much more that burn calories!

During the playing season, stick with a variation of standards sets, not circuits. Prioritize injury prevention (e.g. do rotator cuff exercises every workout, do pulling movements before pushing movements etc). Keep the workouts short (e.g. 20 min workout time) and use low volume (less than 10 sets). Frequency should be about 2 workouts per week total, doing each muscle group only once per week. Look to maintain - plan most of your gains for the next off/pre-season.

Q: I compete in the one-mile run on our track team. Our team practices 5 days a week. Distance runners normally run a couple miles each day, broken into 2 or 3 separate runs. I argue that instead of running several times farther than the event when training for it, that each person establish a time frame in which they want to complete the event and progressively increase their intensity within that frame. What I came up with was a mix of H.I.I.T. and my own progressive wind sprint program. Below is a program for someone attempting to run the mile in under 5 minutes.

During the playing season, stick with a variation of standards sets. Prioritize injury prevention. Keep the workouts short and use low volume.

Week	Wrkt #1	Wrkt#2	Wrkt#3
1.	5x30sec Sprint/30sec Jog	5x30sec Sprint/30sec Jog	5x30sec Sprint/30sec Jog
2.	5x35sec Sprint/25sec Jog	5x35sec Sprint/25sec Jog	5x35sec Sprint/25sec Jog
3.	5x40sec Sprint/20sec Jog	5x40sec Sprint/20sec Jog	5x40sec Sprint/20sec Jog
4.	5x45sec Sprint/15sec Jog	5x45sec Sprint/15sec Jog	5x45sec Sprint/15sec Jog
5.	5x50sec Sprint/10sec Jog	5x50sec Sprint/10sec Jog	5x50sec Sprint/10sec Jog
6.	5x55sec Sprint/5sec Jog	5x55sec Sprint/5sec Jog	5x55sec Sprint/5sec Jog

At this point, the individual would be running for five minutes at close to their previous sprinting speed.

1. Will this work? Why or why not?
2. If so, how should I embed this or another program into my training?
3. What is your opinion of conventional training programs for distance runners?

Beacon

Get Buffed!™

A: What you have proposed is what I termed many years ago 'reverse periodization' i.e. develop the power component of the relevant energy system and then increase the capacity (volume) of the power ability. Charlie Francis used this method very successfully in sprinting. As I understand it, his influence was from methods he had seen used many years before in East Germany. I have also used this concept with success in various sports. Many want us all 'burned at the stake' for our audacity and heresy in not conforming with the old 'aerobic base' trash, volume through to intensity rhetoric.

I believe that you are on track with your approach. I will say therefore that yes it can work, but I can never say anything 'will' work. I would lean towards the approach you have presented.

The program you have prepared is a good literal interpretation of the reverse periodization concept. You will need to implement it to answer your own questions as to how effective it will be. However from my experience I can give you some tips on how you may be able to improve upon it.

- Reverse periodization does not mean you cannot have some exposure to other energy systems within the same week/week. I would see you using the shorter duration interval work early in the week, and using longer duration training methods in the latter sessions e.g. workout 1 = alactic; workout 2 = lactic; workout 3 = aerobic. From wk 1 to wk 6 of your plan you merely shift from the power aspect to the capacity aspect within each energy system. This provides greater variety in training, and avoids the fatigue build-up that may result from the repetitive exposure to the same training stimulus.
- Your progression from micro-cycle to micro-cycle (week to week) looks good in theory, but may not occur in such a linear fashion (note - may not, not will not). You may benefit from building in more progression with this six weeks e.g. 3 x 2 week blocks, with similarity within the 2 week blocks, and greater variety between the 2 week blocks. This variation between 2 week blocks can be based on various points of the power-capacity continuum.

My opinion on conventional distance running programs? What is the highest injury potential in distance running? Overuse injuries, bone density challenges, and so on. Why increase these risks by constantly running more than the race requires when the same may be achieved through lower volume?! I believe most long distance runners greatest obstacle in their approach to training is their mindset. They run more than is needed to soothe their confidence that they are doing enough! (Not that they are the only athletes guilty of this!)

Q: I know that workout schedules should vary according to an individual's recovery ability, but is their any one specific powerlifting routine that you find to be better than the others? Another way to put it would be, if an intermediate-level powerlifter wanted to take his training to the advanced level, say he wanted to go from a class 2 to elite or master, what would you tell him?

> *I believe most long distance runners greatest obstacle in their approach to training is their mindset. They run more than is needed to soothe their confidence that they are doing enough!*

A. You don't get judged a class 2 or 1 powerlifter on the way you train - rather on your competitive achievements. Therefore don't look for programs that correlate to lifting qualification. Look for ways to change the individuals qualification level. So what I would tell a powerlifter wanting to improve his competitive ranking is exactly what I would tell any athlete wanting to do the same. In fact this simple strategy has leveraged power! Find out their weak link and fix it! Sound simple? Too simple to work?

The lifter doesn't have to know how to fix it - they just need to be able to honestly and objectively assess their strengths and weaknesses. OK, so we have eliminated many already from this process! Some wont let go of that circus mirror!

For example, inability to lock out in the deadlift - it may be a weak upper back, it may be lack of form (losing hips) off the ground. In the deadlift it may be the lockout - a solid tricep specialization program may be required. In the squat it may be excessive forward trunk flexion - a lower back specialization program may be needed.

The above are textbook. Lets look at some reality situations. They may train like Tarzan, compete like Jane. Psychological work required! They may get red-lighted on form (e.g. lack of depth in squat, no hold on the chest in the bench) - more discipline and reality required in training.

Find the weakest link - fix it. This is what I tell all coaches. (I don't always tell the athlete, as I don't usually tell them too much. I want them to do, not over-analyze. If they ask, I may tell them. But I would prefer they focus on what I want them to do, not on what they may or may not have been doing inadequately!)

Q: I've just recently started training a marathon runner and have a question on periodization. I'd assume that doing some strength intervals early in the season and progress lighter as the season progress? Most of my background is with shorter distance. Any advice? Your knowledge is most appreciated,

Thanks, Gordon

A: The word periodization is a long-winded way of saying plan. Unfortunately most in the athletic preparation world equate the word with a pre-determined training program. In energy system sports the dominant myth is the need for that so-called 'aerobic base' training prior to any other training. In the strength training field it has been the use of 'light loads' for maintenance during the competitive season. Do one thing for me - separate the word 'periodization' from any pre-conceived training models.

Find the weakest link - fix it. This is what I tell all coaches.

This is how I approach strength training in endurance sports - determine your optimal maximal strength levels and go there. I use strength training to get strong, and modified specific drills for endurance. Most endurance athletes would not be able to tell you what their optimal maximal strength levels are because they are too busy repeating their specific training with strength-endurance methods. Why go there twice?

Work towards what might be your optimal strength levels in your general preparation phase, and maintain this in your competitive phase by lower volume, less frequent workouts - not by lighter loads!

Q: I'm working with an 18 year old, ectomorphic basketball player with some training experience (2 years). We were working about 3 months alternating every 2-3 weeks hypertrophy phases (6-8 reps, 60 min. duration, using supersets and drop sets) and strength-power phases (3-5 reps, 60 min. duration, using different exercises, i.e. front squats, cleans, pulls, compensatory acceleration method and a little bit of plyometrics in the form of complex training). Frequency was 4 times a week. He achieved good muscle mass (and strength) gains but his basketball performance dropped (heavy legs, slowness,...). Is he over-trained? Presently he has a basketball practice every night. I would appreciate any advice!

Ante

A: The word 'ectomorph' is a handy way for colleagues to communicate, but I hope that you don't give the same message to the athlete i.e. this is the body type you are and it won't change. A nice system to pidgin-hole people, but very limiting.

You are using alternating accumulation and intensification with this 18 year old? Why give them a V8 when you are not sure they can manage a 4 cylinder?! Again I am going to be blunt, but only because if I take more than 1000 words to say it, my editor will cut me! Many coaches learn lovely advanced methods, and become proud of their new-found knowledge. That's great - the next step is knowing when to use it! I am not suggesting that this is the cause of the symptoms you describe, but I do believe you are throwing the kitchen sink in when all he asked for was a plate! He will probably gain on less complex methods e.g. linear periodization.

> *It doesn't matter how good a strength program you provide - if the athlete is over-training is any aspect of their training - your work is wasted.*

You say he has achieved good muscle mass and strength gains - to whom are they good? To you? If his on-court performance isn't better then how can you say his gains are good! Strength coaches should never detach themselves from the reality that on-court/field performances measure success, not non-specific parameters size and strength!

That's the bad news. Now for the good news - it is probably not what you are doing in the gym that is causing the performance decrement. It doesn't matter how good a strength program you provide - if the athlete is over-training is any aspect of their training (usually in their specific training courtesy of the head coach) - your work is wasted. This realization led me many years ago to the realization that unless I could

288

control the total training program, I was wasting my time being there.

You would benefit from reading my book *Winning and Losing : Lessons from a decade of physically preparing the elite athlete.* I cover issues such as these in this book. Final point - what are you doing training the athlete 4 times a week in the gym when they are doing specific (on-court) training every day?! When you are not in control, first look at what damage is being done via the training load, then avoid adding to it. If he is training that much on court, 4 strength sessions may be contributing to this over-training!

And if you don't sort it out soon, some smart-arse coach or other support staff will look to blame you for the lack of performance.

Q: Should I do weight training and calisthenics at the same time? I'm a submission wrestler and I've been out of the gym for a while. So I've been doing a lot of push ups, free squats, Chinese push ups, etc...but I'm about to go back to the gym. Is there a way to do both or should I just drop the calisthenics?

Anthony

A: You can do both, but you must ask - am I better of for doing so? If the calisthenics transfer to your wresting i.e. offer you some specific skills, you may choose to retain some, even if only in low volume. But if you are doing calisthenics for strength purposes you may find the strength training makes them redundant.

If you are doing calisthenics for strength purposes you may find the strength training makes them redundant.

Q: I help coach the sprints in track and field. Is their a particular rep range when lifting weights that I should use for my sprinters that would give them a more powerful start.

Also what do think of complex or contrast training. I'm also curious about what the sprinters do down under weights and speed work. Any help would be greatly appreciated.

Yours Truly, Mario

A: In the first instance I would say no - there are no magic rep ranges for the starts - the key is that it causes them to be stronger than they were. This leads ultimately to the use of lower reps. I say ultimately because a raw beginner may get stronger from 15's! And it would not be appropriate to apply the 'magic' power reps to a beginner.

Having provided the broader picture (disclaimers included!) I stress that of all components of the sprint, the part most highly correlated with strength is the start. The means increased strength is important. I say strength, because the first step is less about power than it is about strength. From a stationary start, the stretch-shortening cycle has been dissipated, and the time frame of concentric contraction is the longest in the whole race. This is why I believe a deadlift is perhaps one of the most effective 'start' exercises. It has relatively high velocity specificity (starts slowly then accelerates) and no prior pre-stretch.

I stress that of all components of the sprint, the part most highly correlated with strength is the start.

Contrast and complex training are nice power methods and I do use them. If you want to get into it, the critical issue for you as a coach is to determine what their greatest need is e.g. maximal strength or stretch-shortening cycle? With this answer you can then apply values to training methods e.g. I believe contrast and complex training, generally speaking, apply to the transition phase of mid-acceleration, as opposed to starts (which is more a maximal strength and technique issue) or maximal velocity (which is more a technique and stretch-shortening cycle issue).

Sprinters down under? Until a few years ago, you would have to say that whatever they were doing wasn't working. It is only in the last few years that Australians are seeing a surge in the sprinting events. From what I see most of the training methods are influenced by Americans e.g. Loren Seagrave has been brought over here a few times recently by Australian track and field.

Q: I enjoy powerlifting. You say you can squat and deadlift once a week. What would be a good range of the amount of sets one could do for each without over-training? What if I wanted to do some lat work also, would do it on deadlift day or couple it with bench day? Any help would be appreciated on designing a powerlifting routine.

A : I may have said you can squat and deadlift once a week -

but you don't have to. There is a time and place for lower and higher frequencies. I cannot tell you how many sets would be optimal for you without knowing more about you, but I can generalize. I would never exceed my squat volume on my deadlift day. I may even do less. I rarely exceed a total of 10-12 sets on either day i.e. not just squats or deadlifts - total number of sets for that day.

With regards to lat work, it is traditional in powerlifting to do it on the deadlift day, but I suspect this is more of a reminder to get it done than anything else. Having said that, it is a big muscle group, similar in size to bench, which makes is hard to do it on the bench day. If you had to choose between the two, most times I would do it on the deadlift day. But there will be variations. The tables provided give an idea how lats may be integrated into the total program over four stages leading to a peak. It also shows how squat and deadlift frequencies can be varied.

Stage 1

Mon	Tue	Thur	Fri
Lower Abdom x 2	Upper Abdom x 2	Lower Abdom x 2	Upper Abdom x 2
Back Squat	Incline Bench Press	Deadlift	Chin Ups
Narrow Stance Squat	Seated Row	Front Squat	Shoulder Press
Good Mornings	Decline bench press	Stiff Leg Deadlift	Lat Pull-downs
Singe Leg Squats	Bent over rows	Hip Extensions	DB Shoulder Press
Calf Press	Lying tricep extension	Shrugs	Bicep Curls

Stage 2

Mon	Tue	Thur	Fri
Lower Abdom	Upper Abdom	Lower Abdom	Upper Abdom
Back Squat	Bench Press	Deadlift	Chin Ups
Quarter Squats	Bent over rows	Clean Pulls	Shoulder Press
Explosive Squats	Dips	High Pulls standing on low block	Bicep Curls

Stage 3

Mon	Tue	Thur	Fri
Back Squat	Bench Press	Deadlift	Shoulder Press
Quarter Squats	Close Grip Bench	Deadlift off blocks	Chin Ups
Lower Abdom		Upper Abdom	

Stage 4

Mon	Tue	Thur	Fri
Back Squat	Bench Press	Deadlift	Shoulder Press

Q: I was hoping to get some info. on increasing my vertical. My sport is volleyball. I play in the summer time, and it is about that time for me to start training. I know squats, and power cleans help your vertical, but I don't know how many set's, rep's, and tempo. Or what other lifts will be beneficial to help me in this area. Also the frequency. How many times once a week twice, and how and when to mix in plyometrics. Any info. Or tip's will be greatly appreciate.

Thanks for the time
Xsuavex

A: What it would help to know is how much vertical jump type training you have done in the past and how effective was it. I have developed a progression of training dominance for vertical displacement sports and it goes like this (see table). Once we place you on this progression I can be more specific with my recommendations.

Stage No.	Description	Dominant Training Methods
Stage 1 : Just started in the sport	Just playing the sport and practicing the related drills will increase VJ	Strength training in stage should be stability and technique oriented. VJ gains come from playing the sport.
Stage 2 : After a year or so (e.g. years 2-3)	Now look to go beyond stability training in the gym - go for general strength, achievable through general multi-joint exercises and middle of the road reps (6-12)	VJ gains from playing sport are diminishing. Now just getting stronger generally will give further VJ gains.
Stage 3 : year 4-5	Now are ready to add loading in the gym.	Maximal strength training methods, with exposure for learning purposes to more advanced power drills (e.g. power clean, box jumps)
Stage 4 : year 6-7	High levels of max strength being achieved, now increase component of power training	Power methods dominate i.e. vertical jump, jump squats, plyometrics; integrated with relative strength training methods

Get Buffed!™

Q: I realize I'm a few weeks too late, but can you recommend a good leg routine to improve my mobility around the soccer field? This would be implemented during summer.

Obviously I'd like to increase my running speed, mobility and "skill speed" (dribbling, turning the ball etc.) and this would have to go hand in hand with flexibility. Please note I am unable to squat due to slight scoliosis in my upper spine (due to bad squatting years ago, no doubt).

Also, if this isn't asking too much, could you suggest a decent split to combine leg training/fitness training? I usually stop leg training altogether during the soccer season, as (compulsory) soccer training twice a week, plus a game tends to screw up recovery a bit. Love yer work and many thanx.

Radar

A: I think you will get the best gains for your sport by using a variety of uni-lateral leg exercises. You can expect a greater transfer to the multi-directional game of soccer. Your inability to squat also becomes a non-issue because the exercises I would use do not create compressional or shearing force on the spine. And yes, flexibility exercises should be conducted with each leg session (minimally). I would do two leg workouts per week (one day hip dominant exercises, the other quad dominant). I would recommend, where possible, doing at least a three stage program of 3-4 wks, as in the following table.

I think you will get the best gains for your sport by using a variety of uni-lateral leg exercises. You can expect a greater transfer to the multi-directional game of soccer.

Stage No	Wk No.s	Dominant Strength training goal
1	1-3	Control and hypertrophy
2	5-7	Hypertrophy and maximal strength
3	9-11	Maximal strength, power and reactive strength

Q: I play rugby for my college club team, and I was wondering if you could give some training ideas/workouts (sets, reps, etc.) to those of us interested in the performance aspects of weightlifting. Specifically strength and speed.

Also, since other training besides weights is used when training for sport how much should you reduce the volume of your weightlifting?

Thanks, Brooke

A: I assume you mean performance as to how weightlifting improves rugby? I introduced formalized strength training for rugby in Australia. In the years leading into the 1991 World Cup, I programmed every senior representative rugby player in Australia. One performance advantage Australia had during the Rugby World Cup in 1991 was that they were better prepared physically on average.

What were the other major rugby playing countries doing about that time? The training adviser to one major rugby nation (I won't mention any names) was apparently telling his players that loading in strength training in excess of bodyweight was unnecessary for the rugby player because it was non-specific. As this rugby nation's training methods influence most of the rest of the world, it was not surprising that maximal strength methods were unheard of in rugby up until Australia led the way.

The amount of other training e.g. field training, may require a reduction in strength training volume.

Most Australian representative rugby players do 4 strength session in the off-season or GPP (Nov-Dec), 3 in the pre-season or SPP (Jan-Feb), and 2 for maintenance for the remainder of the year. Free weight multi-joint exercises dominate e.g. squat, bench press and power clean, and the rep range used is between 1-20, with most work being done around the 1-8 range.

To give you an idea regarding strength levels, the average Australian rugby player has a 3RM bench of approx. 130 kgs, 3RM chin of bodyweight plus 20 kgs.

Your second point is important - recognizing that the amount of other training e.g. field training, may require a reduction in strength training volume. This mistake is often made by novice strength coaches - the rugby player experiences significant leg demand during field training. Literal application of say powerlifting programs is asking for trouble. In the GPP, when

Get Buffed!™

other leg activities are lowest, I use 2 lower body days - one for hip dominant exercises (eg. deadlift, clean etc) and one for quad dominant exercises (eg, squats etc.) In the GPP I reduce to one leg day a week, usually a mix of hip and quad dominant exercises. During the competitive phase the frequency of exposure to legs in strength training is about once every 2 wks. Excessive frequency to leg strength training in the rugby players results in high incidence of hamstring, groin and lower back strains, to say nothing about the negative effect on running style and speed.

Q: I'm a college football player and I was wondering what, in you opinion, would be the best mix of exercises to simultaneously enhance speed, power, and strength. Is it necessary to go through different cycles where you utilize different lifts to maximize speed and strength? Well, in general what do you think would be the best lifts (and tempos) for the football player to incorporate into his program?

A: Yes, I believe it is beneficial to go through the different cycles where you utilize different lifts to maximize speed and strength. I recommend progressing through the following phases :

Control » hypertrophy » maximal strength » explosive power

I will use the hip dominant leg day to illustrate my point - see table below.

A few finer points - I don't introduce the power clean for the first time in the power phase - I have been using it (or parts of this exercise) throughout the whole program as a secondary exercise. In fact, I maintain a component of each strength quality in every phase.

The bests lifts for the footballer are just what Bill Starr was saying 20 years ago - squat, power clean/deadlift, bench press etc.

I don't introduce the power clean for the first time in the power phase - I have been using it (or parts of this exercise) throughout the whole program.

Phase	Week No	Primary Exercise	Sets x Reps	Speed	Rest
Control	1-3	Deadlift	2x6	316 (i.e. 6 sec lift)	2 min
Hypertrophy	4-6	Deadlift	2x6	311	3-4 min
Maximal Strength	7-9	Deadlift	2x4	201	4-5 min
Explosive Power	10-12	Power clean	1x3 1x2 1x1 1x3	*	5-6 min

Q: Do you believe that the 40-yard dash is a good test for American football players or does the 20 yard dash seem more suitable? And what kind of rest periods would you prescribe for a session just before the start of the season (pre-competitive period) in training for speed at it applies to football (such as between individual sprints). And isn't football "speed" really a form of speed endurance.

A: How many positions in American football require you to sprint 40 meters? For those that do, it may be a valid assessment of position specific speed. For those who don't, it is a great endurance test!

How many positions in American football require you to sprint 40 meters?

If you are aiming to improve your speed in the pure sense (ie. your alactic power), I recommend full recovery. That is not just full metabolic recovery, but also neural recovery. Expect to use work:rest ratios of in excess of 1:20. If you are aiming to improve your speed endurance you could argue to use shorter rest periods. The question could be asked - if your one off speed is not at the level you would like, just exactly what is it you are creating in speed endurance training - a low of even slower speed?

Q: I was wondering if you would be able to provide a sample micro-cycle for a drug free powerlifter at a height of 5'8", 176 lbs with a bp of 285 lbs, squat 365 lbs and deadlift of 415 lbs. Weak points are triceps, hamstrings, abdominals and posterior deltoids (that I am aware of).

A. I would be basing the majority of your training around the competitive lifts. I would recommend 3-4 sessions per week, no more, and for you to keep your volume low. A sample specific preparatory phase micro-cycle is shown below.

Get Buffed!™

A Day e.g. Mon

Squat   Warm up @ 1x10/1x8/1x6 1x4 / 1x3 / 1x2 / 1x2 / 1x4

Bench press   Warm up @ 1x10/1x8/1x6 1x4 / 1 x3 / 1x2 / 1x2 / 1x4

Close Grip Bench Press   Warm up @ 1x8   2 x 6-8

B Day e.g. Wed

Deadlift   Warm up @ 1x10/1x8/1x6 1x4 / 1x3 / 1x2 / 1x4

Shoulder press Warm up @ 1x10/1x8/1x6   2x4 / 1x 8 / 1x12

Bent over row   Warm up @ 1x10/1x8/1x6 2x4 / 1x 8 / 1x12

C Day e.g. Fri

Incline Bench press Warm up @ 1x10/1x8/1x6 2x4 / 1x8 / 1x12

Chin Up   Warm up @ 1x10/1x8/1x6 2x4 / 1x8 / 1x12

Back squat (no equipment) Warm up @ 1x10/1x8/1x6 2x6

Q: Youth Weight Training. I have a question regarding strength development for my 12 year old daughter who is a very good soccer player at the CA Club level. Incidentally, we are very grounded and are the antithesis of the "BMW/Lauren blanket/pass the cheese and Merlot parents"...anyway, my daughter is real fast and plays hard but at 5 ft., 1 in. and 98 lbs, is weak. Compared to a few of the genetically gifted players, who occasionally "shoulder" her off the ball, she may fall a little more behind a year or two from now in terms of anaerobic strength. She is the fastest player in the league at 40 yds. Or so, but can lose an attempt to get the ball in a 5 yd. effort, I think, due to lack of explosive strength.

TC Louma helped me out a month ago by his encouragement of full squats, which even at 48 years of age are helping my leg strength phenomenally! She sees that and is somewhat inclined to try lifting. I think full squats and presses overhead would help her against naturally stronger girls. Your guidance, please!

GDSEAL

If you are aiming to improve your speed in the pure sense, I recommend full recovery. That is not just full metabolic recovery, but also neural recovery.

A: Without knowing your daughter or seeing the comparisons with other girls she competes against I will have to generalize. There are many reasons to consider strength training the younger athlete, and I will give you perhaps the number 1 reason - many sports involve exposure to loads (e.g. extreme impact or repetitive) that are in excess of the young athlete's ability to absorb through the musculature. Therefore, as in any case where training load exceeds athlete condition, the loading may be dissipated through the joints, or inappropriate muscle balance are developed in an attempt to manage the movement/load. Because of the high levels of hormones in the young bodies, they 'appear' to be 'managing' the training, but I strongly believe that long term problems are being created (e.g. bone surface changes, muscle imbalances, inappropriate movement patters and skills) - that could have been avoided if either the athletes condition was raised or the loading (both impact and intensity/volume) was reduced.

There will come a time when external loading may be necessary - for example, when she can stand on 1 leg and perform a full squat - 10 times!

So yes - I do support strength training for young athletes. Conservative main-stream guidelines for pre-pubescent/pubescent strength training stress minimize the load etc. As far as loading goes, I don't normally align with too much of the main-stream ideas, but I apply the following guideline to any athlete, not just young athlete - why use external loading before developing the ability to manage the load of bodyweight?

Start with appropriate bodyweight, monitor her technique and progress in reps initially. There will come a time when external loading may be necessary - for example, when she can stand on 1 leg and perform a full squat - 10 times!

Q: A friend told me that you know where I could order a copy of "Training for Speed" by Charlie Francis, over there in OZ.

Also I would be interested in knowing about any books that you have published? Thanks a lot for taking the time to help me out.

Yours gratefully,
George

A. Since asking our members in a recent client newsletter if they knew how to get hold of the Charlie Francis books *Train-*

Get Buffed!™

ing for Speed and *Speed Trap,* we have received a number of leads. These include :

www.charliefrancis.com

In my opinion Charlie Francis is not only an expert on speed development, he is one whose rare feel for the training process I have much respect for. And you don't hear this comment too often! Many people know a lot about training. Many promote themselves well. But few have that 'feel' for the athletes response and ability to adjust training accordingly. Of course my respect for Francis is aided by the fact that I share much his philosophies on training.

> *Charlie Francis has that rare feel for the training process. Many promote themselves well. But few have that 'feel' for the athletes response and ability to adjust training accordingly.*

On strength training and bodybuilding...

Q. I'm about 6'3" and weigh 205 at anywhere from 14-16 percent bodyfat. I eat five to six times a day. I usually have about 200 grams of protein, 250 carbs (low glycemic), and I use some flax oil. I train each bodypart once every five days and sometimes use a split of once every six days. I alternate intensification phases with accumulation phases every third workout cycle.

My intensification phase will usually consist of about 10 sets per body part with very low reps and a tempo that will be at least 30 seconds. My accumulation phase will use reps of 6 and above and a total sets of about 10-12 per bodypart. I've used the German Body Comp and Volume programs (which got me stronger, but no size increase). As far as supplements go I use a whey protein powder, multi-vitamin and mineral, and occasionally, when I can afford it, creatine.

I know, I know so what is my question? Well, I can't even touch my goal of 230-240 at about 7-9 percent bodyfat. I know this looks like a bibliography, but I'm just trying to give as much pertinent information as possible. Is there any obvious mistakes you guys see? I would like to hope that my hard work would be paying off, but I haven't made any progress since, I don't when.

Thanks for your time and keep the new info coming!
Josh

Rewrite your program halving whatever was your previous number of total sets per workout.

A. From what you say you are doing some good things to help you achieve your goals - monitoring your diet, carefully planning your training, using supplements etc. Yet no cigar. There may be many reasons for this lack of response. Rather that list them all, I am going to start with the one that stood out the most to me.

You say you are doing about 10-12 sets per muscle group. How many muscle groups in the workout? Try this. Rewrite your program halving whatever was your previous number of total sets per workout. Yes, half. (I find 10 sets per workout on average optimal for most people) In brief, if in doubt, do less. You are unquestionably burning up more than you are putting in.

The bottom line is that you don't need to wait more than 6-8 weeks before concluding whether something is working or not. Actually, gains can often be seen from workout to workout, or week to week - when you refine the process of what works for you!

Q. If you could only work out for say, 20 minutes because you had a train to catch, what type of routine would you do?

A. This type of workout can be an excellent methods of gain on - one thing is for sure, the chances of over-training are reduced! The trap to avoid is this. You will not be able to do as many exercises in the lesser time, so the chances of a muscle group or exercise of line of movement being neglected are great. To compensate for this, create 6-12 week programs (interspersed by recovery weeks) that alternate the exercises, so as to ensure equal exposure.

As far as the workout goes, the exercises and muscle groups you trained in each session would be influenced by the frequency (i.e. how many workouts per week). The sequence of muscle groups and exercises (i.e. what order you would do them in) will be influenced by your priorities.

Don't concern yourself with the fact that you are in and out of the gym before most others around you have completed one of their many intra-workout social experiences.

Basically however, I can see you doing 2-4 exercises, with a total of 6-12 work set in the workout. I would stick to the basic exercises, ones that train multiple muscle groups, for their time efficiency.

Don't concern yourself with the fact that you are in and out of the gym before most others around you have completed one of their many intra-workout social experiences. You will probably grow quicker than them!

Q. You seem to know just about every bodybuilding/strength building method every devised. What single method would you judge to be the most effective in building strength and muscle?

A. That's an interesting question. It raises what I consider to be one of the greatest traps in training theory. Is there a single method that is more effective than all others for building strength and muscle? I don't believe so. And I suggest that those who generalize in this regard deny themselves of the benefits of the methods they disregard.

It doesn't matter whether it is training methods or exercises or equipment - **it is not which one to use, but rather how much time/effort to allocate to each one**. And this raises an even greater challenge. Everyone has the potential to respond differently. There is no guarantee that you will respond the same way as the twenty-three college age general trainers did in the study from which some training guidelines may be extrapolated. And there is no guarantee that what worked for me will work for you. In fact, there is no guarantee that what worked for you a year ago will work again for you now!

Q: You suggest a training frequency of three times per week, and you suggest both squatting and deadlifting one time per micro-cycle. How would you recommend splitting up the body between three workouts while performing squats and deadlifts every week?

Thanx, Josh

There is no guarantee that you will respond the same way as the twenty-three college age general trainers did in the study from which some training guidelines may be extrapolated.

A: In a 3 day a week training program (A,B, C), I would do either squat or deadlift on A day, and the other on C day. You could do some upper body either before or after these lower body lifts on A and C day, depending on what your priority was at the time. By doing lower body twice a week in a 3 day program, this gives the program a slight emphasis on lower body over upper body. If you wanted to reduce this lower body emphasis, do both on B day, freeing up A and C day for upper body.

Q: I work 45-50 hours a week. I have been training for 11 years as a bodybuilder and power lifter. I do not want to diet as strict any more so I'm getting back into power lifting. I do not use any drugs to enhance my recovery ability. Is it possible to train twice a week and still make strength gains? I'm still eating good and taking supplements.

Thanks,
Brian

A: I can understand that desire not to diet as strictly. That one great thing about powerlifting. No-one cares whether you have a washboard stomach. Training frequency is only one factor that affects recovery. There is still volume and intensity. I could say sure, twice week is OK to make gains on (which it probably is) - but you could be doing 2 hour, 40 set sessions!

Hey, two is super-safe, but still be mindful of volume and intensity.

Q: *After reading your interview a few weeks back (on the Testosterone Web site), you touched on something that really has me wondering. You said that for an individual who is genetically predisposed for speed, that a Louie Simmons routine wouldn't work very well because they're only doing what they're good at. Well I am VERY predisposed for speed, but I have a hell of a time increasing limit strength. I can follow a basic bodybuilding program and never run, sprint, jump or do anything explosive but I'll still get faster. My goal is to get much stronger. How should someone with a Donovan Bailey type build and genetic predisposition train? I heard that Bailey could bench press around 210 lbs whereas Ben Johnson could bench over 400 and squat over 600 for reps. I'm basically weak but have a lot of speed and explosiveness, like Bailey. I just need to get stronger.*

A: I don't believe that I used the word wouldn't. And from my refresher of what Nelson wrote I don't see that either. I make an effort to avoid generalizations - because we are all individual. Moving on. How do you know your are predisposed to speed? I would hate to reinforce an assumption. My first task when working with you would be to confirm this hypothesis. What do you mean by limit strength? Again, I don't want to assume a common definition. This is not smart. I read about what Ben Johnson could lift, and I am sure there are words written describing Bailey's strength levels. But unless one of us witnessed it, we have to be guarded in our acceptance of this. Athletes succeed in the same sport relying on different qualities. In this instance, Ben exploited his strength. Carl Lewis, for example, succeeded by exploited his stretch-shortening cycle. You concluded that your goal is to get stronger. That is easy. But the only strength training method you mention is a 'basic bodybuilding program'. Bodybuilding programs should not dominate in the training of the strength athlete! I am confident there are many **strength** programs that will work for you!

Bodybuilding programs should not dominate in the training of the strength athlete!

Q: *I'm a 21-year-old male college student who has been working out for about 2.5 years. During the school semester, I do not have a job and thus have plenty of time to train, eat, and rest properly. So I make good progress. During the summer, I work as a grocery stock clerk 50+ hours a week. The job involves odd hours and a lot of manual labor. I'm constantly exhausted, over-trained, miss meals, miss training sessions, and end up losing weight and strength every summer. I'm a junior now and I don't want this to happen again this summer. Do you have any suggestions that would assist me?*

Sincerely,
Evan Peck

A: Yes. Quit work. Only joking. Good to see you gain experience in various industries. Reminds me of my first year in university. Assuming you are faced with this same work schedule, let's make 'war plans'. I will divide your approach into two : training and recovery.

Recovery : the key to recovery is planning. For starters, with regards to meals, there is no need to miss them. You know what the work involves, so use your experience to plan. If it means you have to eat on the run, use a MRP made up before work. If it means something small that can fit into a pocket and not get in the way of work, arrange some calorie dense food bars. You have no excuses here. Now increase your supplement intake in general, even though you I would recommend less training than during semester. If your sleep is affected by shift work there are many lessons you can take from those experienced in this e.g. if you have to sleep during the day, ensure your room is blacked out; if you are struggling to fall asleep, use melatonin. Shift-work affected sleep is not ideal, because you are constantly resetting your body clock, but the down-sides can be minimized.

Under-train initially, then if you feel the need, progressively increase.

Training : in the past you have lost ground during summer. You need to change your attitude about training. Your initial training focus should be to maintain, not to try and improve. This is something of a switch in attitude, because you normally train to improve. In summer, train to maintain. Your initial goal is simple - not to lose any strength or size. How should you train? Under-train initially, then if you feel the need (and most of that feeling will be psychological), progressively increase. You will be surprised how little you need to do to maintain. Stay with major muscle group exercises. Train small muscles every 5-7 days, larger muscles every 7-14

Get Buffed!™

days. Workouts should not exceed 20 minutes. Use predominantly low reps, high load - you are getting enough volume of high reps, low rest work at work.

Sounds restrictive? Sure is. But you know the alternatives - watch your gains disappear like paint on muscles in a rain storm! Only when you have established successful variables for maintenance should you even consider looking to gain.

Q: I will enter a lean mass gaining phase of training next week. What is the best training program for gaining lean mass? My training is advanced, so I am looking for answers on frequency, splits, reps, volume, tempos, rest periods and exercise selection. I was thinking of giving German volume training a try.

A: Will it work for you? Only you and time can tell. Whilst I feel there is a time and place for high volume training like this, there are a number of aspects of this program that I do not usually recommend. For example, program duration e.g. beginners 6 wks. I feel that most people will over-train if they use these demanding methods for more than 2-3 weeks. That is clean of course. With anabolics, more over-training is tolerated. Most bodybuilders are walking examples of this! And frequency e.g. 5 day cycles - again, an excellent recovery ability required.   In conclusion, there are aspects of this program that I use, I would just recommend it differently. You be the judge - I look forward to your feedback as to how it went.

Will it work for you? Only you and time can tell.

Q: I really like the ten sets method, (what some call the German Volume Program), and I have a few questions for you regarding it.

1)   *What would be the best way to utilize it in regards to the Olympic lifts? Would it be better to do partial movements such as high pulls or the full movements like the snatch?*
2)   *I know some like to use antagonistic supersets, so how would a movement such as the snatch be paired up?*
3)   *Is it possible to use this system on a two-day split - where Monday and Thursday, and Tuesday and Friday are the same or would this volume of work be too much in a single week?*
4)   *Would it be possible to use it on a four-day split? Day 1 being Chest and Hamstrings, Day 2 Back and Shoulders, Day 3 Quads, Calves and Abs, Day 4 Arms. This would be done Monday, Tuesday, Thursday, and Friday.*

Thanks for your help,

Andrew

A. Andrew -

1. The range of movement is less important. The key would be to lower the reps i.e. the more complex the movement, the lower the reps. A full snatch done in this manner may be 10 x 4, whereas a snatch pull may be 10 x 6. The additional question re. Olympic training is whether a reduction in number of sets is advisable due to fatigue issues e.g. instead of 10 x 4 snatches, maybe 6 x 4.

2. Not all exercises benefit neurally from working them in this manner (exercises done in antagonist supersets). Additionally, the larger the muscle group involved, the smaller the paired muscle group should be. In the case of snatch, perhaps finger flexions?! Note that many lower body exercises involve both extensors and flexors. If you think about the snatch for a while, you may well ask yourself which lower body muscle group didn't get worked, that could be considered an antagonist? Don't alternate set for the sake of it. Have a reason.

Note that many lower body exercises involve both extensors and flexors.

3. I believe the so-called GVT is excessive in volume. To clarify, I suggest it is nothing more than a protocol thrown together and then attached a tag that involves the word of a European country. I feel that unless you have an overnight intravenous drip of little goodies, it may be too much. Either vary the workout volume within the week, or use this program for a lesser number of weeks.

4. You have asked 2 questions here - firstly would it be possible to use it on a four-day split and secondly what would happen if the muscle groups were allocated in this manner. It is possible to use it in a four day split, but refer to my above response. As for that muscle group allocation - your arms aren't worked until day 4!

Q: Where does the size come from? I am a 38 year old male and have been lifting on & off since high school. A little over a year ago I decided to finally taking working out seriously. I am 5'10" 195 lbs. I have had pretty good improvements in strength, I'm benching about

325, squatting around 650, and have seen improvements in tone and definition, but I'm not getting any bigger. I'm currently trying the "oscillating wave" program and varying workouts between low volume and high volume days. HV days I call 5 x 5, five sets five reps, on the low volume days I either go 3 x 12-15 or 3 x 20. Got any advice for al old guy like me?

Kerry

A: I find that one of the most common limiting factor to gaining muscle size is the simple old 'calories in vs. calories out', otherwise known as calorie balance. I narrow this down to three things :

1. Inadequate calorie intake : count your calories for a period of 3-5 days. While you are doing that you may want to record your specific nutrient intake (i.e. grams of proteins, carbs and fats). But first eliminate the possibility that your total calorie intake is inadequate. Considering your age, I don't believe you will need what you may once of benefited from (say when you were 17 years old) but anything less than 3,000 calories per day may not be enough.

2. Poor meal timing : after calories, the issue I would be most interested in would be your meal timing i.e. how many meals in the day and how far apart they are. Whilst nearly everyone who has ever touched a dumbbell can tell you the advice of eating every 2-3 hours, it no longer surprises me how many people don't do what they know.

3. Over-training : this is a big issue for you, especially considering your age. I doubt you will benefit from doing in excess of 4 workouts a week, or more than 15 sets per workout. But I don't need to know the answer - you already have got some messages - what you are doing isn't working. When in doubt, do you do more, or do less? I usually go the less path.

PS. I note that you are doing 3x12-20 on your low volume days? This is actually higher volume than your 5x5 days! Maybe you meant low intensity?!

Q: I would like to know the proper way to warm up for a workout (sets, reps, intensity). I know this is a pretty vague question, but I'm stumped as whether to do cardio or light reps or whatever. Should I warm up differently for different muscle groups? I would also like to

I find that one of the most common limiting factor to gaining muscle size is the simple old 'calories in vs. calories out'.

know how to warm up for maxing out to one's full potential if the procedure is any different. Thank you in advance.

A: I break the warm up into general and specific. Cardio or similar is general, whilst warm up sets are specific. With lower body workouts, I recommend both. With upper body workouts, the general is optional. With regards to specific warm ups (i.e. warm up sets), I like to do a warm up set for every exercise that significantly changes the joint involvement. For example, I would recommend a warm up set for an incline bench that followed flat bench, even though similar muscles are used (not everyone endorses this approach, but after 30 plus years of lifting you will learn to look after your joints!). This only changes when the reps are high - in which case the joint has time to adjust during the first half of the set. The use of and number of warm up sets is influenced by the reps in the work set - the lower the reps in the first work set, the more warm up sets needed and vice versa. Yes, the warm up sets should be different for 'max lift (maximal strength) sessions. Here, the aim is to keep the volume of the warm ups sets low, so you would in essence do less reps in each warm up set, and perhaps take bigger jumps.

I like to do a warm up set for every exercise that significantly changes the joint involvement.

Here are some more points :

- you should avoid taking fatigue from warm up into the work sets;
- in hypertrophy training, I usually do higher volume warm ups than neural training;
- when training an injured joint, I am very particular about my warm up; and
- the bigger the muscle group, the more relevant a general warm up is e.g. I recommend say cardio warm-ups prior to leg days, but don't push this on upper body days.

Further guidelines for warm up sets are given in my book *How To Write Strength Training Programs : A Practical Guide.* (available at www.kingsports.net)

Q: I am very intrigued by your suggestion of no more than 20 sets per workout. I like to work on a 2 on 1 off routine. Will this work effectively? And I am more interested in building size. Is this effective? And lastly I am very curious about your suggestion of gradu-

ally increasing the intensity of workouts. Will this really help build up size and strength?

Thanks
Stone cold

A: Two days on and one day off (which I assume you meant) is effective. Going three straight on is not so (for the majority)! However just watch for cumulative fatigue - only 1 day off may not eventually or from time to time be enough. Again, for most people, I would recommend a 2 day off period at the end of at least every second or third 2 days on.

Regarding building size, the frequency of training is not enough on its own to determine the training effect, but you are on track in frequency.

Will gradually building up the intensity of the workouts really help you build size and strength? Anything initially, if different than what you normally do, will probably get a good response. However I suggest that the method I recommend will continue to produce gains over years, for a number of reasons including :

1. it reduces the likelihood of residual and cumulative fatigue from over-training;
2. it matches your inter and intra-muscular improvements (skill) with load increments.

Anything initially, if different than what you normally do, will probably get a good response.

Q: *Since we can not train all out year round, what's the best training cycle to recover after a 6-8 week program? The only things I've heard of doing are the following.*

Start a cycle by going 10% below max weight, then every week add wt until your back to your max weight in about three weeks. Once your at your max weight at the third week finish off the last 3-4 weeks at your max. Or go all out for 6-8 weeks then cut your training volume in half for three weeks then start over on a new cycle.

Everybody has training programs but no one talks about recovery. I'm hoping you can help me so I don't over-train. A recovery cycle is something I could never get down. PLEASE HELP?

Thanks, Zach

A: You have two choices in recovery - full or part recovery. The full recovery method discourages any specific formal training, allowing only low-intensity informal activity. The part recovery method involves a reduction in volume and or intensity. After a 6-12 week strength program I recommend a full recovery period of one week. In short time frames I might use a part recovery method for a week e.g. 3 wks on, 1 wk part recovery.

It is amazing how many lifters fear taking a week off. As if gains made over years will disappear in a week! Quite the opposite. Training theorists often muse over the apparent benefits of short-term detraining. Whilst no-one has really narrowed this down as to why - who cares!? It is effective - do it! (there is the added benefit in that during the recovery week you can catch up on areas you usually compromise due to training)

After a 6-12 week strength program I recommend a full recovery period of one week.

Q: Thanks for emphasizing the psychological aspect of training. A new, very demanding job has cut my training time back to a max of only three days a week and I just haven't felt that my workouts were very productive...should be doing more, y'know. After reading your suggestion that three days a week were plenty for a full time worker, I went back to the gym with a completely different attitude. The result? Much better workouts, more progress. So would you please elaborate on the three day a week plan? In general terms what kind of body split, how many sets per body part, time between sets etc, do you recommend?

ZZD

A: Great to hear you felt more comfortable with reduced volume training considering changed work demands. There are endless ways to break this up, but I will generalize. In your case, I would cycle between 5-15 total work sets per workout, and cycle between 1 minute and 5 minutes rest between sets.

Q: I am familiar with an undulatory approach to accumulation and intensity phases and the need for variety, but I am confused as to your opinion of the low, medium and high effort days that other sport scientists prescribe during each micro-cycle. Do you recommend that athletes avoid increasing the workload every training session and therefore, workout with a greater frequency and less DOMS than other high effort, 5 day cycles. Do your training princi-

ples include a "two steps forward, one step back" approach for con-
tinued improvement or should an athlete seeking mass and strength
increases ALWAYS go to the gym and attempt to better their last
performance. Are 'low-effort' days a waste of time?! Thanks for mak-
ing yourself available to your readers' questions. Please answer this
question for I'm sure I'm not the only one overwhelmed with the
buzz of 'periodization'.

Brian

A: The 'low, medium and high effort days' you refer to as being recommended by some are recommended for different reasons than the undulatory approach. The heavy-medium-light
system is attempting to integrate with the fatigue curve
throughout the micro-cycle. A recognition of fatigue, yet a desire to keep training. The undulatory approach is based on
Schmidtbleicher's theory that the absence of volume during an
intensity phase may cause loss in hypertrophy, and the absence of intensity in the accumulation phase may cause loss of
strength.

Based upon the above rationale, these two methods are presented for totally different reasons. I believe your question focuses mainly on the pro's and con's of the light-medium-heavy
system. In brief, I don't use it that much. I feel it is a bit of a
waste of time. I prefer to do better every time I repeat the
same workout. However a major difference in my program
design is that general I don't repeat the same muscle group in
a micro-cycle. For example, may do two leg workouts in micro-cycle, but one is a quad dominant (e.g. squat or similar)
and the other a hip dominant (e.g. deadlift or similar). So I
don't have as much need for the heavy-medium-light system.

*I believe that the
few athletes who
need to repeat
the same muscle
groups in the
week are those
who are focusing
on the technical
component of
lifts e.g. Olympic
lifters and power
lifters.*

I believe that the few athletes who need to repeat the same
muscle groups in the week are those who are focusing on the
technical component of lifts e.g. Olympic lifters and power lifters.

As far an any comparison with other peoples program design,
I may be a bit more conservative in volume and frequency but
not necessarily intensity.

*Q. I've read these charts that are supposed to tell you how big you
are capable of getting by measuring the diameter of your wrist. Is*

there any truth to that?

A. Wrist circumference as a predictor of muscle mass potential was a topic that has drawn some attention by many including US anthropometry researchers Willoughby. Some theorize similarly about the size of the calf. Having big wrists and calf are nice, but I don't accept the hypothesis. Especially not in these days of extreme chemical contribution. Without naming any, I know some pro bodybuilders over the last decade who were not limited by their very small wrists! Whilst I do believe it is an encouraging sign to have large wrists, I don't see this as being either a guarantee or a limiting factor.

Q. My buddy had a book that had gave you a formula that was supposed to tell you what ideal or maximal lifts you should be able to perform. For example, at my 180 pounds, it said I should bench 328, squat 466, and deadlift 545. Is there really any goals I should set based on my body weight?

Whilst I do believe it is an encouraging sign to have large wrists, I don't see this as being either a guarantee or a limiting factor.

A. It is all relative. If you narrowed it down by saying I compete in this sport at this level - are there any strength expectations - I would say yes. But generally speaking, no. Any tables giving figures such as the ones you refer to are either displaying a great imagination on the author's part or based on a sample group - but what was the group? If the sample group was national level weightlifters and powerlifters, you could suddenly feel very inadequate. But if it was based on the average person found making friends in a commercial gymnasium in Anytown USA, it would be easy to think you were Clark Kent in his after-hours leotard.

Q: I am writing with reference to your 6/1/6/1/10-20 workout. My question is: how do you determine what weight to use on the single? If the single rep is a genuine predetermined one rep max there must always be the chance that it will be missed which would I assume adversely affect the next set. Is it perhaps more important that you increase to a weight that is close to maximum and requires high intensity than trying to achieve a limit single? Also what precisely is the purpose of the twenty rep set. Is it necessary for those of us interested only in strength?
Regards, Peter

A: No, the single is not a pre-determined 1 rep max. This is an error in this method. If you go too close to max, the residual fatigue negates the load contrasting effect, as you have suggested. The aim of this single is to merely provide a loading contrast, and to elevate the neural activity. The purpose of the 20 rep set is as follows :

- it is in the traditional hypertrophy bracket, therefore adding a potential hypertrophy response;
- you can do more reps at a given weight in this back off set than you would if you approached it prior to the heavier loading - therefore you are gaining an adaptation further along the neural-metabolic and FT-ST fiber continuum;
- you also create increased ATP storage training effects, which is important for many sports.

I think you can give credit for this training method to the eastern European weightlifting training methodology. It's a sensationally powerful method - if used wisely.

Q: I really want to get bigger and I think I am doing the wrong exercises because I am not getting any bigger, so I was wondering if you could send me your top three exercises for each muscle, I would appreciate it.

Thanks,

zp

You can do more reps at a given weight in this back off set than you would if you approached it prior to the heavier loading.

A: I could give you what you want, but the exercise selection is rarely the greatest limiting factor. I would say lack of intensity or over-training are the most likely problems. If you are doing more than 10 sets per workout (yes, that is right, 10 sets per workout, not per muscle group!!!), cut back to this and see how it goes. If you are going to failure on each set, try stopping a bit short of failure. Make sure your diet approximates a bodybuilding diet (there is no shortage of info on this in the mags) and minimize stress in life. Let me know how you go with these suggestions. Maybe then we can look at exercise selection.

Q: At what point will age inhibit strength gains? I am 40 years old, 5' 10", 185lbs, 10% body fat, I work out 3 times per week alternating between upper and lower body per workout. I utilize compound movements as much as possible. I have been working out for 10 years.

I have started the 1,6 rep scheme. For example:
Warm up - 5 sets dumbbell squats of 60, 65, 70, 80, 90lbs for 5 reps
Dumbbell squat 1 rep = 100lbs
Rest 3 minutes
Dumbbell squat 6 rep = 85 lbs
Rest 3 minutes
Dumbbell squat 1 rep = 105lbs
Rest 3 minutes
Dumbbell squat 6 reps = 90lbs
The squats were full squats

The next morning my knees were sore. I have never had problems with my knees in my life. Is this a sign that at this age I can no longer go heavy?

Iaradzikoski

A: No, I don't believe this is a sign that you are 'too old to go heavy'. But I do believe that due to your age, and the lowered recovery ability associated, that you will need to go more carefully. What I recommend is to ease your way into loads in future - instead of going to what you know to be your max or near max capabilities, use more sub-maximal loads initially. You may be frustrated by this go slow approach, but it will give your body (joints in particular) a chance to adapt. If you don't take this advice seriously, your final condition may well be one where you are 'too old to go heavy.' Hope this helps!

> *I recommend ease your way into loads - instead of going to what you know to be your max or near max capabilities, use more sub-maximal loads initially.*

Q: I've heard every problem from injuries to growth stunting arises when teenagers weight train. Once and for all, how should us teenagers train without breaking our necks or getting our balls cut off?

Thank you
Chris

A : Chris - Most of the claims regarding teenagers are bogus. In fact, your bodies (from a growth i.e. hormonal response perspective) are in a better condition than a person in their 20's! Train like any other adult - but don't make the same mistakes most do. Because if you have started training younger than the prior generation, the error in training induced injuries will surface for you at a relatively younger age. I see the most common mistakes being failing to stretch (to develop and maintain appropriate muscle length and tension) and de-

Get Buffed!™

veloping imbalance (through focusing too much on some muscles and ignoring others). In the last point, I don't refer to visual balance or aesthetic balance - I refer to muscle balance to prevent use injuries around the joint e.g. more chest work than upper back, more lower back than abdominal training etc.

So go and train as per your older peers - just smarter!

On stretching.....

Q: Can you recommend some good stretching programs? How about some resources (books and videos) that provide the scientific basis for stretching for hypertrophy, strength, power and injury prevention?

Thanks,
Rick

A: Up until a few years ago, there was a real shortage of material on stretching. This is changing, but compared to other forms of physical preparation e.g. strength training, there is still a big hole.

Human Kinetics publishing have a number of books and videos on stretching. Try to get a hold of their catalogue. And I have a 3 options for you, from basic to more advanced they include :

Up until a few years ago, there was a real shortage of material on stretching.

- a single video titled 'Ian King's Guide to Individual Stretching', which gives you the how-to do an total body stretching routine; this is available at www.getbuffed. net, and you can find more info about this and the *Get Buffed!*™ range;
- a three video series on stretching which is aimed at the practical side - put in the video and do as you see type of thing. This is called the 'Flexibility Training Video Series' and is available at www.kingsports.net;
- A two day seminar edited down to video called the 'Strength Specialization Video Series'. This is aimed more at industry professionals. But of course if very practically oriented! This is also available at www. kingsports.net.

As far as 'providing the scientific basis for stretching for hypertrophy, strength, power and injury prevention' - there is perhaps a handful of scattered research articles on these topics. Stretching has yet to become a 'hip' topic for the sport science researchers.   Others may recognize what I say when I describe the shift in research interest from endurance to strength in the early '80's. Academics were one day a endurance specialist - the next day an expert on strength training.

Well, it hasn't happened yet in stretching, so don't expect an avalanche of 'scientific' support. If you understand what I mean when I call sport scientists sport historians, you will understand that sometimes you will benefit from being onto something before it becomes 'universally and scientifically supported'.

Q. You said that for every hour of lifting an athlete should spend an hour stretching. What type of stretching do you recommend? Are there any good books on stretching out there?

A. There are lots of good books on stretching. Human Kinetics for example, a large US publishing company, have a range of books/videos on stretching (e.g. McAtee, R., *Facilitated Stretching*). Also, M.J. Alter has a number of stretching books (e.g. *Science of Stretching, Sports Stretch*, Leisure Press, Illinois); also Bob Anderson (*Stretching*, Shelter Publications, Calif.) I am a bit biased - I like my 3 part video series on stretching. It has been a very effective tool for me to teach athletes and coaches my basic philosophy on stretching. The tapes have a large component of 'monkey see, monkey do' - which means just do what I am showing you for as long as I am doing it etc. A sort of live one-on-one session. Makes it user-simple. You can now get the individual stretching tape as a single video by ordering the 'Ian King's Guide to Individual Stretching' (at www.getbuffed.net).

During the latter half of the 90's, static stretching has become non-chic, with the 'you must be doing more specific types of stretching' mentally sweeping the world.

What types of stretching do I recommend? During the late '80's/early 90's I preferred to do my bulk of stretching statically, i.e. passively, and by using PNF. This was OK then because ballistic stretching was considered evil, and the PNF research study mill was in overdrive. During the latter half of the 90's, static stretching has become non-chic, with the 'you must be doing more specific types of stretching' (i.e. dynamic and ballistic) mentally sweeping the world of those that can't think for themselves. I use them all, but believe that static stretching has a valuable role to play, which means I am not politically correct. Wonder what next decades trend will be?!

Ian King was born and raised on an island in the Pacific. It was there he developed a passion for sport. In addition to being involved in many sports, he began his strength training career at the early age of seven years old.

For the bulk of his adult life Ian has been committed improving the sporting success of elite athletes. His involvement with athletes in over 10 countries and over 20 sports has provided a rare and ideal opportunity to develop successful physical preparation methods applicable to the multi-year development of the athlete.

He has prepared athletes for every winter and summer Olympic Games since 1988, and every Commonwealth Games since 1984, as well as World Championships and World Cups in numerous sports. However he doesn't count the medals - he believes that credit should stay with the athlete.

Ian has taken the lessons he has learnt from training elite athletes over many years and applied them to training programs to benefit every person committed to developing their bodies through strength training. He is sharing the methods he developed from both his personal and professional experience. Ian belief's in training that training should be fun and rewarding, that training is for life, and that there is a little part in all of us that has a desire to *Get Buffed!*™

Get Buffed!™ is range of strength training educational material by Ian King. Drawing from his extensive personal and professional experiences in strength training, Ian has created a collection of educational material to help you Get Buffed!™ Ian's goal is simple—to elevate the training results of everyone using strength training. The training methods being shared with you in the Get Buffed!™ range have been extremely well received. Why? Because they work!

The Get Buffed!™ Newsletter   Free subscription to readers of this book

The Get Buffed!™ Newsletter! is packed with TONS of invaluable information. We are covering tons of topics that will help and inspire you achieve your goals to use your time and efforts more effectively than ever before - to create a physique that is more than you could ever have imagined! Subscribe to this newsletter by emailing to info@getbuffed.net with the words SUBSCRIBE GET BUFFED in the subject field.

Ian King's Guide To Control Drills $29.95 USD

This video has Ian King demonstrating, with the use of an athlete, his approach to control/stability training. Control drills, as Ian calls them, can be quite complex and challenging to describe their execution in the written word - especially to do them in the special and unique way that Ian has his athlete's doing them! Make sure you are executing the movements in the way Ian intended by using this video series in conjunction with the program from the *Get Buffed!*™ book!

Ian King's Guide To Abdominal Training $29.95 USD

This video has Ian King demonstrating, with the use of an athlete, his approach to abdominal training. Abdominal exercises can be quite complex and challenging to describe their execution in the written word - especially to do them in the special and unique way that Ian has his athlete's doing them! Make sure you are executing the movements in the way Ian intended by using this video series in conjunction with the program from the *Get Buffed!*™ book!

Ian King's Guide To Individual Stretching $39.95 USD

This video has Ian King demonstrating, with the use of an athlete, his approach to individual stretching. Flexibility exercises can be quite complex and challenging to describe their execution in the written word - especially to do them in the special and unique way that Ian has his athlete's doing them! Make sure you are executing the movements in the way Ian intended by using this video series in conjunction with the program from the *Get Buffed!*™ book!

Ian King's Guide — 3 video package $87 USD

Save about 13% on buying the above 3 single *Ian King's Guide to...* videos by ordering them as a 3-pack!

Ian King's "Killer Leg Exercises for Strength and Mass" $39.95 USD

Ian King's "Killer Leg Exercises for Strength and Mass" is jam-packed with special techniques that will keep your leg training fresh and muscles growing. This video covers all the exercises used in the 'Limping' program as posted on the T-mag web site (see the **Articles** section for easy access to these programs). This video is only available by ordering directly from http://www.biotest-online.com/

Get Buffed!™ Video Series $137 USD

This video has Ian King demonstrating all the exercises in this four day split, 12 week (4 stage) *Get Buffed!*™ program! So if you have done this program, or are doing, or plan to do it, and you want some expert coaching - it doesn't get any better than this! Make sure you are executing the movements in the way Ian intended by using this video series in conjunction with the program from the *Get Buffed!*™ book!

Get Buffed!™ Total Package $227 USD

The *Get Buffed!*™ *Total Package* is the most cost effective way to get the full range of Ian King's *Get Buffed!*™ material. The *Get Buffed!*™ range is aimed at the end user in strength training and bodybuilding/shaping - those who just want to know how to do it themselves! The *Get Buffed!*™ *Total Package* includes five (5) products - a mix books and video tape. In all you get $277 worth of product for $227, a saving of fifty ($50) dollars!

New product developments are continually being developed. To learn more, go to www.getbuffed.net or email us at info@getbuffed.net.

King Sports International
www.getbuffed.net
info@getbuffed.net
Ph +1-775-327-4550 Fax +1-240-465-4873
1135 Terminal Way, Suite 209, Reno NV 89502, USA